THE ART OF THE LP

CLASSIC ALBUM COVERS 1955—1995

STERLING and the distinctive Sterling logo are registered
trademarks of Sterling Publishing Co., Inc.

Library of Congress Cataloging-in-Publication Data Available

10 9 8 7 6 5 4 3 2 1

Published by Sterling Publishing Co., Inc.
387 Park Avenue South, New York, NY 10016

© 2010 Essential Works Limited

Distributed in Canada by Sterling Publishing
c/o Canadian Manda Group, 165 Dufferin Street
Toronto, Ontario, Canada M6K 3H6
Distributed in the United Kingdom by GMC Distribution Services
Castle Place, 166 High Street, Lewes, East Sussex, England BN7 1XU
Distributed in Australia by Capricorn Link (Australia) Pty. Ltd.
P.O. Box 704, Windsor, NSW 2756, Australia

Produced for Sterling Publishing by Essential Works
www.essentialworks.co.uk

Publishing Director: Mal Peachey
Managing Director: John Conway
Editors: Fiona Screen, Dipli Saikia
Proofreader: Tatiana Bissell
Designer: Michael Gray
Reprographic Assistants: Marin Finerty, Jessica Cash

Sterling ISBN 978-1-4027-7113-2

For information about custom editions, special sales, premium
and corporate purchases, please contact Sterling Special Sales
Department at 800-805-5489 or specialsales@sterlingpublishing.com

THE ART OF THE LP

CLASSIC ALBUM COVERS 1955—1995

Johnny Morgan and Ben Wardle

STERLING

New York / London
www.sterlingpublishing.com

CONTENTS

INTRODUCTION

Observant readers will already have noticed something particular about this book: it ends in 1995. What? you may exclaim. Surely, there must have been some respectable album artwork produced after that date. There was indeed, but chiefly by then the vinyl album—for which so many classic designs had been produced—was on its last legs. It had become the lesser of the three formats to house recordings, third in line after the cassette.

But by then, artists as well as designers had pretty much gotten used to making music for the CD format. There are plenty of great CD designs from this period but these are perhaps for another book—although we couldn't resist dropping in a couple from the period after 1995 which work particularly well on vinyl. See if you can spot them.

This volume focuses on the rich period from 1955 onward. Album sleeves, or at least ones with artwork designed to make them look individual, didn't really exist until the 1940s. You can probably date them to the time that Columbia Records employed Alex Steinweiss as art director in 1939, when he put together an illustrated cover for an album of Rodgers & Hart 78 rpm records.

Before that, hard to believe though it is, 78s were packaged in brown sleeves with plain cardboard covers. Steinweiss is quoted as saying that they reminded him of tombstones. Much 1980s heavy metal artwork might perhaps have prompted similar comments from him.

An album cover provides a record, and frequently an artist, with a visual identity. Of course, its primary concern is to be attractive to the potential purchaser of the record, but it also endures as a landmark in an artist's career path, preserved forever as it first appeared. What other mainstream business sells products housed in exactly the same packaging for its entire life? Look for any album on Amazon and,

with few exceptions, you'll see a packshot of a CD of it dressed in the same artwork as it was on the day it first came out.

Like any business, the music industry was always commercial, capitalist, competitive and cynical. In the mid-20th century, the industry first created an enormous source of income when jukeboxes spread across America; it then made another fortune when people began to buy their own home "jukeboxes" and 7" singles sold in the millions. By the late 1950s, the business was looking at any and all ways of selling more music in different formats to as big an audience as possible. When Elvis wiggled his hips on the *Ed Sullivan Show* and turned the Western world onto rock & roll, the biggest singing star at the time was Frank Sinatra. He had pioneered the selling of millions of long-playing records by condensing ten-song mini-operas onto one disk. It was not lost on Elvis's manager Colonel Tom Parker as he skillfully molded the career of his protégé.

While the conventional music business believed that in order to sell a pop music long player you needed to project the star openly, smiling invitingly at the camera, Sinatra had broken the rules and created mini-movie scenes for his album covers. Some were rendered in paint or pencil, others had sets created for a photo shoot. One Sinatra cover featured in this book has Frank looking away from the camera, seated among a throng of other people. He's definitely not smiling. Elvis isn't smiling on his debut cover either: his eyes are closed as he's captured mid-performance in the emotion of playing an instrument. As with so much that Elvis did before joining the army, it proved to be groundbreaking and trendsetting, even in black and white.

Colonel Tom and the businessmen at RCA Victor who made such decisions helped to create the proto-rock & roll album cover image. They didn't know it at the time, of course, but then rarely do such instances of creative genius come out of deliberate intention.

Not that there hasn't been a wealth of deliberation and intention put into scores of album cover designs over the fifty-year period that this book covers. There have been some truly great, inventive, artistic and inspired minds used to great effect in the art departments of record companies in America and Europe. There have been many other books on album artwork before this one, but in considering the organization for this book it struck us that it was time someone put artwork into a different context, rather than simply categorizing it by musical genre or decade. Like pop music itself, cover art is concerned with universal themes; it attempts to project an image, an idea, a feeling or a mood. Sometimes this may have nothing to do with the music on the record it houses.

Confronted with a bland-looking bunch of musicians with no obvious sex symbol members, art departments have frequently had to be inventive in selling an act. Would Pink Floyd or Chicago have sold quite as many records without their unique artwork?

Within these pages we have arranged sleeves within thematically created sections; each theme concerns the artwork and not necessarily the music on the records. While designers often worked with the musicians on their cover art, it's just as true that record companies often produced artwork with very little input from the recording artist. Indeed, sometimes the art department would design a sleeve without even hearing the album. That said, most successful album cover designs work because of the involvement of the musicians.

We have also included some sleeves that for various reasons are not blessed with aesthetic success (marked ❶). For every great sleeve, which set a style and example for others to follow, there were misguided attempts at copying the form, possibly because of overambition or perhaps by simply having a bad idea. These examples make such a mess of things that they deserve a showing. We can all learn from our own and others' mistakes. Though in the case of a couple of designers and bands, that has sadly not proved to be true.

We have attempted to give the appropriate level of credit to those photographers, designers and artists whose work deserves it. It's not surprising that many of them began what became illustrious careers by first working on album sleeves. There are many photographers here who went on to have solo exhibitions at galleries and museums, or who produced cover images for major international magazines. There are also designers who went on to create world-recognized brand identities and international commercials. Yet their first work was to project an idea of what a record would look like if you could see the sound it made.

For every inclusion, readers will no doubt shake their heads in disbelief at the omission of their favorite. We've included what we think are perennial classics but tried to steer a little away from the usual suspects and throw in a few unfamiliar ones. No list is ever definitive and for everyone out there who is scoffing at the absence of *Abbey Road*, *Pet Sounds* and their like we make no apologies. Deal with it. One of the great things about the 12" vinyl long-playing record is that it means so much to so many people.

Uniquely, the packaging of those circular pieces of plastic, which held roughly 20 minutes of music per side, has proven to be as enduring and important to people as the music in the grooves. Hopefully looking through this book will prove exactly why that is.

Johnny Morgan and Ben Wardle
2009

ROCK & ROLL

Whether linked with "roll" or not, rock is not really about music. Closer to its heart is the sheer exuberance of youth, sex, rebellion, aggression, and more sex—a transient transistor blast that's gone as soon as the goose pimples on the back of your neck start to fade. Surely trying to capture that in a cardboard sleeve so it can be shoved into a record store rack is impossible?

Ironically, record stores—now an endangered species—have always been museums. They're surely the only commercial outlets whose stock is a history lesson. Aside from being shrunk down to a 5" CD, Elvis Presley's debut album is still there in its black-and-white sleeve with the pink and green lettering. And so is Eric Meola's 1975 photograph of Springsteen leaning on saxophonist Clarence Clemons sporting an Elvis badge, as well as Ray Lowry's 1979 homage to Elvis artwork for *London Calling*.

Regardless of its origination and roots, the spirit of rock & roll is all about Elvis—and with him, as Nik Cohn says in *Awopbopaloobopalopbamboom*, it was all about sex: "There was no more pretence about moonlight and hand-holding, it was hard physical fact." So despite frequent depiction of instruments, rock & roll artwork has little to do with actual music: what you see on the sleeves—the tight jeans, the mean stares, the shades and the leather jackets—all come from the King, never mind that most of his own sleeves feature him grinning like a puppy dog.

Rock & roll is youth obsessed, but it's simultaneously making constant reference to Presley and its past. And sex. Never forget that the phrase was a euphemism for the act of procreation long before Elvis entered the Sun studios.

Elvis Presley The Sun Collection

1975
RCA Starcall
England
Sleeve design uncredited

By 1975 Elvis Presley was in dire need of a credibility makeover. After the brief return to form that his 1968 NBC TV special had marked, when he appeared slim, happy, hungry to perform and in good form as he jammed with old buddies Bill and Scotty, it was a short time before he grew fat and looked bored. He was almost permanently resident in Las Vegas where he could earn top dollar for the same over-the-top show night after night, always wore rhinestone-encrusted jumpsuits and threw ridiculous "karate" shapes as he went through the motions singing MOR pop. RCA's decision to release these original Sun Studios recordings reminded the world what we'd first fallen in love with. And the cover, despite being a mid-price release with every penny spared in production, perfectly recollects the young, hip Elvis in proto-rocker garb. Before long young bands in England were appearing in black shirts wearing thin white ties and young punks were adding rock & roll wear to their wardrobe. The drawing is a scene from a show that never happened.

Elvis Presley
Elvis Presley

1956
RCA Victor
America
Photography by William "Red" Robertson

The photograph was taken during Elvis's performance as bottom of the bill on the *Andy Griffith Show* at Fort Homer Hesterly Armory in Tampa, Florida. The photographer, co-owner of the Robertson & Fresh agency, was hired by Elvis's manager Colonel Tom Parker for a flat fee. The vivid pink and green lettering was added by an unidentified hip young thing in the RCA art department. In the full photograph and cropped out of the final cover image is a line of screaming girls above Elvis's head. The movement and immediacy of the image has been attempted countless times in the decades following this album's release, but rarely with such success.

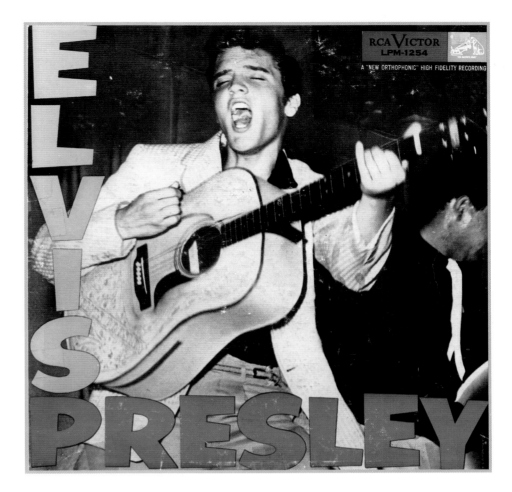

The Clash
London Calling

1980
Epic
America
Sleeve design by Ray Lowry
Photography by Pennie Smith

The photograph was taken instinctively by Pennie Smith, as she was backing away from the advancing Clash bassist Paul Simonon; she realized that he was going to do something extraordinary and captured him mid-swing of his guitar. Cartoonist Ray Lowry, who was with the band on the road in America when this shot was taken, was asked if he'd design the album sleeve. The result was what he described as "a genuine homage to the original, unknown, inspired genius who created Elvis Presley's first rock & roll record." He also added "the strange potency of the pink and green lettering and the sheer vibrancy of the Elvis picture" as another inspiration.

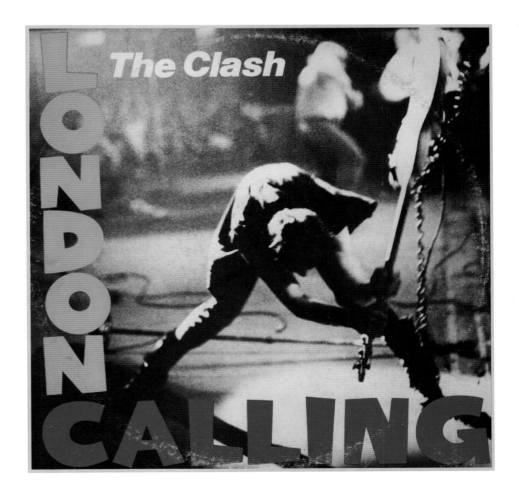

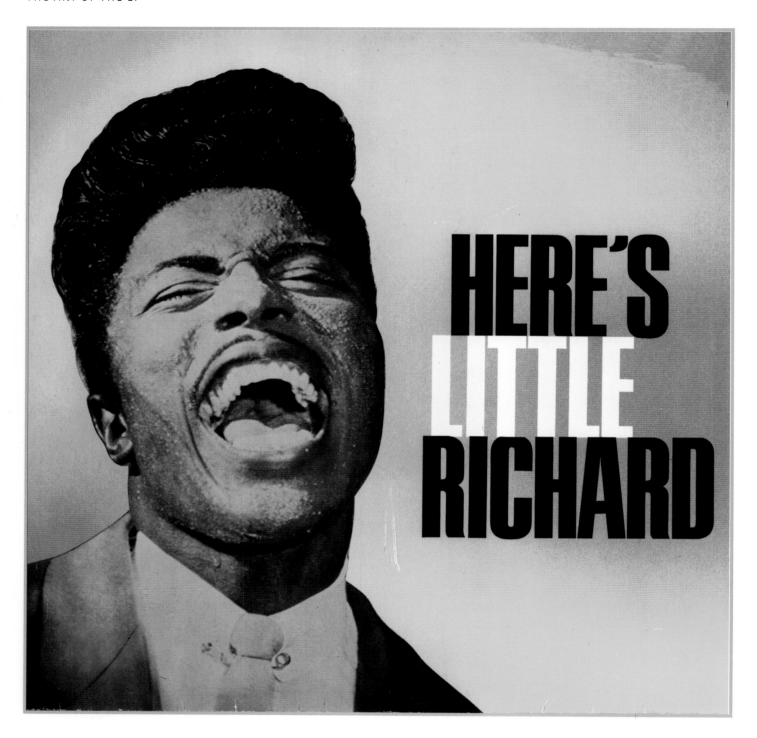

1957
Specialty Records
America
Sleeve design by Thadd Roark,
Paul Hartley

Little Richard *Here's Little Richard*

Once Elvis had let the rock & roll cat out of its bag, all the other rockin' cats came bouncing out too. Among the first was the self-styled Georgia Peach, Little Richard Penniman. When his appearance singing the title tune of *The Girl Can't Help It* hit cinemas around the world in 1956, his high camp, high-kicking, piano-pounding performance made him an instant star. After a string of hit singles including "Tutti Frutti," "Long Tall Sally" and "Rip It Up," his record label decided that if the Presley kid could release an LP—which were then normally sold to adults wanting to hear classical music, show tunes or crooners—so too could Richard. And like the Presley album (see p. 11) the LP cover would have the singer in mid-performance. It was a brave move in some ways, given how the civil rights movement was only just gathering pace and white kids were still not expected to listen to, let alone buy, music performed by an African American. But the infectious spirit of the pompadoured shouter comes across loud and clear here and his in-your-face attitude became a much-copied image.

CRUISIN' WITH GENE VINCENT AND THE BLUE CAPS

Rockstar
RECORDS
RSR-LP 1007

Cruisin' with GENE VINCENT & The Blue Caps

Capitol Photo

1983
Rockstar
Germany
Sleeve design by Divine
Photography by Capitol Studio

Gene Vincent Cruisin' with Gene Vincent & the Blue Caps

Not all of the first wave of rock & roll stars had matinee looks and clean-living reputations. When Gene Vincent, a Virginia boy, visited the UK in 1959, his limp (the result of a motorcycle accident) and haggard physique (the result of mixing painkillers with alcohol) presented the perfect opportunity for pop TV producer and visionary Jack Good to create a truly threatening rock & roll idol. Good gave Vincent a black leather suit and told him never to smile, to make his limp more pronounced and to scare the girls into loving him. The boys liked the idea of Vincent too and pretty soon he had a huge following of like-minded and copycat-dressed fans. In the early 1970s a British faux rock & roll Glam outfit named the Rubettes stole the Blue Caps' look completely. Morrissey's longtime musical collaborator and cowriter Boz Boorer has been a lifelong fan of Vincent, going as far as playing the guitars (like the one shown here) that he played. The fact that this record was released in 1983 demonstrates how long and far the appeal of Vincent, who had only one big hit, "Be-Bop-A-Lula," spread.

13

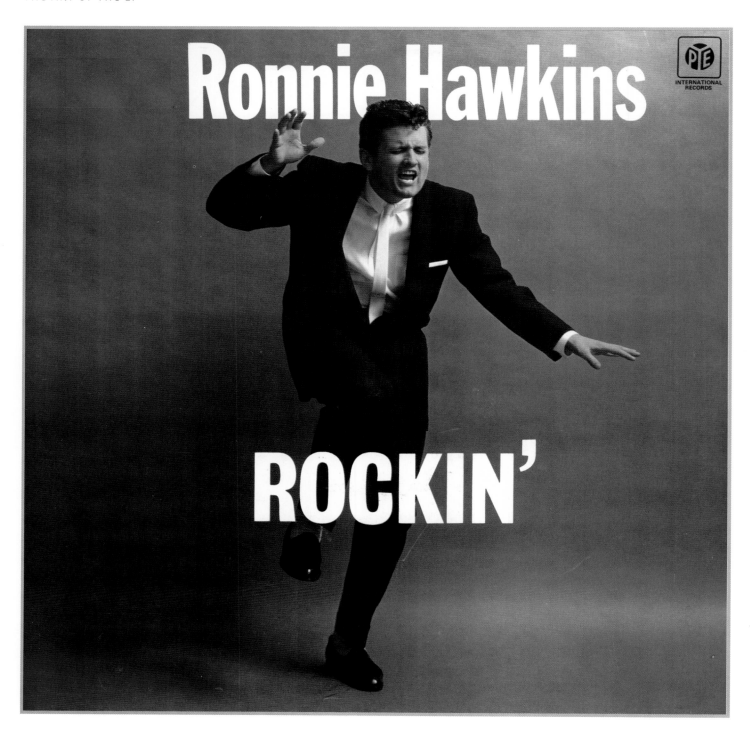

1959
Roulette Records
America
Photography by Mel Sokolsky

Ronnie Hawkins *Rockin'*

Although originating from Arkansas, Hawkins moved to Canada before his first hit single (a version of "Hey! Bo Diddley," in 1958), and rarely left there after that. Hawkins soon gathered a band of promising musicians around him, including future members of the Band (Bob Dylan's backing band) plus future members of Janis Joplin's Full Tilt and David Clayton Thomas, better known as the singer of Blood, Sweat and Tears. He was a charismatic and engaging performer and band leader. Despite beginning his career as a typical teen idol after scoring a hit single with "Mary Lou" in 1958, The Hawk soon became notorious as a rocker. He may have dressed snappily, and there were few snappier suits at the time than the one he's wearing here, but his performances were high energy. Again, as with Elvis, Hawkins's debut album captures him "mid-performance," although this photo was clearly taken in a studio. The image is staged in a way that pre-dates and prefigures the kind of action fashion shoot that would become common in the late 1960s, where models would "dance" in a studio.

CR 300002

16 TRACK ALBUM

Jerry Lee Lewis Jerry Lee Lewis

1981
Charly Records
England
Sleeve concept and art by
Jacques Parnell

Some twenty-five years after rock & roll had first become popular there
was something of a revival in Europe. Part of the revival was due to the
reissue of classic rock albums such as this (and the Gene Vincent one on
p. 13). While Jerry Lee (and Chuck, Little Richard and Bo Diddley) could
often be seen performing live across the Continent, they were by then
middle-aged and tired, their shows often lacking the physicality of their
original recordings and performances. Reissue labels like Charly had grown
out of the UK punk movement, run by original rockers who loved this stuff.
The labels lovingly repackaged recordings that they'd license for little
money because the original owners of the recordings didn't see any worth
in releasing them. Instead of a "classic" photo of the stars of the fifties
on the cover, Charly would use Frenchman Parnell to recreate what would
have been a fabulous scene in a small club, with Killer looking you straight
in the eye, nursing a shot while cool guys gave slinky girls in tight dresses
diamond bracelets. Those, it is saying, were happy days.

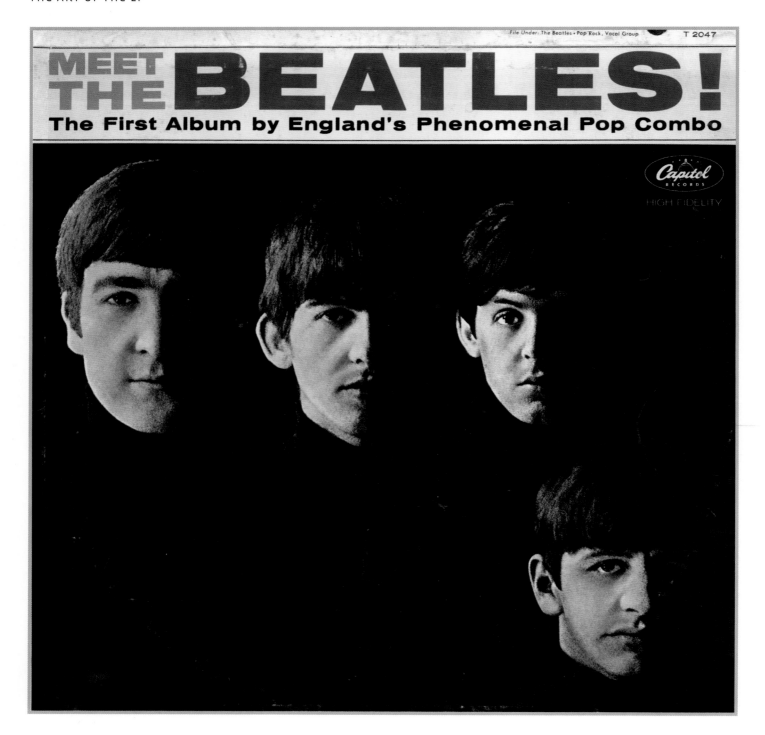

File Under: The Beatles • Pop Rock, Vocal Group   T 2047

MEET THE BEATLES!
The First Album by England's Phenomenal Pop Combo

Capitol RECORDS

HIGH FIDELITY

1964
Capitol
America
Sleeve concept by the Beatles
Photography by Robert Freeman

The Beatles Meet the Beatles!

It wasn't the first Beatles album, nor the first released in America—that had been *Introducing . . . the Beatles*, which was in stores two weeks before this went on sale. It is the first Beatles album on Capitol, though. The cover photo had appeared on the band's second UK album, entitled *With the Beatles* and released in November 1963. They had shown photographer Robert Freeman some photos taken by an old Hamburg friend, Astrid Kirchner (she'd dated deceased ex-Beatle Stuart Sutcliffe); Freeman had an hour in a Bournemouth hotel to capture the biggest band in Britain at the time. So he closed the curtains, lined them up and snapped, darkening the blacks and lightening the whites in his darkroom later. The stunning, stark image and composition was so unlike the public conception of the lovable mop-tops at the time, and showed exactly how much they, not the record label or manager, were in control of their image. It has been copied endlessly since, by bands who would like to touch the hem of the Beatles' garments (see p. 17).

Queen Queen II

1974
EMI
England
Photography and art direction by
Mick Rock
Sleeve concept by Mick Rock and Queen
Typography by Ridgeway Watt

Queen's sophomore album gave them their first big hit "Seven Seas of Rhye," but arguably its greatest legacy is Mick Rock's cover image. Even those unfamiliar with the album will recognize the imperious, uplit image of the band from the video to 1975's "Bohemian Rhapsody," in what is now acknowledged as the very first pop video. Glam rock photographer Rock had done much to define Marc Bolan and David Bowie's looks and his shot of Queen—possibly inspired by the *With the Beatles* cover (see opposite)—was itself subsequently copied many times. The sleeve concept is credited to both the photographer and the band since the album is conceptual in nature, having a "white" side and a "black" side—the front cover clearly representing the "black." An image of the band in white appears inside the album's gatefold sleeve. Ridgeway Watt's regal Queen logo had been used on their debut album but really comes into its own here.

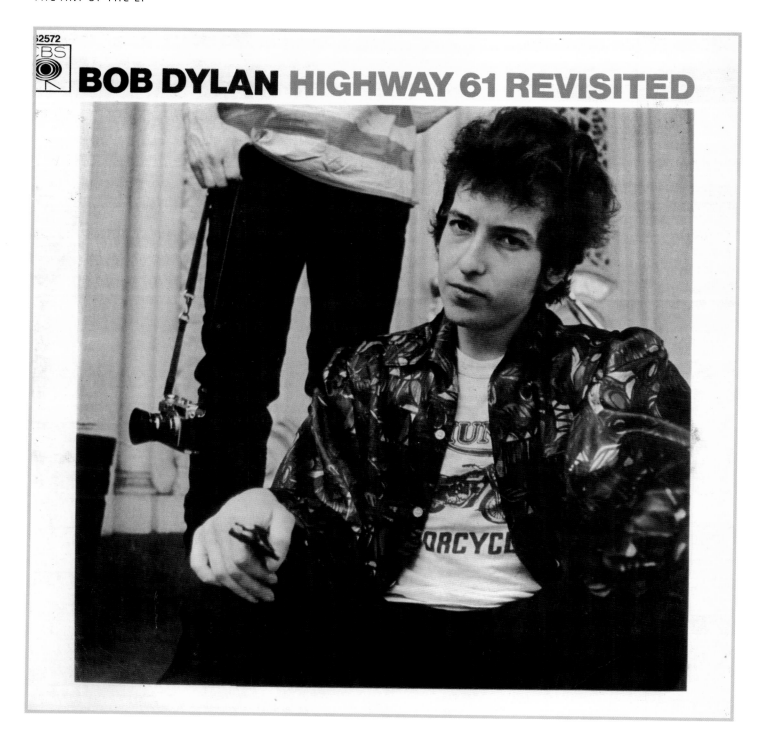

BOB DYLAN HIGHWAY 61 REVISITED

1965
Columbia Records
America
Photography by Daniel Kramer

Bob Dylan Highway 61 Revisited

This was Dylan's sixth album but the first to be fully recorded with a complete electric backing band. Only half the songs were recorded with a band in *Bringing It All Back Home*. Before the recording of this album began, Dylan was booked to play two sets at the Newport Folk Festival on Sunday July 25, 1965. The first was performed solo and acoustic. Come nighttime, a full electric band featuring Mike Bloomfield and Al Kooper plugged in with Dylan; uproar ensued. The album also features members of the Butterfield Blues Band from that night, and is considered a rock classic. With the release of "Like a Rolling Stone" Dylan became a pop star as well as a folk idol, the single making #2 on the Hot 100. The cover, shot by Kramer, who also photographed *Bringing It All Back Home*, captures an unsmiling Dylan, possibly not posing, wearing a T-shirt depicting a British Triumph Bonneville motorbike. Brando rode a Triumph in *The Wild One*. The guy with the camera in the background adds to the feeling of a documentary photograph. Folk singers don't ride motorbikes, but rock & rollers do.

THE JIMI HENDRIX EXPERIENCE ELECTRIC LADYLAND

The Jimi Hendrix Experience Electric Ladyland

1968
Track Records
England
Sleeve design by David King
Photography by David Montgomery

The models who answered the call for this shoot were paid approximately $10 each, and another $5 if they took off their panties as well as everything else. There are nineteen women in total, all invited to a London studio after being approached in various clubs and pubs by designer King (who also worked for the *Sunday Times* magazine) and photographer Montgomery. The idea was for the women to be shown in as unglamorous a light as possible, and to make a feminist, anti-*Playboy* magazine statement. As Spinal Tap's David St. Hubbins would ask fifteen years later, "What's wrong with being sexy?" Inevitably, the sleeve was banned pretty quickly, making it much sought after by adolescent males the world over who were too young to be sold a copy of *Playboy*. Apparently Hendrix hated the cover, the darkness of the image being his major concern. Unfortunately, endless metal and rock groups have since used it as their touchstone in attempting to project their rock & roll credentials.

Robert Johnson **King of the Delta Blues Singers**

1961
Columbia Archive Recordings
America
Design and painting by Burt Goldblatt

The mythology that has grown up around Robert Johnson is entirely down to the pioneering 1961 Columbia release of his mid-1930s recordings by John Hammond. It was Hammond who gave his next signing, Bob Dylan, a promo copy of the record and Dylan became the first of many pop musicians to be inspired by it. Artwork must have represented a challenge for Columbia as there was no precedent for marketing archive material, particularly of unheard-of black blues men. Burt Goldblatt was a safe pair of hands, though. One of the finest cover artists in the business, he had designed all the sleeves for prestigious New York jazz label Bethlehem. He was equally at home with photography, drawing, typography and painting, which he claimed was born out of necessity because the budgets were so small. His overhead view of the anonymous blues guitarist playing outdoors in the bright sun captures the poetry of Johnson's recordings and is at least partly responsible for this album becoming so widely accepted.

Free Heartbreaker

1972
Island Records
England
Sleeve design by Julian Glover and
Dick Polack
Photography by Dick Polack
Graphics by CCS Associates

Free formed in England in 1968 and made up part of the burgeoning British Blues explosion, which also gave the world Led Zeppelin, Black Sabbath and Deep Purple. Centered around the guitar playing of then 17-year-old Paul Kossoff and the extraordinary voice of Paul Rodgers (who would go on to form Bad Company before replacing Freddie Mercury in Queen), Free's heavy but sparse blues-oriented songs scored them hit singles, most memorably "Alright Now" and "Wishing Well," which is taken from this, their seventh and final album together. Kossoff's heroin addiction would make him unreliable and ultimately lead to his death of heart failure at the age of twenty-five. Yet for the five years that Free existed they helped to write the rules for emerging rock bands: their recordings may be sparse and well edited, but live they could and did rock out whenever possible. The stark, negative quality to the cover image here is a perfect poster for the image of rock & roll bands of the early 1970s. Rodgers' mic stands at the Elvis angle (see p. 10), and the fist raised in salute and head bowed say, "Let's rock!"

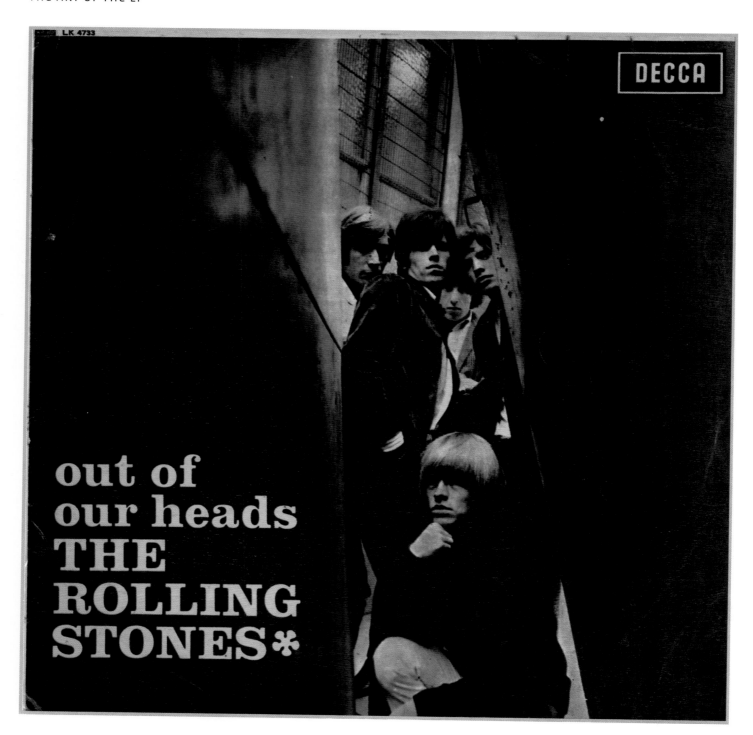

1965

Decca Records

England

Photography by Gered Mankowitz

The Rolling Stones Out of Our Heads

The fifth UK album by the Rolling Stones was issued in September 1965, a month after it had come out in the U.S.—where it not only had a different track listing but also a different sleeve. This shot—taken by Gered Mankowitz—so impressed the U.S. that the band used it for their next release *December's Children (And Everybody's)*, which came out later that year. London-born Mankowitz had been commissioned by Stones manager Andrew Loog Oldham and he later claimed that his "main qualifications were some nice snaps of Marianne Faithfull, being a nice guy, and being the son of Wolf Mankowitz"—the latter being the author of pop impresario play *Espresso Bongo*, which had been a big influence on Oldham. The very first session produced this shot. Even though the Stones had already worked with luminaries like David Bailey, this photograph wholly defined the bad boy image they would retain for the rest of their career. It also set the tone for similarly minded boy gangs who became bands.

The Who Who's Next

1971
Track Records
England
Sleeve design by Kosh
Photography by Ethan Russell

Ever since the Rolling Stones got fined for it in 1965, there's always been something rock & roll about public urination. But it's not often you see a band indulging in it on an album cover. According to photographer Ethan A. Russell, the Who were unable to pee. The picture was taken at Easington Colliery in Northeast England, which the band chanced upon returning from a gig. Often seen as a reference to the monolith in Stanley Kubrick's *2001: A Space Odyssey*, the cover was voted second to *Sticky Fingers* in VH1's Greatest Album Covers of All Time in 2003. And how did Russell mock up the urination? Easy—rainwater was tipped from an empty film canister.

The Clash The Clash

1977
CBS
England
Photography by Kate Simon

Very much the punk version of the Rolling Stones, the Clash were always focused on the aesthetics of rock & roll. No doubt inspired by the 1976 debut by the Ramones (see p. 167), photographer Kate Simon did the shoot for their debut in a grimy urban environment, and like the Stones on *Out of Our Heads*, uses a constricted view to dramatize the framing. The location was actually opposite the door to the band's Camden Rehearsal Rehearsals studio. While Simon's photograph is iconic (she has shot everyone from Andy Warhol to Bob Marley), the Clash's artwork is completed by the grainy treatment.

Frampton Comes Alive!

Peter Frampton
Frampton Comes Alive!

1976
A&M Records
America

Sleeve design by Stan Evenson
Photography by Richard E. Aaron
Art direction by Roland Young

By the end of 1976 this was the most successful double live album to have been released. Today it's still one of the best-selling live albums ever, and it was a complete surprise when it hit the top slot of the album charts in April 1976. Frampton, formerly the guitarist with British psychedelic popsters the Herd and then Humble Pie with former Small Faces leader Steve Marriott, became a rock superstar with this album. The cover, taken from the front pit of the stage by veteran rock photographer Aaron, captures Frampton in a state of near nirvana, his eyes glazed and two spotlights on either side of his head acting like a semi-halo. The foldout cover displays his Gibson Les Paul Black Beauty to perfect effect. The cover set the look for similarly minded, West Coast–influenced rockers for generations to come.

SIDE ONE:
Introduction
Something's
Happening
Doobie Wah
Show Me The Way
It's A Plain Shame

SIDE TWO:
All I Want To Be
(Is By Your Side)
Wind Of Change
Baby, I Love Your Way
I Wanna Go To The Sun

SIDE THREE:
Penny For Your
Thoughts
(I'll Give You) Money
Shine On
Jumping Jack
Flash

SIDE FOUR:
Lines On My
Face
Do You Feel
Like We Do

This stereo record can be played on mono reproducers provided either a compatible or stereo cartridge wired for mono is fitted. Recent equipment may already be fitted with a suitable cartridge. If in doubt consult your supplier.

AMLM
63703

Grand Funk Railroad Live Album

1970
Capitol
America
Sleeve design by Mark Amerling
Photography by Mark Amerling, Joe Sia

In 1971 Grand Funk (as they were mostly known) broke the Beatles' record for ticket sales at Shea Stadium, selling out in seventy-two hours. They were a great live band, and their shows were among the loudest and longest in rock history up to the late 1970s. This was the band's fourth album release in two years, and their first live one (there have been four in all). It made #5 on the Billboard Hot 200 albums chart and was certified double platinum. The photo, taken at the Atlanta International Pop Festival in July 1970, perfectly captures the movement, power and sound of the band. The black-and-white photo lends a documentary and authentic feel to the cover, and the nonironic title adds to the sense of no-nonsense boogie in which Grand Funk specialized. You know before hearing any of this album how the music on it is going to sound.

1978
Atlantic
England
Design by Bob Defrin
Photography by Jim Houghton

❗ AC/DC If You Want Blood You've Got It

The fact that this is an inarguably tasteless and tacky design has no influence on the legions of AC/DC fans who buy countless shoulder bags and T-shirts with its image emblazoned upon them. Released in 1978, AC/DC's first live album is a great record, most of which was recorded in the Glasgow Apollo on their Powerage tour earlier that year. But rather than use any authentic live shots of the band's performance, they chose to create a mock-up of guitarist Angus Young (in his trademark schoolboy outfit, no less) being stabbed with his own Gibson S.G. Graham Parker's live album of the same year (see p. 120) also featured a mocked-up, blood-related image but does it with a style that wouldn't have suited AC/DC's characteristic over-the-top approach. AC/DC's artwork was never great but, as seen here, their unmistakable logo frequently carried them through. Designer Defrin went on to create a few unforgettable album covers, three of which are in this book as examples of How Not to Do It. . . .

The Faces A Nod's as Good as a Wink . . .

1971
Warners
England
Sleeve design by Graphreaks
Models by Edwin Belchamber
Photography of models by
Rodger Banning

Despite what you might think from the cover, this is not a live album. The Faces were formed in 1969 from the ashes of the Small Faces when Steve Marriott left to form Humble Pie with Peter Frampton, and when Ronnie Wood and Rod Stewart left the Jeff Beck Group. The "Small" was dropped and the Faces became one of the best live bands around. Which is why this cover, with its front image of the band and the crowd so close to them as to look as if they're also on stage, was so appealing to fans at the time. The rear image of hand-knitted models of the band perfectly captures the Faces' humor and wit. With this release, their third, they had their first big hit single, "Stay with Me" (#17 in the U.S., #6 in the UK) but were becoming better known for their lead singer, Rod Stewart, who had hit #1 on both sides of the Atlantic with "Maggie May," and with his "solo" album *Every Picture Tells a Story*, on which all the Faces appear. The great thing about this cover, though, is that there's no clear star of the show; they look like a band having fun. Try to make them all out on the stage.

Rolling Stones Sticky Fingers

1971
**Rolling Stones Records/Atlantic
America**
Cover concept by Andy Warhol
Graphic design by Craig Braun
Photography by Billy Name

Sticky Fingers in many ways represents the ultimate in major rock band artwork: witty, extravagant, salacious and self-indulgent, it grows increasingly iconic as the genre ages—it was voted Greatest Album Sleeve Ever by VH1 in 2003. This was the Stones' first album on their newly formed Rolling Stones Records, so who better to turn to than pop artist Andy Warhol (see pp. 225, 242, 254). He conceived having a real zipper mounted on the crotch of a pair of very well-filled jeans. Once unzipped, the card underneath would reveal a pair of underpants overstamped with Warhol's signature logo. Warhol "Superstar" and photographer Billy Name took shots of many men, including Factory star Joe Dallesandro; but one thing is certain—the crotch is not Jagger's. Craig Braun put it all together and almost got sued by Atlantic when the zipper was found to be damaging the vinyl (usually on the track "Sister Morphine"). Braun's solution was to get it shipped with the zipper at half mast. The album also marks the debut of the infamous Tongue and Lip logo, by young British designer John Pashe.

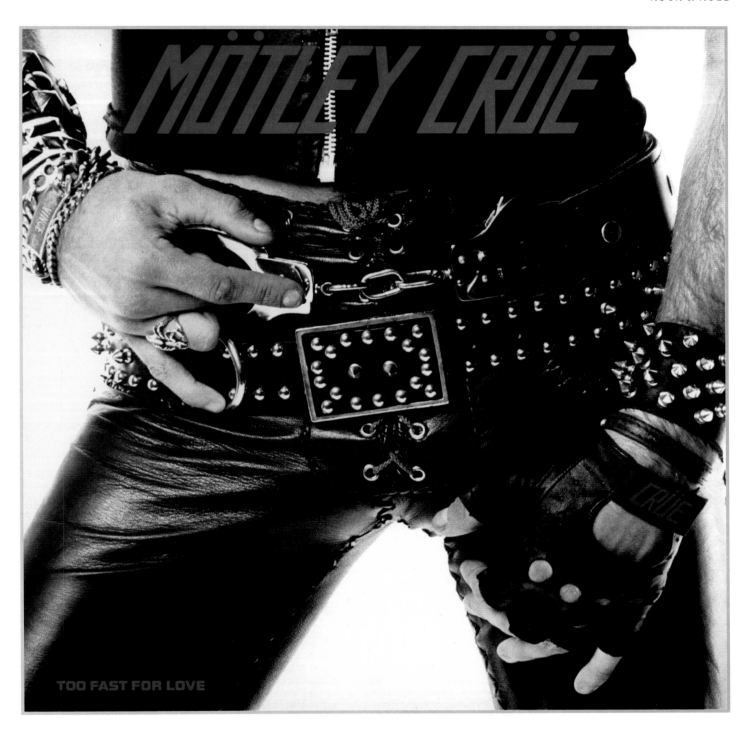

TOO FAST FOR LOVE

Mötley Crüe Too Fast for Love

1982
Elektra
America
Sleeve concept by Coffman & Coffman
Productions
Photography by Michael Pinter

You gotta love a band who, with their first album, emulates one of the greatest and most recognizable cover designs of all time, right? As they're situated on these pages you can see the comparison, and the fact that the original is more subtle and more witty. Though to be fair to the Crüe, the early 1980s were not a time for subtlety if you wanted to make it in the shiny leather trousers, makeup and poodle-perm world of LA metal. Which is also why this is a great R&R cover. From the crude joke of the title through its crude repro of the Stones' iconic image, this is full of attitude and machismo. The Crüe also gets points for not having a Derek Smalls-type pickle moment too. The cover was apparently the idea of the band's managers, (Allan) Coffman & (Barbara) Coffman, who so believed in the band that they formed a record label (Leathür Records) to release the first version of this album, using the same artwork. Allan Coffman died of a brain tumor in 1992, but his inspired creation lives on here in the form of Crüe singer Vince Neil's crotch.

THUNDER ROAD

Bruce Springsteen: guitar, vocals, harmonica
Garry Tallent: bass guitar
Max M. Weinberg: drums
Roy Bittan: Fender Rhodes, glockenspiel
Clarence Clemons: saxophones
Background vocals: Roy Bittan,
Mike Appel, Steve Van Zandt

TENTH AVENUE FREEZE-OUT

Bruce Springsteen: guitar, vocals
Garry Tallent: bass guitar
Max M. Weinberg: drums
Roy Bittan: piano
Clarence Clemons: tenor saxophone
†Randy Brecker: trumpet, flugel horn
†Michael Brecker: tenor saxophone
**Dave Sanborn: baritone saxophone
Wayne Andre: trombone

NIGHT

Bruce Springsteen: guitar, vocals
Garry Tallent: bass guitar
Max M. Weinberg: drums
Roy Bittan: piano, harpsichord, glockenspiel
Clarence Clemons: saxophone

BACKSTREETS

Bruce Springsteen: guitar, vocals
Garry Tallent: bass guitar
Max M. Weinberg: drums
Roy Bittan: piano, organ

°BORN TO RUN

Bruce Springsteen: guitar, vocals
Garry Tallent: bass guitar
Ernest "Boom" Carter: drums
*David Sancious: keyboards
Danny Federici: organ
Clarence Clemons: saxophone

SHE'S THE ONE

Bruce Springsteen: guitar, vocals
Garry Tallent: bass guitar
Max M. Weinberg: drums
Roy Bittan: piano, harpsichord, organ
Clarence Clemons: saxophone

MEETING ACROSS THE RIVER

Bruce Springsteen: vocals
Roy Bittan: piano
Richard Davis: bass
†Randy Brecker: trumpet

JUNGLELAND

Bruce Springsteen: guitar, vocals
Garry Tallent: bass guitar
Max M. Weinberg: drums
Roy Bittan: piano, organ
Clarence Clemons: tenor saxophone
Strings arranged and conducted by Charles Calello

†Appear courtesy of Arista Records
*Appears courtesy of Epic Records
**Appears courtesy of Warner Reprise

PRODUCED BY BRUCE SPRINGSTEEN, JOHN LANDAU, AND MIKE APPEL
°PRODUCED BY BRUCE SPRINGSTEEN, AND MIKE APPEL

© 1975 CBS Inc. / ℗ 1975 CBS Inc. / CBS is a trademark of CBS Inc. USA. INTERPAK I BY SHOREWOOD PACKAGING CO. LTD. ENGLAND.

1975
Columbia
America
Sleeve design by Andy Engel and
John Berg
Photography by Eric Meola

Bruce Springsteen Born to Run

Photographer Eric Meola apparently took over nine hundred shots during the session for *Born to Run*, "but when we saw the contact sheets, that one just sort of popped . . . ," he later wrote in *Born to Run: The Unseen Photos*. Meola's decision to let the band relax and play while he shot them was clearly prudent. The final picture captures the relaxed camaraderie of Springsteen's band—saxophonist Clarence Clemons happily playing on as a grinning band leader leans affectionately on his shoulder, as well as the classic rock & roll cool of Springsteen himself, in white T-shirt, black leather jacket, tousled hair. And low-slung guitar. The narrow font was unusual for the time but now adds to the sleeve's timelessness.

BRUCE SPRINGSTEEN

BORN TO RUN

R.S.O. DELUXE 2479 201
CASSETTE NO. 3216 196

COCAINE
WONDERFUL TONIGHT
LAY DOWN SALLY
NEXT TIME YOU SEE HER
WE'RE ALL THE WAY

THE CORE
MAY YOU NEVER
MEAN OLD FRISCO
PEACHES AND DIESEL

THIS SOUND RECORDING WAS MADE BY THE ROBERT
STIGWOOD ORGANISATION LIMITED OF 67 BROOK
STREET, LONDON W.1. FIRST PUBLISHED IN THE
U.K. 1977. ©ROBERT STIGWOOD ORGANISATION 1977.
RECORD MANUFACTURED AND DISTRIBUTED BY
POLYDOR LTD. 17-19 STRATFORD PLACE,
LONDON W1N 0BL.

IMPORTANT NOTICE
COPYRIGHT EXISTS IN ALL RECORDS ISSUED BY
POLYDOR LIMITED. ANY UNAUTHORISED
BROADCASTING, PUBLIC PERFORMANCE, COPYING
OR RE-RECORDING OF SUCH RECORDS IN ANY
MANNER WHATSOEVER WILL CONSTITUTE AN
INFRINGEMENT OF SUCH COPYRIGHT. APPLICATION
FOR PUBLIC PERFORMANCE LICENCE SHOULD BE
ADDRESSED TO:- PHONOGRAPHIC PERFORMANCE
LIMITED, GANTON HOUSE, 14-22 GANTON STREET,
LONDON W1V 2LB.

1977
RSO Records
America
Sleeve design and art direction by
David Stewart and Nell for El and
Nell Ink
Photography by Watal Asamuma

Eric Clapton Slowhand

After his previous two album releases had failed to match the success
of *461 Ocean Boulevard* of 1974 (in similar fashion as live album *E.C. Was
Here*; see p. 59), Eric Clapton changed musical directions slightly, away
from his blues roots and into a more country style for *Slowhand*. It worked
and this album not only made #2 on the Billboard charts but went on to
give him three huge hit singles: "Wonderful Tonight," "Lay Down Sally" and
"Cocaine." Perhaps the cover design helped to persuade old Clapton fans to
try him again. It's all about the guitar, and while the graphics echo those of
Springsteen's *Born to Run* (see previous page), the photo doesn't feature
Clapton's face; neither does he have a pal to lean on. Just the guitar.

ERIC CLAPTON
SLOWHAND

Cheap Trick, In Color.

Cheap Trick In Color

1977
Epic Records
America
Photography by Benno Friedman
Design by Jim Charne and Paula Scher

A great record in a very disappointing sleeve. Why? Well first, Cheap Trick's debut had defined their look, with the kids'-printing-set logo, the handsome singer Robin Zander and the gurning geek guitarist Rick Nielsen. Second, that sleeve was in black and white. Now with their second effort, *In Color*, they leave the less aesthetically pleasing band members to the back cover (in black and white, riding bicycles—get it?) and concentrate on creating a classic rock & roll shot—handsome, long-haired men, looking mean and tousled on motorbikes. Except, importantly, part of the band's appeal was Nielsen and the contrast between his escaped-lunatic-with-guitar look and Zander's pretty-boy appeal. Plus—and here is the big one that renders this sleeve null and void—Zander and bassist Tom Petterson have their bike stands down. Neither very rock nor very roll, the stabilizing effect of the stands preventing any kind of movement at all, in fact. The result is that they look like girls on an amusement park ride and not mean, butch bikers. Although, maybe that was what they wanted, after all?

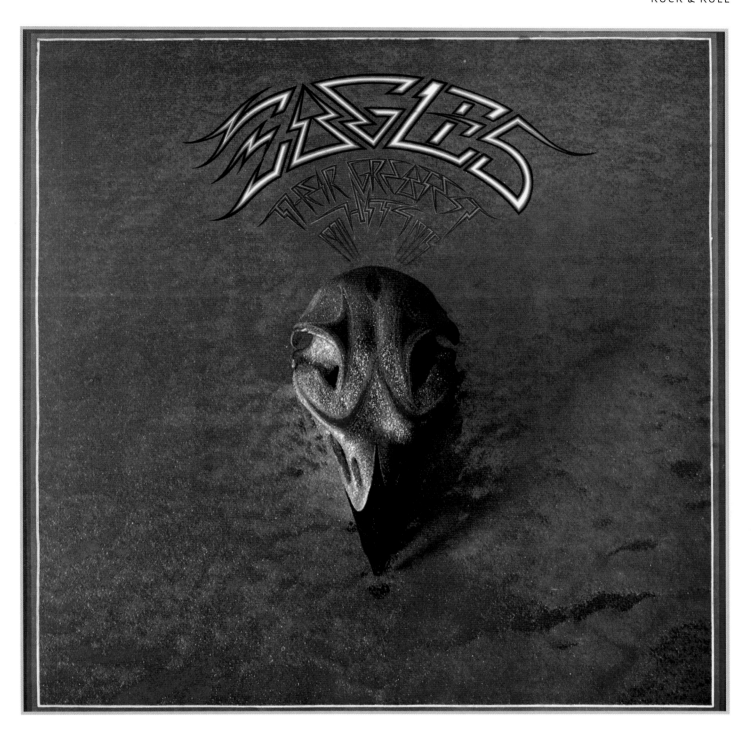

The Eagles Their Greatest Hits 1971—1975

1976
Elektra
America

Art direction and sleeve design by
Boyd Elder and Glen Christensen
Photography by Tom Kelly Jr.
Lettering by Henry Diltz

At the time of writing this album had supposedly sold 20 million copies in America alone. And there's not a single photograph of the band to be found anywhere on this remarkable sleeve. The eagle skull, painted as if a part of some ancient ceremony, is wonderfully photographed and San Francisco photographic legend Henry Diltz supplied perfect lettering. The blue is that of the sky or sea in California. It's enigmatic, appealing and so much simpler than the scores of Prog Rock covers that attempted a similar style in the wake of this album selling its first million copies.

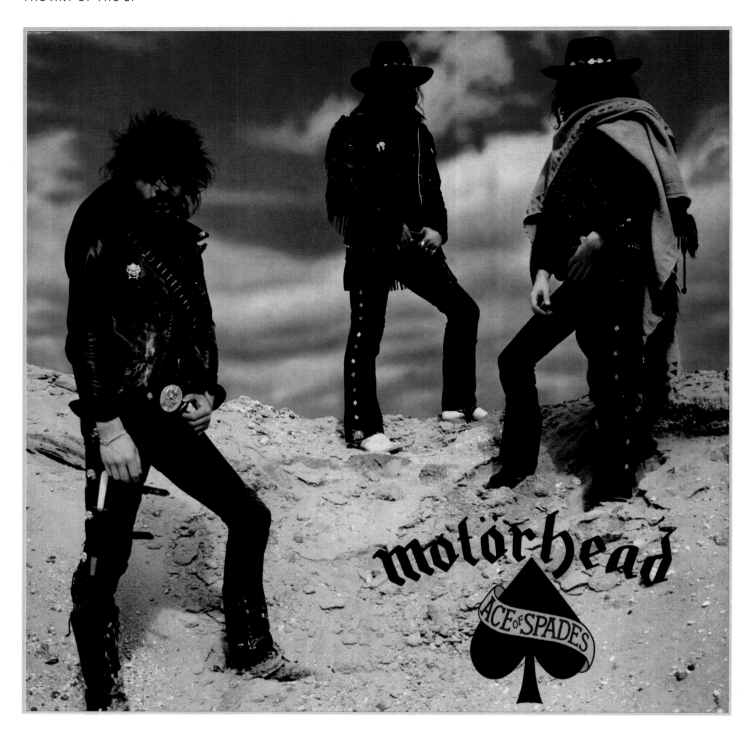

Motörhead Ace of Spades

1980
Bronze
England
Sleeve design by Martin Poole
Photography by Alan Ballard

The first Motörhead album to really make them big, *Ace of Spades* (their fourth) was also the first to feature the band on the cover. Usually precedence was given to their distinctive logo with its umlaut over the *O*. Asked by *Wave Magazine* if this German diacritical mark should affect pronunciation of the band's name, Lemmy said, "No . . . I only put it in there to look mean." Which is also the reason for this shot—Wild West outlaws standing in the desert. Although, again, all is not quite what it seems. Apparently the shoot took place in a sandpit just outside London. Regardless, the black leather and outlaw biker chic displayed here went from being a gay fancy dress look in the late 1980s to a cliché of rock & roll attire, greatly helped by Motörhead's rise to the status of rock gods. Along with the logo, the other thing that all Motörhead sleeves have in common is the band's "War-Pig" icon. The logo was designed by Joe Petagno for their debut and he carried on creating versions of it until he fell out with the band in 2007. Here it appears on drummer Phil "Philthy Animal" Taylor's badge.

1979
Epic/CBS
America
Photography by Reid Miles
Design by Paula Scher and
Steve Dessau

Cheap Trick Dream Police

Oh no! They've done it again! One could argue that the reason the massively successful Cheap Trick never quite took off in Britain was because the aesthetically superficial record-buying public there just couldn't get their heads around the terrible artwork. Well, that and there being no FM rock radio to play their music nonstop. In their homeland, this is the band's biggest-selling album to date, regardless of the fact that it came housed in some low-rent sci-fi fantasy episode, involving band members in various states of discomfort. In fact, the only band member who looks in any way happy about the proceedings is Rick Nielson (top left), whose exhibitionist disposition one suspects was perhaps partly responsible for the sleeve concept. Surely, it can't all have been Reid Miles'sj idea? The photographer, Blue Note owner and architect of some of the greatest sleeves ever cannot be held fully responsible for this one!

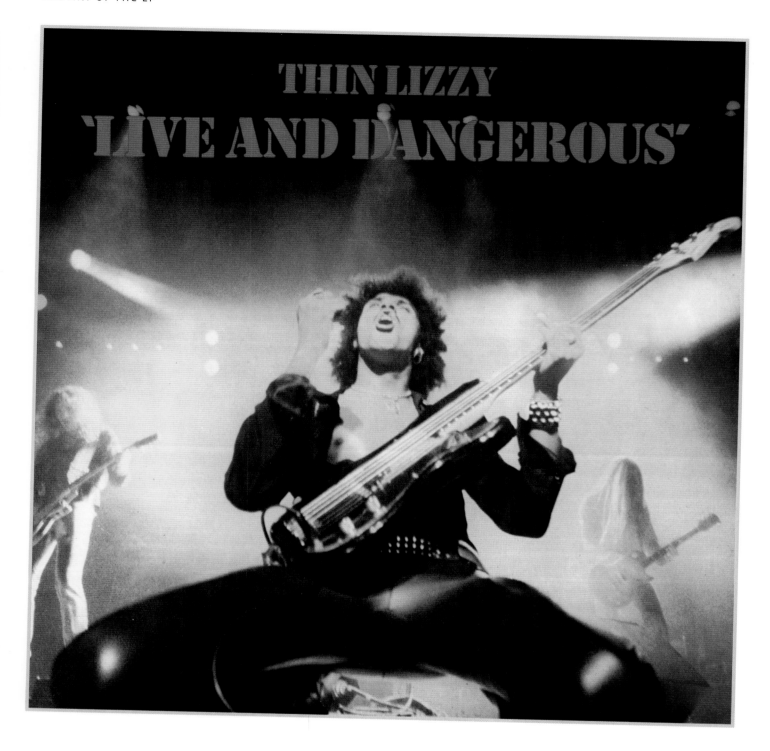

1978
Vertigo
England
Cover concept by Thin Lizzy and
Chalkie Davies
Artwork and layout by Chris O'Donnell
and Sutton Cooper
Photography by Chalkie Davies

Thin Lizzy Live and Dangerous

Irish rockers Thin Lizzy enjoyed a reputation as hard-living, hard-rocking "boys," and their biggest hit, "The Boys Are Back in Town," is still used as a musical cliché to announce the entrance of football teams, boxers, wrestlers or any similarly macho collection of males onto a stage. Bassist, singer and songwriter Phil Lynott was the most high-profile black rocker of the age and he enjoyed a reputation for being a party animal. That's him, crotch out, bass flying, face contorted, with lights projecting him out on the front of the sleeve. Scrunch your eyes and it could almost be Hendrix, right? That was the idea, anyway. It's hard to believe that by this time the Sex Pistols, Clash, Ramones and Television had changed the whole notion of what a "guitar hero" should or shouldn't be, but Lynott had joined forces with Cook and Jones of the Pistols once they'd disbanded, and played a few low-key live gigs with them as the Greedy Bastards. Lynott died in 1986, of multiple organ failure caused by long-term drug abuse. He was thirty-six years old.

1987
Paisley Park/WEA
America
Sleeve design uncredited
Photography uncredited

Prince Sign o' the Times

Less than ten years had passed since the sleeve opposite, but so much had changed. In the late 1970s black musicians like Lynott playing rock music for a living were rare. Funk, disco and dance-oriented music yes, but not screaming lead guitar of the kind that—irony of ironies—Jimi Hendrix had made popular. Thin Lizzy were looking like relics from the past by the time they made it big, and Prince was beginning to put his screaming guitar solos over beats and rhythms that James Brown, Parliament/Funkadelic and Chic would have been proud of, but appealing to white audiences like no other African American had since Sly Stone got busted. The difference between then ('78) and now ('87) is perfectly summed up by this cover image. The "stage" is a mess of neon, drum kit, flowers (is that Elvis's face on the right, peeking from the bass bin?), keyboards and Cadillac, while Prince, or half of him, stands so close to the camera that he'll never be in focus (never categorized, perhaps?). His custom-built guitar lays dead center between him/us and the stage.

Stray Cats Stray Cats

1981
Arista Records
England
Sleeve design by Malcolm Garret for
Assorted iMaGes
Photography by Gavin Cochrane

It's often seemed like the more things change in rock & roll, the more they stay the same. Twenty-five years after the release of the first Elvis Presley album, three young Americans, none of whom were born when it was released, traveled to England. They played the kind of rockabilly style music that Elvis, Scotty and Bill liked, and which continued to be played long after Elvis had joined the army by the likes of Link Wray, Johnny Burnette and Carl Perkins. At the end of the 1970s the British rock & roll revival was in full swing and the Cats got a lot of bookings because of it. They signed to a UK label and made this, their first album. The look, with exaggerated quiffs, skin-tight drainpipe jeans and biker jackets, match the vintage stand-up slap bass and semi-acoustic guitar with snare drum beat (they all stood to play). The look found its way into non-Rockabilly bands too: look at photos of Echo & the Bunnymen, the Cure or Thompson Twins from that period for proof.

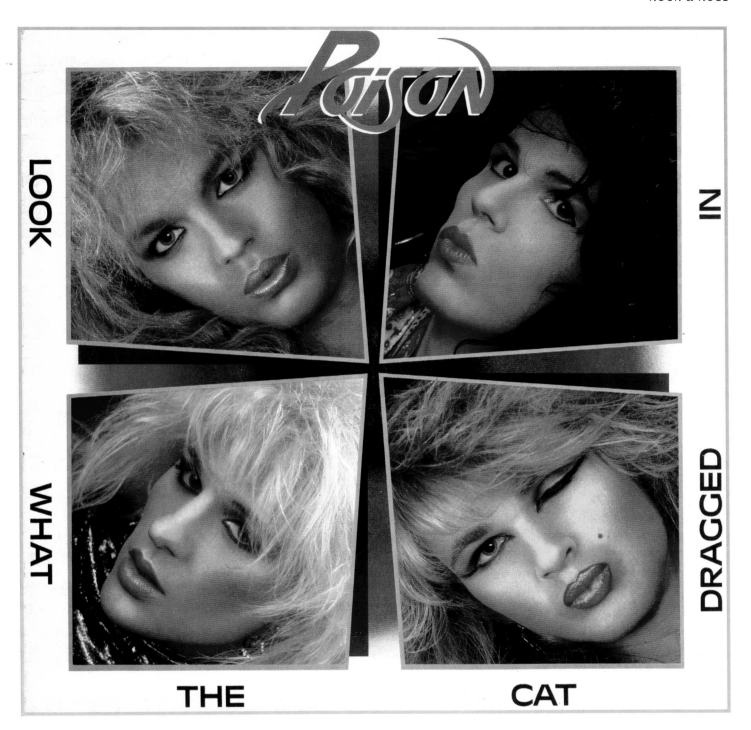

Poison Look What the Cat Dragged In

1986
Enigma/Capitol
America
Sleeve design uncredited
Photography uncredited

While in Britain young Americans were remembering Bill Haley and Elvis, in Los Angeles they were discovering the New York Dolls. A wave of "glam metal" acts came out of LA in the 1980s, among them Mötley Crüe, Quiet Riot and Twisted Sister. Then came Poison, who wore more makeup and teased their hair higher than any rocking boy band had since Johansen, Sylvain, Thunders and Killer Kane back in the early 1970s. This, their debut release, manages to pastiche the final Beatles album cover, *Let It Be*, make a joke about the way they look in its title, and put the band across as pouting, lipsticked, fun-lovin' guys. It could only be an album by an LA glam metal act of the 1980s and it could only go on to influence successive generations of wannabe gender-bending rockers from the West Coast.

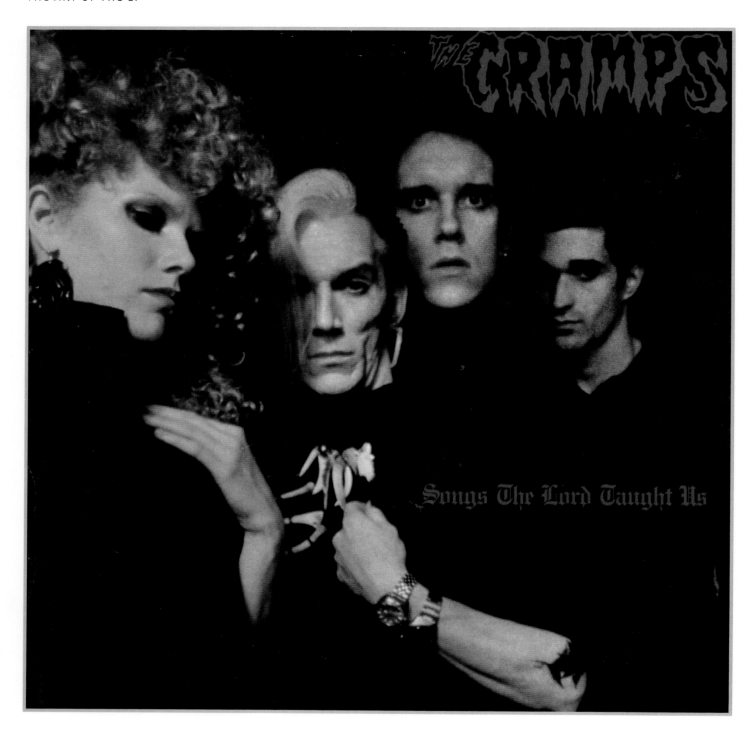

1980
Illegal Records
England
Sleeve concept by the Cramps
Photography by David Arnoff

The Cramps Songs the Lord Taught Us

The source of the Goth, this album influenced a whole wave of similarly gothic-minded rockers in how to look and sound. An original part of the 1976 CBGB's punk scene, the Cramps' high-octane rockabilly sound didn't go down as well in the U.S. as the more metal-sounding Ramones or arty Television and Patti Smith. So they found an English record label and the new wave of rockabillies took them to their hearts. Cramps songs about zombies and voodoo were so much more frightening and thrilling than the cartoon camp horror of the Damned. The Cure's Robert Smith, Siouxsie Sioux, Nick Cave and Bauhaus's Pete Murphy were among the first to find inspiration in the antics of Lux Interior (sadly deceased in 2009) and his wife Poison Ivy, but others soon followed: America's Gun Club always had more success in the UK, for instance, where they'd play headline over acts who looked like the Cramps, such as Sisters of Mercy and Sex Gang Children. The influence of the Cramps and this record was still being felt, thirty years after it was recorded.

LL Cool J Radio

1985
Def Jam
America
Sleeve design uncredited

LL Cool J was the first rapper to follow Run DMC with an album release. Run DMC's artwork was prescient in that it featured a photo of the rappers in street pose with a logo above, a formula that was to become the norm until the early 1990s. Def Jam's first album has a much more conceptual sleeve and the then 17-year-old LL does not even appear. This more bold approach did not adversely affect album sales and it seems a shame that its gauntlet was never picked up by subsequent rap releases. LL Cool J's stripped-down rap style, "reduced," as the sleeve credit ironically states, by producer Rick Rubin, is reflected perfectly in the simple cover, a close-up shot of the then ubiquitous "boom box," as originally used on the street by every aspiring rapper. Movie director Spike Lee used one just like it as the star of his *Do the Right Thing* (1989), in which the destruction of the boom box (blasting Public Enemy's "Fight the Power") sets off a chain of events resulting in murder and riot. The boom box became the symbol of a whole new wave of rock & roll resistance for the next ten years.

SƐX

"What's wrong with being sexy?" asked Nigel Tufnel in *This is Spinal Tap*, when the sleeve for *Smell the Glove* is accused of being sexist. It's a neat joke because even if artists are aware of any linguistic distinction, the parameters of taste and acceptability are changing constantly. There are several provocative sleeves in this chapter, some of which could be considered sexist, certainly. Those scantily clad German girls whom Bryan Ferry "scouted" for *Country Life* perhaps. Or Jane Birkin's revealing a camel toe on *Histoire De Melody Nelson*. Others, however, might consider these sleeves artistic and, yes, sexy. We do, for example.

As stated in the previous section, rock & roll has always been about sex, and the artists responsible for the following sleeves clearly saw it necessary to make that link more obvious. That is, if they had anything to do with the sleeve design, which wasn't always the case—or so some of them would later claim.

It helps if the artist in question is a beautiful woman, perhaps—the early 1960s girl singers probably did not even reflect that they were selling sex, but as the genre became more sophisticated, canny stars recognized that they were the whole package, not just the music.

Like food, sex can be served according to taste; there is little in common between, say, Ohio Players' *Fire* and Suede's debut—one objectifies/celebrates the female form, the other is a close-up shot of two disabled lesbians kissing. Sex in sleeve artwork is very much like the act itself: when done right there is nothing better; when done wrong, nothing worse.

What follows are some examples of how it is done right, plus a few examples of how it is done wrong.

Aerosmith *Pump*

1989
Geffen
America
Art direction by Kim Champagne,
Gabrielle Raumberger
Logo design by Andy Engel
Photography by Norman Seeff

Released off the back of the band's big return to form, *Permanent Vacation*, *Pump* came out when Aerosmith was very much back in vogue. But rather than repeat the sort of cover art used on that album—simply a repeating image of the band's logo—with *Pump* they opted for a witty representation of the title. The 1940s pick-up trucks in mid-coitus pretty much work on their own, without the additional reminder of the album title on the smaller truck's door and the inevitable band logo in the top left. Aerosmith is always best when singing about sex and this album opens with possibly their finest song on the subject: "Love in an Elevator," which contains some pretty close-to-the-bone lyrics for a hit single. How pleasing then that they chose not to go down the common heavy rock artwork route of producing a literal interpretation of the songs. There's a certain irony in the cover photo being taken by Norman Seeff, who is best known by rock fans for his portrait of Carly Simon in her nightie used on the cover of *Playing Possum* (1975), one of the "sexiest" sleeves of the decade.

1958
Liberty
America
Sleeve design uncredited
Photography uncredited

Julie London Julie

Even before rock & roll had hit America, record companies had used what were euphemistically called "cheesecake" photos of pinup girls on the cover of the most unlikely recordings, in an attempt to sex up the record; there are some serious and well-regarded classical recordings that employed the technique. Some of the better uses of the female form to sell odd records are to be found in the pages of this book. Here is an unusual cheesecake cover, insofar as it is the singer herself posing, legs akimbo in a nicely symmetrical net-back chair. Julie London, born to vaudeville parents, became a stage trouper at the age of fourteen and graduated to being a GI pinup in World War II before being discovered working in a London hotel (hence her stage name) by Alan Ladd's wife, an agent. Julie scored a worldwide hit with "Cry Me a River" in 1955 but could never follow it up. After Elvis hit, Julie turned from pop songs to jazz singing, and this is her first jazz record. Not that she was going to go all serious and reserved on her public. Not while she had those legs to show off.

1959
Jaro International
America
Sleeve design by Mauro Studios

Babs Gonzales Tales of Manhattan

Newark, New Jersey—born Gonzales' real name was Lee Brown, and he was the pre-eminent Bop scat-vocalist of the 1940s. As leader of Three Bips and a Bap he sang nonsense words over the horn playing of Charlie Parker and Dizzy Gillespie. In 1951 he formed a band with James Moody and played cooler Bop for a couple of years, developing his Beat Poet schtick, which is given full vent on this recording. Accompanying Babs here are Kenny Burrell on guitar, Roy Haynes on drums and Les Spann on flute. The cover says it all, though: the beautiful woman who looks like Claudia Cardinale exiting a car on what looks like the Upper East Side of Manhattan. She's dishevelled, the light suggests it could be early morning, and the man in the car whom she's just left is wearing shades. This is the cool philosophy of Manhattan as written about by Capote and O'Hara in *Breakfast at Tiffany's* and *BUtterfield 8* (O'Hara's story being the first to tell the tale of supposedly respectable young women who make their way in New York from party to party.) Babs's "Broadway 4am" sums it up perfectly.

the world of reggae vol. 1. **claude sang**   sugar

1970
Sugar Records
Jamaica
Photography by David Wedgbury

Claude Sang The World of Reggae Vol. 1

A decade after Babs Gonzales used the Italian-looking model to sell his jazz poetry, Jamaican singing star Claude Sang chose a Jamaican model to sell his *World of Reggae Vol. 1*. English Reggae label Trojan had been using semi-naked Afro-Caribbean models to sell their *Tighten Up* compilations since 1968 (see p. 58), but Claude—or photographer David Wedgbury—has gone for a far softer, more romantic image than their action shots. The model here is shown in a romantic light (despite also showing her chicken pox scars), and the sexiness comes from her vulnerability, not her brazenness. Photographer Wedgbury was the in-house photographer at Decca Records and shot, among others, the cover of the John Mayall's Bluesbreakers album on which Eric Clapton is reading the *Beano*. Sang was never as big a star as Johnny Nash or Jimmy Cliff outside of his native Jamaica, but at home he was something of a Tom Jones-style crooner. The reggae on this album is very pop, the songs closer to London's Tin Pan Alley in spirit than the Kingston yards that inspired Cliff and Bob Marley.

51

The George Shearing Quintet
On the Sunny Side of the Strip

1960
Capitol
America
Sleeve design and photography
uncredited

By the end of the 1950s there was an adult audience for light jazz music
who bought into the glamor of sophisticated swing. Record companies
worked hard to reach this audience. Blind pianist George Shearing had
been making cool, sophisticated and untroubling jazz successfully ever
since migrating from his native London to America in 1947. His chic appeal
is enhanced by clever marketing on this album, with two elegant couples,
dressed in evening wear and either on their way to or from a smart club
and jazz supper. The physical contact between the men and women is
a deliberate nudge toward what will be happening between them—and
by extension all fans of such sophisticated boom-boom—when they get
to their rooms. "The Strip," as it was becoming known from TV shows
and advertisements selling the good life, was in reality dirty, noisy and
dangerous at night. Although clearly not the night this album was recorded
at the Crescent Club.

SUMP'N
ELSE

Jerry
Allen

1966
Columbia Records
England
Sleeve design by Denis Preston
Photography by Michael Joseph

Jerry Allen Sump'n Else

This very cool and hip young woman is "selling" an album of organ music, played by a middle-aged man who is more used to playing cinema organs at end-of-pier shows on the British coast than the sort of fashionable music suggested by the cover. Jerry Allen had briefly been a TV star in the mid-1950s when he cohosted something called *Lunchbox* for independent TV channel ABC. On the show he and his trio would accompany various pop balladeers of the day as they sang their latest hit. The success of albums of muzak, on which pop hits of the time are played by competent musicians, was led by big band leaders such as James Last or Mantovani, whose records sold in the millions around the world. This was one of Allen's attempts at becoming a middle-of-the-road superstar. The cover is remarkable for its hipness, doubly so considering the record it is selling. The girl is wearing the right gear for an American market, where the British Dolly Bird—as personified by Jane Asher (Paul McCartney's then girlfriend) and Twiggy—was hugely influential in fashion and makeup trends.

Dick Hyman & Harpsichord Happening!

1969
Command
America
Sleeve design by Enoch Light
Photography by Color Library
International

A gifted pianist, arranger and composer, Dick Hyman (born in 1927 in New York) played many forms of jazz piano on hundreds of recordings, many of them in his own name and on Enoch Light's Command label, as here. Hyman also composed or arranged, played piano on or conducted, recordings of many of Woody Allen's New York-based movies from the early 1980s on. So why the cheesecake to sell his records? Look at the date of release. It could easily be ten years earlier, and in many ways for fans of Dick's records it was always ten years earlier. By the end of the 1960s audiences could watch full-frontal nudity on stage and screen, read pornographic books (if over 21) or take part in naked happenings in public places. By contemporary standards, this modestly attired woman is positively over-dressed, but she's still selling muzak—and showing some cleavage. In the 1970s women would become increasingly less dressed on album covers of similar releases.

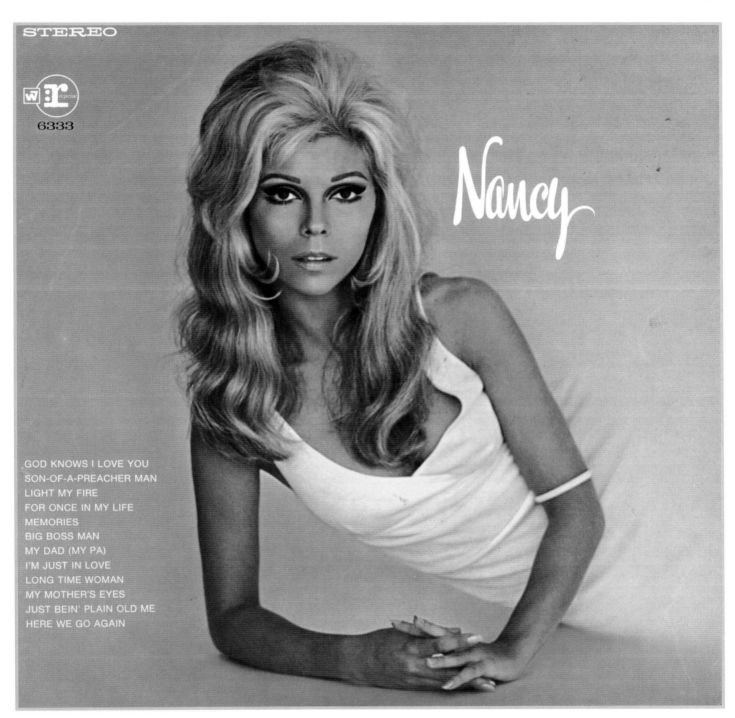

STEREO

r

6333

Nancy

GOD KNOWS I LOVE YOU
SON-OF-A-PREACHER MAN
LIGHT MY FIRE
FOR ONCE IN MY LIFE
MEMORIES
BIG BOSS MAN
MY DAD (MY PA)
I'M JUST IN LOVE
LONG TIME WOMAN
MY MOTHER'S EYES
JUST BEIN' PLAIN OLD ME
HERE WE GO AGAIN

1969
Reprise Records
America
Art direction by Ed Thrasher
Photography by Ron Joy

Nancy Sinatra Nancy

Compare this pose with that of Julie London on page 49. Or that of the model opposite. All three are using sexuality to sell a record, all have a certain amount of bare flesh on display. Only this one doesn't look slightly ridiculous, though. Frank's daughter may look dated by her hair and makeup, but she also looks composed, in control, and her direct stare at the viewer is unflinching, unapologetic. Confrontational, almost, which wouldn't be surprising given who she was and what her public persona was at the time. Ever since scoring a big hit with "These Boots are Made for Walking" in 1966, Nancy had released records in which the female narrator of the song often displayed feminist principles. Or at least wouldn't take no mess from her man. Here is a strong woman, who is also sexy; it can be done. Art director Thrasher was an old pal and employee of Frank Sinatra and would go on to direct several iconic sleeves. Photographer Ron Joy was a well-known pop band photographer in LA who made a name for himself after capturing the Beatles on film in 1964.

1963
Brunswick
America
Sleeve design uncredited
Photography uncredited

Brenda Lee All Alone Am I

Known as "Little Miss Dynamite" for her small stature and big voice, Brenda Lee had her first big hit in 1958 when she was just fourteen. By the time of this, her eighth album, she was a seasoned singer and performer, but still only nineteen years old. The title track of this album gave Lee a #3 hit single in November 1962, and was based on the melody of an Academy Award-winning movie theme, *Never on Sunday*. Greek actress Melina Mercouri played a prostitute in the movie which, being underage at the time, Lee wasn't allowed to see. This photo of the singer almost smoulders. Alone in a spotlight, surrounded by blackness, clearly she's alone, but what does she do while alone? Her enigmatic pout and the almost painterly way her left hand wavers across her shoulder combine to create an artistic image of longing.

1971
Music for Pleasure
England
Sleeve design by BWD Productions
Photography uncredited

❗ Various Smash Hits '71

In 1967 an enterprising Australian named Bill Wellings came up with the great idea of getting session musicians and singers to record note-perfect versions of the hit singles of the day, and released them on budget-priced vinyl records. Of course it featured a scantily clad female on the cover and sold well enough that by 1970 Wellings's company BWD Productions had launched Hot Hits using a similar format (and cover style; Volume 12 features a woman in a fishnet dress straddling a tennis net holding a racquet with clearly no idea which end to hit the ball with). Some of the BWD covers are great. Of the others this has to be a contender for the "What is that?" award. The woman is wearing a bikini bottom with an enormous diaper pin in it, the baby wears a matching diaper and looks very unhappy. On the reverse, they are wearing different but still matching diapers. What is the message here? Sex makes babies? Women are often somebody's mother? Women were once babies too? The lack of retouching means her legs are the color and consistency of tangerines. Sexy it ain't.

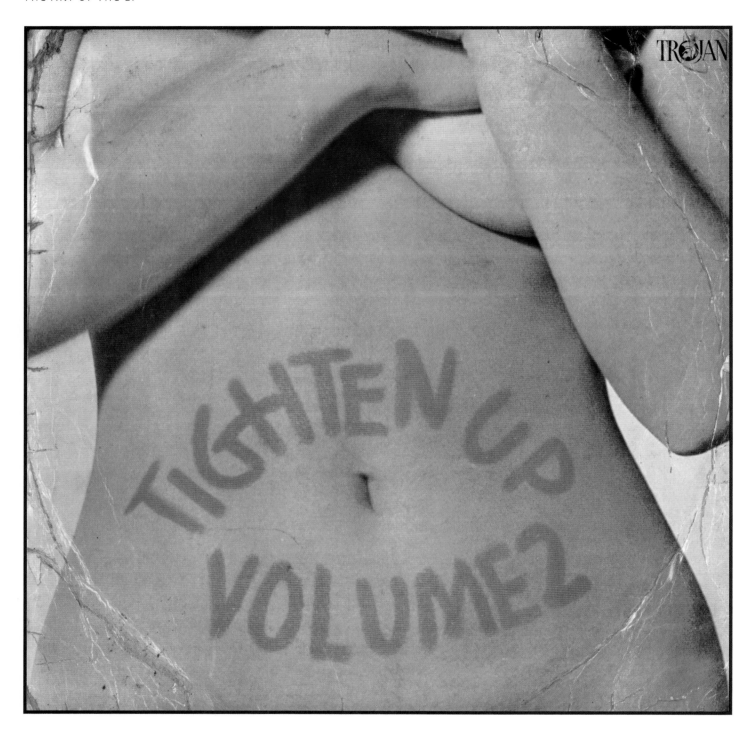

1971
Trojan
England
Sleeve design by CCS Advertising
Photography by Tim Fulford-Brown

! Various Artists *Tighten Up Volume 2*

The follow-up to Trojan's 1969 compilation, this is the album that many British reggae fans remember as the one that initially got them into reggae music. The compilations were budget priced and contained the label's recently released hottest tracks. As with Island's *Club Ska 67* (see p. 103), those at the label must have debated long and hard as to how to market reggae compilations given the lack of established visual code. Volume 1 simply had a picture of black women in tribal headdress on the front, so perhaps this one is more well known because of its appallingly tacky sleeve. But seen in the context of what its purpose was—to be sold in budget-priced record stores, filed alongside chart compilations, which invariably featured a bikini-clad girl grinning on the front—the sleeve makes sense. Sex sells! the marketing department must have shouted at the reggae purists at Trojan who complained.

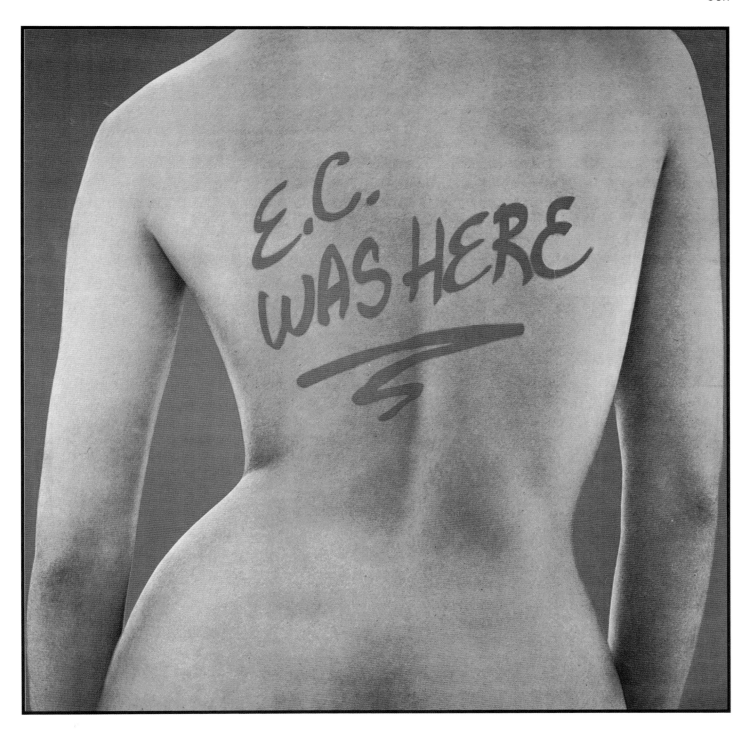

1975
RSO/Polydor
America
Sleeve design by El & Nell Ink
Photography by Frank Moscati

⚠ **Eric Clapton** E.C. Was Here

This live album is a return to Clapton's blues roots after he had kicked heroin. Clearly he still wasn't thinking straight, though. El and Nell's credited "art direction" is nothing more than a simple idea that had already been done (see previous page) and which objectifies women crassly. There is no excuse for this cover, which makes reference to the graffiti that had appeared around the country several years before: "Clapton is God." No doubt the defense offered for the idea is that the graffiti on the woman's back signifies the "love 'em and leave 'em" macho pose which has become such a cliché in rock lore. The mid-seventies were not the most enlightened time, yet Clapton would soon suffer for other unenlightened comments, about immigration, which then had him branded a racist. If you manage to get past the artwork, however, the album has the pureness and soul that is absent in the cover—the reverse has a photo of an enormous cleavage.

Ohio Players Fire

Their first Mercury release focused on a woman's legs, in a kneeling position. Here is what could be a still from an expensive porno flick of the time. The symbolism is crude, but the #1 on her helmet is a statement of intent and achievement from the Players: the title track made #1 on the pop as well as the R&B charts the same week that the LP reached the top of the album charts. With a hit single and that cover, it was always destined to be a success.

1974
Mercury Records
America
Sleeve design by Len Willis
Photography by Stan Malinowski
Art direction by Jim Ladwig/AGI

Donald Byrd Street Lady

1973
Blue Note
America
Art direction and photography by
Mike Salisbury

In 1972 jazz trumpeter Donald Byrd recorded and released a now seminal jazz funk album entitled *Black Byrd*. The black-and-white cover image of a turn-of-the-century-era jazz band of that album is initially in complete contrast with this, supposedly a documentary photo of real prostitutes at work somewhere in America. Yet both images reveal the trumpeter's concern with the stereotypes of black Americans held by many at the time. In contrast to the glamorized subjectification of women employed by the Ohio Players, art director Salisbury—who went on to suggest that Michael Jackson wear just one white glove, and to invent the Levi 501 branding— uses no studio method to reveal a very different view of the female form. As with the Players' sleeves, this also folds out to reveal the cover star in full: she's wearing hot pants and platform boots designed to attract men willing to pay for a "good time." She's either supremely in control or a victim, but she sure ain't glamorous. Salisbury uses a woman selling sex to sell the album, while the Players use the idea of sex to sell theirs.

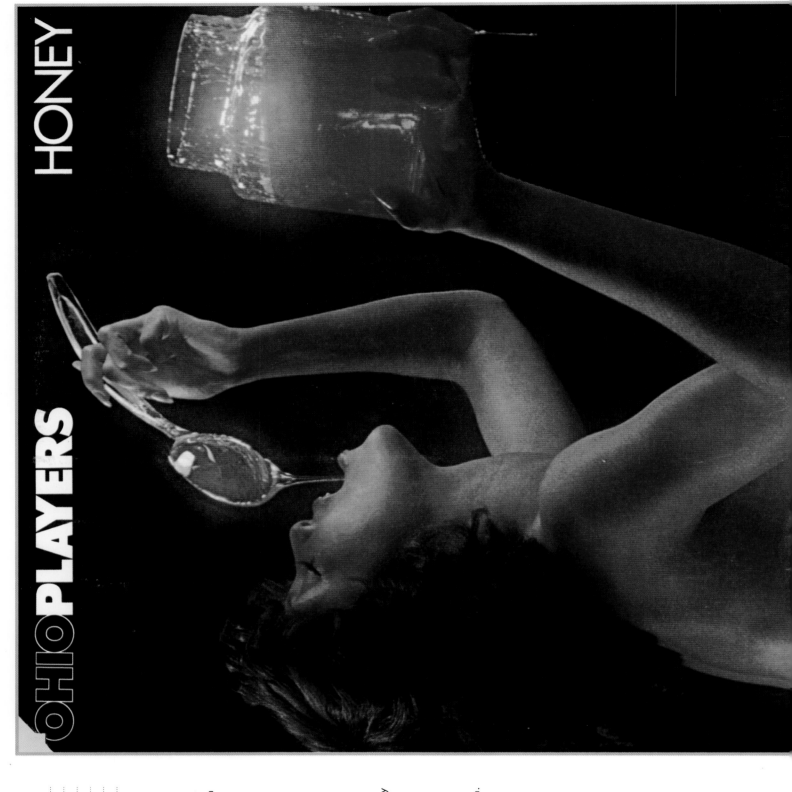

HONEY

OHIO PLAYERS

Ohio Players Honey

1975
Mercury Records
America

Sleeve design by Joe Kotleba/AGI
Photography by Richard Fegley
Art direction by Jim Ladwig/AGI

Having found their funky groove with a series of extended early disco albums on an independent label in the early 1970s, in 1974 the Ohio Players signed to a major label and changed their album cover model too. For their previous four LPs the Players had used a bald-headed female in various states of undress and in clinches with a man. For their first Mercury release, *Fire* (see previous pages), they used a different woman and a prop—the firehose. In 1975 they used the model seen here, who has a problem eating honey without spilling it—presumably why she's naked. Having dropped the S&M theme used on their earlier releases *Pain*, *Pleasure*, *Ecstasy* and *Climax*, the Players went straight for soft-core food porn, and then clunky—but funky—symbolism. Is it sexist? Or is it sexually liberating? Either way it won a Grammy for the sleeve.

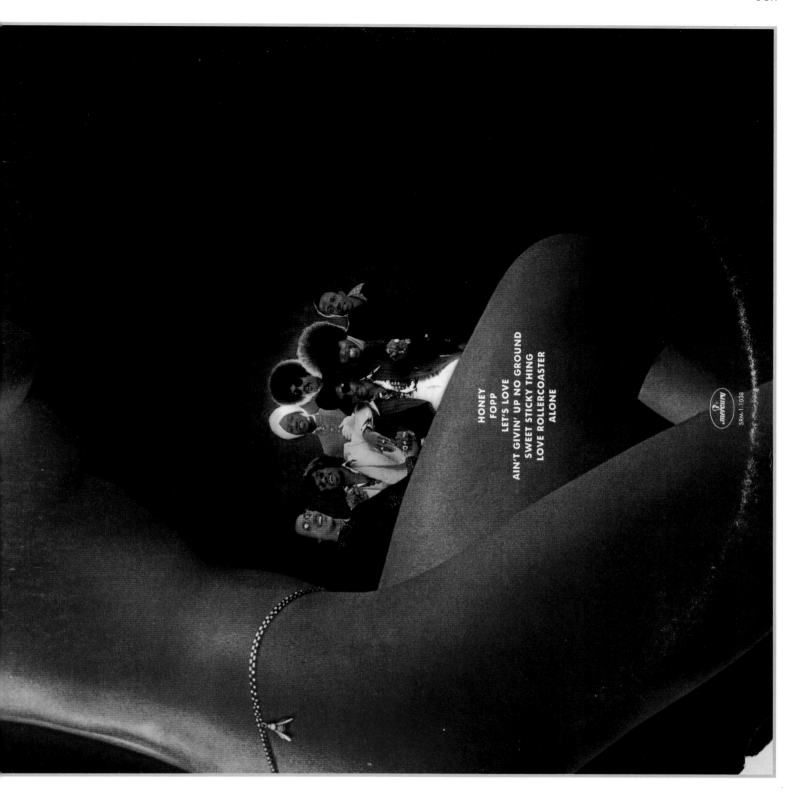

1974
Swan Song
America
Sleeve design and photography
by Hipgnosis
Retouching by Richard Manning

The Pretty Things Silk Torpedo

The Pretty Things were the first band signed to Led Zeppelin's vanity record label, Swan Song. They have remained true R&R rebels throughout their forty-five-year career. For this, their debut Swan Song release, the hot design company of Hipgnosis was given the job of producing the cover. The band was on a tour of America at the time and so didn't see the cover until it was finished. Despite the juvenile obsession with sex that Hipgnosis had at the time—see the various Scorpions covers in this chapter—and the silly symbolism of the torpedo here, the finished product is rather elegant and appealing, in a vaguely nostalgic way. Sadly, the cover model was dead of a drug overdose within two weeks of the shoot.

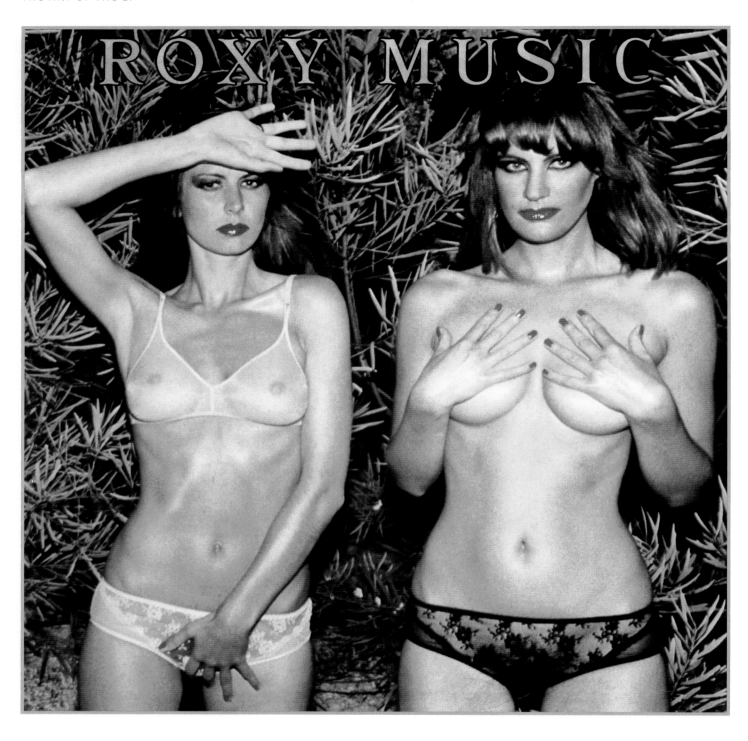

ROXY MUSIC

1974
Island
England
Sleeve design by Bryan Ferry
Photography by Eric Boman

Roxy Music Country Life

The previous three Roxy Music albums had all featured scantily clad women on their covers so presumably Bryan Ferry saw no reason to stop for *Country Life*. The models, both German fans, were "discovered" by the singer in Portugal where he had gone to write lyrics. They were enlisted for the cover as well as to help him out with some translation of the lyrics to "Bitter Sweet." In the end Constanze Karoli (possibly the sister of Can's Michael Karoli) and Eveline Grunwaldget got a name check in the publishing credits but no credit for their modeling. The sleeve is the most provocative of all Roxy's sleeves, particularly when one looks at where Constanze's hand is going. Indeed, U.S. retailers objected to it and the cover was changed to a photo of the trees without the girls. It became Roxy's biggest selling album in the U.S. to date.

Pixies

Demtro las piñones y las holas 'riqueña. Oh my golly! Oh my golly! Caminamos bagala luna caribe. Oh my golly! Oh my golly!
Besando, chichando con Surfer Rosa. Oh my golly! Oh my golly! Entonces se fue en fus madera. Oh my golly! Oh my golly!
Rosa, oh oh ohh Rosa! Rosa, oh oh ohh Rosa! Yo soy playero pero no hay playa. Oh my golly! Oh my golly!
Bien perdida la Surfer Rosa. Oh my golly! Oh my golly! La vida total es un porkeria. Oh my golly! Oh my golly!
Me hecho menos más que vida. Oh my golly! Oh my golly! Rosa, oh oh ohh Rosa! Huh! Huh! Rosa, oh oh ohh Rosa! Huh! Huh!

The Pixies Surfer Rosa

1987

4AD

England

Sleeve design by Vaughan Oliver
at v23

Photography by Simon Larbalestier

Despite hailing from Boston, Massachusetts, the Pixies were signed to British label 4AD and as such based their initial operation out of the UK. Thus, the very Spanish-looking set where photographer Simon Larbalestier took this cover shot was built in the pub over the road from the record company's headquarters in Southwest London. Putting semi-naked women on alt-rock album sleeves was not fashionable in the 1980s and there was obviously sensitivity about it: "I told them I liked nudity," said singer Black Francis to writer Joy Press at the time. "I like body lines—not necessarily something in bad taste, didn't even have to be female, just body lines. . . ." The composition, sepia tone, peeling paint, torn poster, crucifix, guitar headstock, and fairy lights are like a landscape of the Pixies' fraught songs. And the topless flamenco dancer, "the surfer rosa" of the song "Oh My Golly," welcomes you on the start of your musical journey.

The Runaways The Runaways

1976

Phonogram

America

Photography by Tom Gold

Design by Desmond Strobel

The Runaways were the first all-girl band to sell substantial numbers of records. What is interesting about the artwork to their debut is that their unique aspect is not exploited: where are the other four members? Perhaps the marketing guys at Phonogram were worried that an unsuspecting public would balk at the sight of an all-girl band—after all, Fanny (see p. 349) had flopped a few years earlier. Despite all this, the sleeve works—largely because lead singer Cherie Currie has such a great look. It is said that each member of the band modeled herself on her own icon—that is, Joan Jett on Suzi Quatro, Lita Ford on Jeff Beck. Currie was supposedly David Bowie, although here her look is veering much more toward Farrah Fawcett on speed. Remember also that this was over a year before Debbie Harry emerged as the voice and look of Blondie. The Runaways' most famous song, "Cherry Bomb," was about Currie, and because of that song and this sleeve image, she is how the band is best remembered.

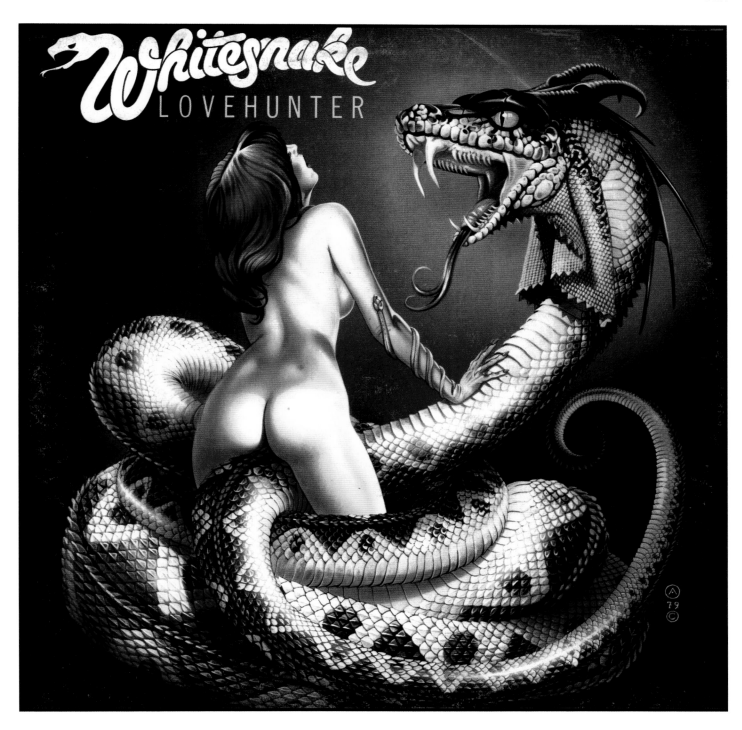

1979
Sunburst Records
England
Art direction by John Pache
Illustration by Chris Achilleos
Logo by Jim Gibson

🛈 Whitesnake Lovehunter

Here is proof that *This is Spinal Tap* is a documentary and not a work of fiction. Whitesnake was formed out of Deep Purple by singer David Coverdale and keyboard player Jon Lord. The cover was inspired by Lord's failed solo effort of 1976, *Sarabande*. The illustrator, of Cypriot descent, was amazingly still creating "artworks" in which women were objectified and demeaned in equal measure thirty years after he drew this dumb image. His works of fantasy art are used on sci-fi book covers and in comics—sorry, "graphic novels"—in which dragons and mythical beasts fight "Amazons" whose ridiculously overdrawn breasts never quite fall out of their skimpy tops, regardless of how many times they wield their enormous swords or axes. Whitesnake was looking for—and finding—an audience whose emotional and social development ended at around age thirteen. They must have been so proud to have been voted 85th Best Metal Band by the VH1 channel in 2008.

1975
Chrysalis
England
Sleeve design and photography
by Hipgnosis

UFO Force It

This was the first album by metal band UFO to chart in the U.S.—perhaps it was the wordplay in the title—bludgeoned home by designers Hipgnosis, which helped. The couple in the tub, their state of undress making it unclear as to their sex, are alledgedly a couple of British performance artists, Genesis P. Orridge and then wife Cosey Fanni Tutti, leaders of the electronic experimental musical outfit Throbbing Gristle. It could well be that the one with the ponytail is Genesis, who is at the time of writing transgendered, living in Brooklyn and occasionally performing with the latest incarnation of the band he/she formed after TG, Psychic TV. He and his revolving band of collaborators, musicians and artists have continually sought to stretch boundaries of gender identification, sex and attitudes toward both. If it is Orridge and Tutti in the photo (and there is doubt), it makes this cover far more interesting than it at first seems. Hipgnosis was going through a decidedly shady patch of sleeves at the time. This is borderline, only avoiding the ❶ by Orridge's participation.

1979
Atlantic
America
Art direction by Sandi Young
Photography by Chris Callis

Foreigner Head Games

Another bathroom punning title (see opposite); another sexually intriguing visual. The band was an immediate success from the get-go. Originally formed around two Brits—Mick Jones, ex of Spooky Tooth, and Ian McDonald, ex of King Crimson—and an American, Lou Gramm, they added one more Brit and two more Americans (hence the name) and released a self-titled debut album in 1977 that sold four million copies. The follow-up album (*Double Vision*) sold five million copies, and this, their third, entered the album chart at #5. It also sold over five million. *Head Games* was the first Foreigner album to have an interesting cover, which wasn't repeated. It was art directed by in-house designer Sandi Young and photographed by Chris Callis, who had taught himself how to take photos before being drafted into the army, to serve in Vietnam. His photos of the conflict earned him an extra year working for the Army Press Corps before he got to shoot fashion and band portraits, first in LA, then in New York. It's Callis's work which marks this out as an unusual and outstanding cover for such a traditional, MOR rock band.

EKL-318
MONO

goodbye and

TIM BUCKLEY

1967
Elektra
America
Sleeve design by William S. Harvey
Photography by Guy Webster

Tim Buckley Goodbye and Hello

Photographer Guy Webster specialized in shooting rock bands on the West Coast—he took the cover image of the Doors for their first album—in his Venice studio. William Harvey was art director for most of Elektra's rock releases, and between them they usually came up with simple, appealing covers. This, with Buckley smiling, presents the singer-songwriter as a relaxed and handsome-looking guy. His first album cover had been an almost complete contrast, with Buckley standing (leaning against a wall) unsmiling and wearing a rather formal outfit, a houndstooth sports jacket slung over his shoulder. That worked for the debut (photo and art direction by Harvey) and Buckley earned a reputation as a serious singer-songwriter at the age of nineteen. A year later, though, Buckley was more relaxed about what he was doing. The sunshine yellow front cover uses the same photo on the reverse, but with a sky blue background, with the button in the singer's eye bearing the word "hello." The year of its release Buckley appeared on the final episode of The Monkees TV show.

Amarcord Nino Rota
(I REMEMBER NINO ROTA)

INTERPRETATIONS OF
Nino Rota's Music
FROM THE
Films of
Federico Fellini

ARRANGEMENTS BY
Carla Bley
David Amram
Muhal Richard Abrams
William Fischer
CHRIS STEIN & MICHAEL SAHL
SHARON FREEMAN

SOLO PERFORMANCES BY
Jaki Byard
Steve Lacy
BILL FRISELL
DAVE SAMUELS

1981
Hannibal Records
England
Sleeve design by M&CO New York
Photography by Franco Pinna (from
Fellini's Films © 1976 Diogenes Verlag
AG Zurich)

Various Artists Amarcord Nino Rota

Nino Rota (1911—1979) was an Italian composer who worked with Fellini, supplying the score for his greatest works, including *La Dolce Vita*, *8½*, *Romeo & Juliet* and *Satyricon*. Rota also composed the score for Francis Ford Coppola's *Godfather* trilogy and wrote ten operas and five ballets. Producer and fan Hal Wilner pulled together a bunch of great jazz musicians, among them Jaki Byard, Carla Bley, Wynton Marsalis and Bill Frisell, to record their versions of Rota's music for the first of a long line of tribute albums that Wilner would go on to create (including ones dedicated to Mingus, Disney and Kurt Weill). In some ways, to include this cover is cheating, because the image, a still taken on the set of Fellini's *Amarcord* (translation: "I remember") by set photographer Pinna, was not taken for the use of the album sleeve. However, the use of it by Tibor Kalman (via his M&CO firm) is as inspired as was his work on the Benetton *Colors* magazine. The saturated red color, dark glasses and finger-on-lips pose of the actress is almost erotic.

BOZ SCAGGS SILK DEGREES

Boz Scaggs *Silk Degrees*

1976
CBS Records
America
Design by Ron Coro, Nancy Donald
Photography by Moshe Brakha

At a Grammy Museum exhibition of his work in 2009, photographer Moshe Brakha said, "I was friends and neighbors with many of the most popular punk and garage bands in Los Angeles. I knew punk music from the day it was born—it was the music of my generation." Strange, then, that it would be Boz Scaggs's smooth pop that put him on the map. *Silk Degrees* was Skaggs's most successful album: not only did it reach #2 in the Billboard chart but it was nominated for a slew of Grammys, including Best LP Package. But what of the photo? It's not surprising that after he had photographed many of his punk friends (although they were from the East coast; he shot the Ramones' *Leave Home*, p. 275), Moshe made a career in award-winning TV advertising. As with a commercial, this image contains everything the viewer needs to invest for his own fantasies. All we see of the girl are red nail-polished fingers but this, and the fact that they are crossed, suggests all sort of adulterous, noirish plots much more exciting than Scaggs's polished seventies pop rock.

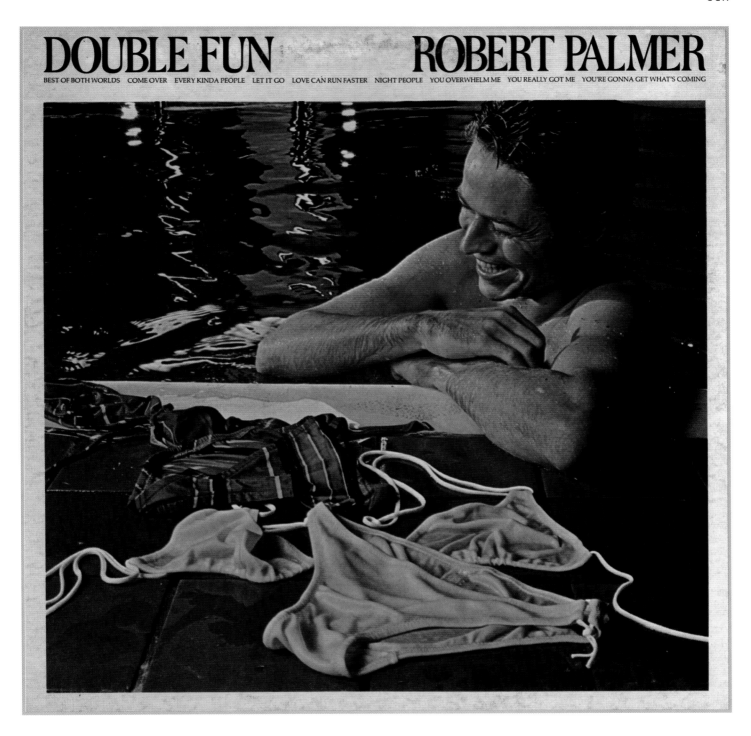

DOUBLE FUN   ROBERT PALMER

BEST OF BOTH WORLDS   COME OVER   EVERY KINDA PEOPLE   LET IT GO   LOVE CAN RUN FASTER   NIGHT PEOPLE   YOU OVERWHELM ME   YOU REALLY GOT ME   YOU'RE GONNA GET WHAT'S COMING

1978
Island
England
Photography by Hiro
Art direction by Tina Bossidy,
Robert Palmer

Robert Palmer Double Fun

Like *Silk Degrees* (opposite), the cover to Robert Palmer's fourth album lets the viewer tell his or her own story. In this case, however, the title and image leave a little less to the imagination. Then living in the Bahamas, Palmer was probably leading a life not dissimilar to the one in the photograph. But somehow he managed to remain likeable as an artist— perhaps because men aspired to be him and women wouldn't have minded being the bikini owners. The photographer who made it all come together was almost sixty at the time. Shanghai-born Hiro had been an award-winning photographer on *Harper's Bazaar* from 1956 to 1975, frequently delighting and outraging with his juxtaposition of objects; in 1963 he caused a stir by placing a priceless diamond necklace on a cow's hoof for a fashion shoot. As a freelancer he took the cover shot for the Rolling Stones's 1976 album *Black and Blue* and his clean style and signature use of color made him an ideal choice for Palmer's concept picture.

SPC-3586

FERRANTE & TEICHER
getting together

OH! CALCUTTA! • RAINDROPS KEEP FALLIN' ON MY HEAD • FOR ONCE IN MY LIFE • HAIR
SOMETHING • LEAVING ON A JET PLANE • GOOD MORNING STARSHINE • THEME FROM "Z" • LAY LADY LAY

PICKWICK STEREO

1970
Pickwick Records
America
Art direction by Frank Gauna
Photography by Chuck Stewart

 Ferrante & Teicher Getting Together

Ferrante and Teicher were Americans born in the 1920s who formed a piano duo in the late 1940s and went on to record hundreds of light classical, pop and movie-score easy listening albums. They also, amazingly, inspired John Cage through their experimentation in the 1950s with prepared pianos—or so it is claimed by some fans of the duo. No one knew what they looked like, which suited them just fine, since it meant that they didn't have to "age" in front of their fans, of whom there were enough to put the pair in the Top Ten pop charts four times with instrumental versions of movie themes (the last being *Midnight Cowboy*). As fashions changed, F&T changed their repertoire, and their cover stars. This is a particularly shocking cover: is that the beginnings of a sad "swinging" party we're witnessing? And either those unfortunate women in bikinis must be freezing, or the apparently disinterested man must be sweltering in his fisherman's sweater. Or perhaps the women are hungry cannibals and are preparing him for the pot? There are also far too many fonts on there.

The Cars Candy-O

1979
Elektra
America
Art direction by David Robinson
Artwork by Alberto Vargas

Just as Saul Bass was to
leave semi-retirement for
the Smithereens (see p. 140),
because his kids were fans, so
it was with legendary *Playboy*
and *Esquire* artist Alberto
Vargas, whose niece was a fan
of the Cars. The idea to use
the 83-year-old artist came
from vintage pinup collector
and Cars drummer David
Robinson. Robinson was the
band's very own art director
and organized the photo
shoot on which the eventual
painting was based. A little
bonus for the drummer was
that he got to date the model
afterward. Her name? Candy
Moore.

Serge Gainsbourg
Histoire de Melody Nelson

1971
Phillips
France
Photography by Tony Frank

By 1971 Serge Gainsbourg
had already established
himself as a pop writer
and performer of immense
talent. His reputation was
also one based around his
frank approach to sex in his
work—particularly in the
international hit "Je t'aime,"
which featured his wife Jane
Birkin allegedly experiencing
orgasm. And here is Birkin
again on the cover of *Histoire
de Melody Nelson*, portraying
the titular nymphet. The
album is considered to be
Gainsbourg's most influential
(inspiring a catalog of
hipsters from Air to Beck), but
its reputation is aided by its
cover star, and the fact that,
as many have pointed out,
she's not wearing underwear
underneath her tight jeans.

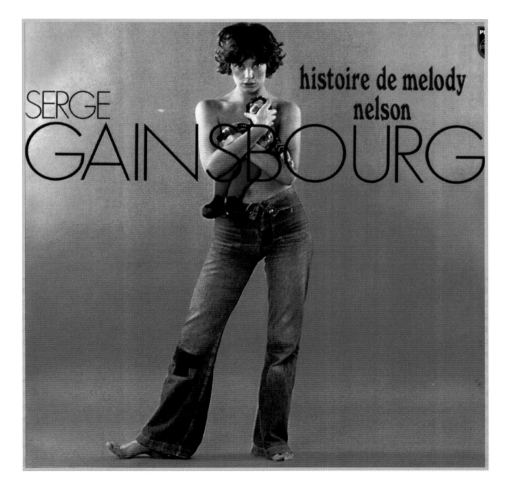

1979
Harvest/EMI Records
England
Sleeve design and photography
by Hipgnosis

Scorpions *Lovedrive*

Album cover design specialists Hipgnosis made their name with the surreal scenes that they created for Pink Floyd. They also came up with some innovative ideas for other rock bands of the early 1970s, and were obviously much in demand for their services. With all that work and creativity going on in their offices, obviously sometimes they must have slipped up and proposed something to a band that was meant to be meaningful, but instead looked like a joke. The band possibly didn't realize that it was rather demeaning, but because it was by Hipgnosis, agreed to use it as the cover of their new album. Or perhaps the band didn't get to approve the cover and instead some new employee at their record company, who was too junior to argue with the design geniuses, approved the image, and sent the artwork off to be printed. This is neither funny nor clever nor big, yet it is now considered to be "iconic" in album cover design circles. Sometimes we should be grateful for the rise of download culture, which has no specific artwork.

SIDE 1
Loving You Sunday Morning   5:35   (R.Schenker/K.Meine-H.Rarebell)
Another Piece Of Meat   3:30   (H.Rarebell-R.Schenker/H.Rarebell)
Always Somewhere   4:54   (R.Schenker/K.Meine)
Coast To Coast   4:40   (R.Schenker)

SCORPIONS
Klaus Meine   Vocals
Rudolf Schenker   Guitars
Matthias Jabs   Guitars
Francis Buchholz   Bass Guitar
Herman Rarebell   Drums

SIDE 2
Can't Get Enough   2:35   (R.Schenker/K.Meine)
Is There Anybody There? 3:55   (R.Schenker/K.Meine-H.Rarebell)
Lovedrive   4:48   (R.Schenker/K.Meine)
Holiday   6:31   (R.Schenker/K.Meine)

℗ 1979 Breeze-Music

FA 41 3080 1

5 099941 308011

Special thanks to Michael Schenker for playing lead guitar on:
Lovedrive, Another Piece Of Meat and Coast To Coast, and a special
thank you to Mother Dierks for looking after us so well.
Michael Schenker appears by courtesy of Chrysalis Records Ltd.
Cover design and photos by Hipgnosis.
Recorded at Dierks-Studios, Cologne, from September to December '78.

Produced by Dieter Dierks for Breeze-Music.

SCORPIONS
P.O.Box 5220
3000 Hanover 1

Fame

MARKETED AND DISTRIBUTED BY MUSIC FOR PLEASURE LIMITED HAYES MIDDLESEX

79

1980
Harvest/EMI Records
England
Sleeve design and photography
by Hipgnosis

Scorpions Animal Magnetism

So, a year later (see p. 79), the same big design firm sent over the photos for the next album, and the German Metal band thinks . . . what? That the equation of woman and dog photographed at a man's crotch level is an improvement on the image of a man's hand pulling chewing gum away from a "posh" woman's breast? Obviously they do. Maybe they laugh at the dog's head disappearing on the back cover. Hah hah hah, he's got da bone! Or maybe not. The man at the big design firm is quoted as saying, "That one was funny. I don't think we figured it out. We just knew there was something rude somewhere." You think? Still, at least it's (marginally) better than the odious image of a naked ten-year-old girl on the cover of their *Virgin Killer* album (1976), which was obscene and rightly banned everywhere; that had been designed "in-house" at their previous record company.

SIDE ONE
MAKE IT REAL
DON'T MAKE NO PROMISES
(Your body can't keep)
HOLD ME TIGHT
TWENTIETH CENTURY MAN
LADY STARLIGHT

SIDE TWO
FALLING IN LOVE
ONLY A MAN
THE ZOO
ANIMAL MAGNETISM

SCORPIONS
KLAUS MEINE vocals
RUDOLF SCHENKER guitars
MATTHIAS JABS guitars
FRANCIS BUCHHOLZ bass guitar
HERMAN RAREBELL drums

Recorded and mixed at DIERKS STUDIOS, Cologne
Strings and horns on Lady Starlight recorded
at MANTA SOUND Studios, Toronto, Canada.
Cover design and photos by Hipgnosis
Colour prints by Maintide
Produced by DIETER DIERKS for BREEZE MUSIC
℗ 1980 Original sound recording made by Breeze Music Ltd.
Available on tape
scorpions
p.o. box 5220
3000 Hannover 1
West Germany

EMI Record

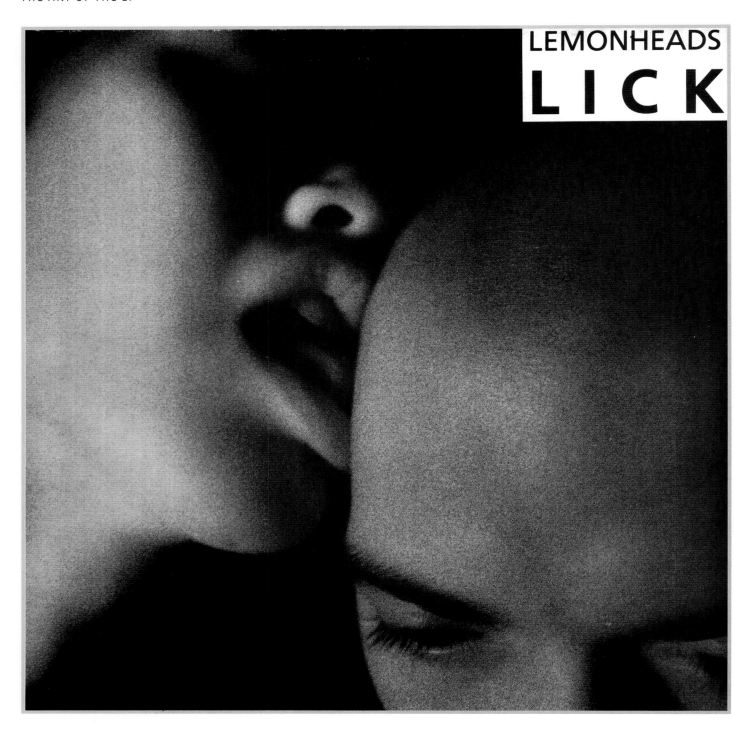

LEMONHEADS
LICK

1989
Rough Trade
England
Photography by Jesse Peretz
Graphics by Jane Gulick

The Lemonheads Lick

The third Lemonheads album was the last indie release before they signed to major label Atlantic. Despite having one of the most handsome and photogenic front men in the world, the band avoided putting him on the sleeve—as was and remains the fashion in alt-rock. Instead a photograph taken by band bass player Jesse Peretz was used. Perhaps because of the resigned look in the eyes of the shaven-headed lick recipient, the picture is deeply sexy, plus the lighting, tone, and the sheer surprise of the image all combine to make it striking and beautiful. Harvard-educated Peretz tried his hand at video directing once the band had signed to a major label, found he was good at it, and moved on to directing bigger acts like the Foo Fighters and Jack Black as well as shooting commercials for Nike and Playstation. Peretz directed the feature film *The Ex* starring Zach Braff and Amanda Peet in 2007.

1993

Nude

England

Sleeve concept by Brett Anderson

Photography by Tee Corinne

Artwork by Peter Barrett and
Andrew Biscomb

Suede Suede

Forced to change their name to the more prosaic the London Suede in the
U.S., and subsequently never really taking off, the Brett Anderson-led
fourpiece was nonetheless a hugely influential band in their native UK.
The cover to their debut album was—like all the band's artwork at that
point—chosen by front man Anderson. The original image he wanted was
of two wheelchair-bound lesbians kissing, from a 1991 book called *Stolen
Glances: Lesbians Take Photographs*, edited by Tessa Boffin and Jean Fraser.
The photographer, Tee Corinne, was also a feminist activist and writer.
Given the band's other sleeves (e.g., fashion model Verushka dressed as a
man on the sleeve for the single "The Drowners"), it is likely that the simple
controversy of the picture is what appealed to Anderson. In the end the
band opted for a cropped image and benefited hugely from the ambiguity
achieved—are they boys or girls? Are they fused together forever? This
sleeve promises all the romance, weirdness and sexual freedom that every
adolescent music fan seeks.

1984
EMI Records
England
Sleeve design by Kocklowski/Missmahl/
Pieczulski
Photography by Helmut Newton

❗ **Scorpions** Love at First Sting

Look closely at the photograph and you might notice that the man is tattooing the semi-naked woman with the half-smile on her face. He is dressed in the height of 1980s Eurotrash fashion—leather pants and cowboy boots, hair gel and quiff. She looks like a high-class hooker or model, maybe used to posing for Helmut Newton, the king of the objectification of female models. The image looks like an amateur's version of a Newton photo, but in fact it's the work of the man himself. Newton shot a few album covers, none of them particularly successful or memorable, none as objectionable as this. Would the Scorpions ever learn the difference between sexy and sexist? Of course not. *Savage Amusement* from 1988 features a woman who is part scorpion.

1978
A&M
England
Sleeve design by Nick Marshall
Art direction by Michael Ross
Photography by George Greenwood
(Official Mr. Universe Photographer)

Squeeze Squeeze

After releasing one EP (*Packet of Three*, 1977) independently, South London's Squeeze signed to A&M and, as was the tradition in those days, were packed off to the studio with a top producer. The producer in question turned out to be ex-Velvet Underground Welshman John Cale who, after having produced debuts for the Stooges and the Modern Lovers, clearly thought he had free reign to get the band to do exactly what he wanted. Apparently he wanted them to call the album *Gay Guys* and forced them to write a whole batch of new songs to fit in with that theme. The artwork probably partly stems from that, as well as relating to the song "Sex Master." Regardless of the fact that the sleeve, or indeed the music, doesn't really reflect the true nature of the band's whimsical commentaries on suburban life, which would flower on sophomore album *Cool For Cats*, it remains a new-wave classic: garish, cheap and sleazy.

1994
Flying Nun/Elektra
America
Sleeve design by Reiner Design
Consultants Inc.
Photography by John Kuczala

Ween Chocolate and Cheese

A fine parody, or celebration, of the Ohio Players' covers of twenty years earlier, this is a very witty take on the genre. Ween is not a "normal" band in any way. There are two members—Gene and Dean Ween—and they play all the instruments on a wide and eclectic range of musically styled numbers, the lyrics of which veer between the inane and profane to the funny and poignant. Photographer Kuczala is well known for manipulating images of the famous into satirical situations—Hillary Clinton smoking a cigarette on the stage of a stand-up club, Paris Hilton with puppet strings, Rupert Murdoch taking a sledgehammer to a newspaper vending machine, etc. The band claims that it wanted the sleeve to feature a "gay sailor" image, but the record label was nervous about the possible inclusion of a song about HIV. Gene and Deen also claimed that they never met the model, supposedly named Ashley Savage, though that is likely to be a false name. The boxing belt-style with band logo and the crop top are repeated with a rear view of the model on the other side of the sleeve.

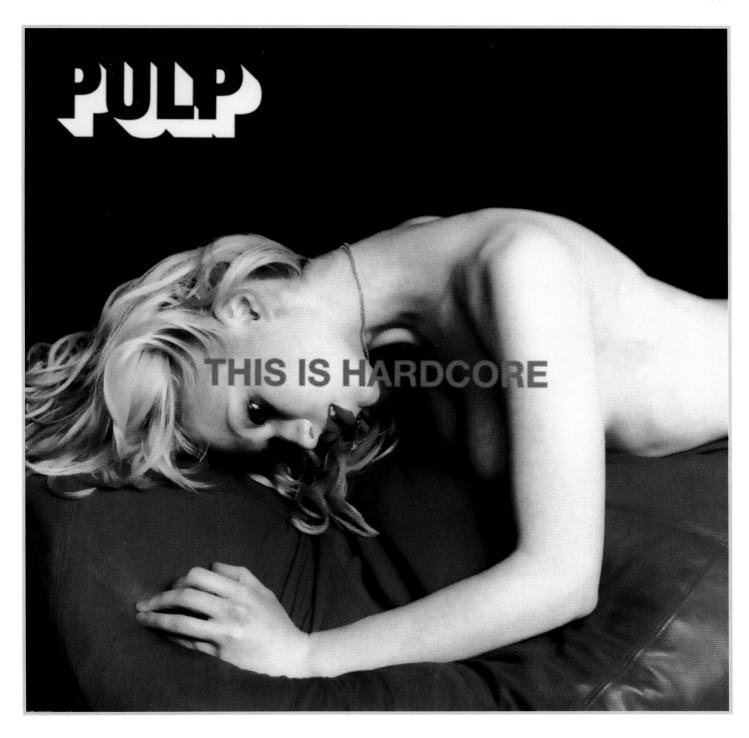

Pulp This Is Hardcore

1997
Island
England
Art direction by John Currin and
Peter Saville
Photography by Horst Dikegerdes

Island Records wanted to ensure that Pulp's follow-up to their mega-selling *Different Class* album would be just as successful. So no expense was spared in the packaging: they hired provocative American painter John Currin and top British designer Peter Saville (see p. 128) to create videos and artwork. The album is filled with disgust for the seediness and decadence that had come hand in hand with the band's Britpop fame, and the movie still-like images throughout the glossy CD booklet (one small advantage that the format has over vinyl) reflect this disgust. At first glance the naked blonde lying facedown on a pink pillow appears to be pure soft porn until you notice the model's zonked-out eyes and realize the double meaning of the word hardcore in the title: this is an ugly, exploitative world and Pulp is fed up with it. The album failed to live up to commercial expectations.

ART

All sleeve design qualifies as art. But then, isn't that box of cereal on your kitchen table art too? Or that can of Choc Full o'Nuts coffee? The companies producing these products certainly all had designers slaving away, making them look as pretty as possible. So where's the distinction? Well, in this chapter we've included sleeves that don't feature simple photography or branding but which offer a unique vision—a worldview—rendered in artistic fashion.

Inevitably this worldview will frequently be the vision of one person, rather than a committee of bass players, managers and record company marketing departments. Along with obvious visionaries like Saul Bass, Mati Klarwein, Barney Bubbles, Peter Saville and Andy Warhol, there are the unsung heroes of artwork such as photographer Brian Griffin, whose work with Depeche Mode was so distinctive; or Paul Cannell, whose untrained genius left us the legacy of Primal Scream's saucer-eyed sun.

While design talent naturally runs throughout this book and many of the names you will see mentioned in this chapter recur in others, here you will find artwork where the designers were pretty much left to their own devices. We have also included a few sleeves where the temptation to use a classic work of art proved too great—visual sampling, if you will: come forward Bow Wow Wow, the Pogues and New Order.

Still, perhaps the original artists would be pleased to know that their work was helping to shift units for record companies. It works just like that pretty Choc Full o'Nuts packaging in front of you.

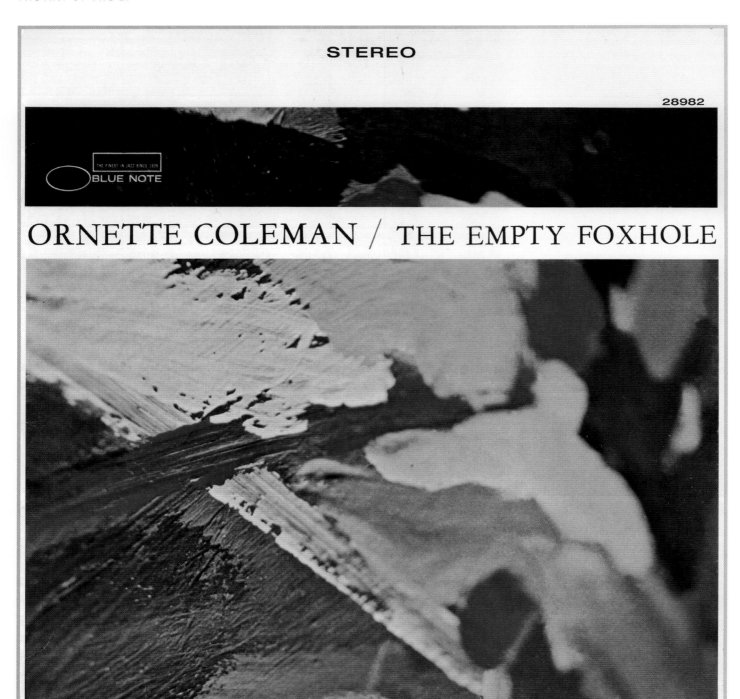

STEREO

28982

THE FINEST IN JAZZ SINCE 1939
BLUE NOTE

ORNETTE COLEMAN / THE EMPTY FOXHOLE

1966
Blue Note
America
Sleeve design by Reid Miles
Painting by Ornette Coleman

Ornette Coleman The Empty Foxhole

In the 1960s it became something of a trend for musicians to put examples of their other artistic output, namely their paintings, on to the covers of their albums. The results were mixed, to say the least (see p. 114). For every one example of a genuinely interesting, well thought out, artistically successful work used as cover art, there were at least six others which, while being of interest for the insight into the egotistically deranged mind of the artist concerned, would never have been contemplated for use by any sane or self-respecting cover designer (or recording artist). That Reid Miles at Blue Note readily agreed to the use of Coleman's artwork for this, the avant-garde saxophonist's third album for the label, says it all. The album became notorious for Coleman's use of his then ten-year-old son Denardo as drummer for the trio session. That, along with the use of the artwork, could have provided well-founded accusations of the label pandering to the monstrous ego of Coleman. Yet the cover stands up to close inspection rather better than the record it houses.

1957
Blue Note
America
Sleeve design by Reid Miles
Illustration by Andy Warhol

Kenny Burrell Volume 2

While most Blue Note album covers are easily recognizable for their use of powerful, impressive photography and bold graphics, this album, combining the rare talents of in-house sleeve designer Reid Miles and founder of the label and photographer Francis Wolff, is a little different. Reid joined the label in 1956 and, eager to try new ideas, he asked a young, New York-based graphic artist to draw the idea that he had for guitarist Burrell's second record for Blue Note. Andy Warhol went on to draw covers for the RCA label before, in 1962, making his mark with his debut art exhibition, after several years spent designing and drawing shoes for a shoemaker. It's been said that the perspective of the drawing suggests that Warhol was inspired by Ben Shahn, the social-realist painter who was then hip in New York, and that the blotted lines are familiar to students of Paul Klee; though it's equally as likely that David Stone Martin, who had designed a number of cool and best-selling Norman Granz-produced jazz album covers of the same period, was as much of an influence.

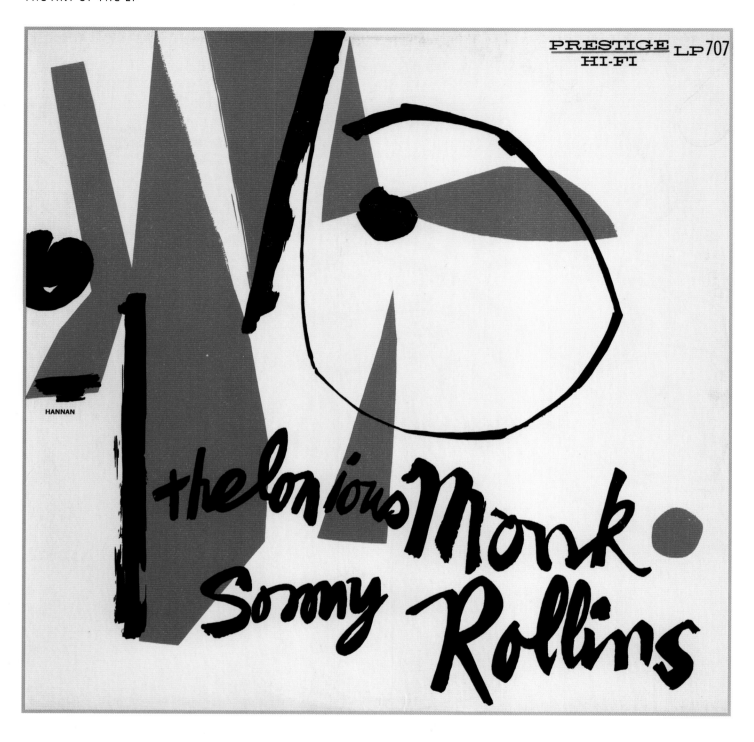

1954
Prestige Records
America
Sleeve design by Tom Hannan

Thelonious Monk, Sonny Rollins
Thelonious Monk, Sonny Rollins

This is a rare and exhilarating example of a sleeve design perfectly redolent of the music it is selling. Designer Hannan would create covers for both of Sonny Rollins' other major releases for Prestige Records, *Saxophone Colossus* and *Tenor Madness* (both 1956), as well as designing the Miles Davis Quintet with J.J. Johnson album *Walking* (featuring a set of traffic lights) and the Phil Woods, Donald Byrd album *Youngbloods* (also both from 1956). Yet it is this sleeve which more than any of the others suggests the sound, freedom, freshness, and oblique angles of modern Jazz in the mid-1950s. It could almost be a painting by one of the New York school of modern artists such as Franz Kline or Robert Motherwell.

Charles Mingus Mingus Ah Um

1959
Columbia
America
Sleeve design by Neil Fujita
Painting by Neil Fujita

By the end of the 1950s the yet-to-be major record labels had begun signing jazz musicians and releasing their albums around the world. One of the results of the meeting between the high art of jazz music and the high commerce of the record labels owned and run by businessmen was the consolidation of album cover design. Because Blue Note, Prestige, and Verve, et cetera, were run by jazz fans who wanted their records to look as good as the music they contained, there was no real set rule for the design of the cover. However, Fujita, the head of design and packaging at Columbia, insisted that album titles and artists' names should be at the top of the sleeve, in order that buyers could see them easily when flipping through record retail racks. He demonstrated beautifully how to present the perfect jazz album package on this Mingus album—even contributing the cover painting himself.

1955
Brunswick Records
America
Sleeve design by Saul Bass

Original Soundtrack The Man with the Golden Arm

Movie soundtrack artwork is often a chopped-down version of the cinema one-sheet poster. Not so with Saul Bass. Arguably the most renowned of all movie art designers, New York–born Bass is best known for his work with Alfred Hitchcock, for whom he designed the title sequences and poster art for *Vertigo*, *Psycho* and *North by Northwest*. But it was in his work with Otto Preminger that he defined his bold, deceptively simple style. This was their second collaboration: the controversial story of a heroin addict. Bass became notorious for his title sequence, which animates white lines to Bernstein's punchy jazz. As the credits and music for this movie conclude, the lines (representing veins? prison bars?) morph into the addict's arm, as you see above. This artwork differs from the poster in that it features no stars of the movie, just Bass's lines (colored) and his now iconic arm motif.

KL 5175 **KURT WEILL'S THE SEVEN DEADLY SINS**
(Die Sieben Todsünden)
A ballet with song
Text by
BERTOLT BRECHT
Sung by
LOTTE LENYA
with Julius Katona, Fritz Göllnitz, Ernst Poettgen
and Sigmund Roth as The Family
Orchestra conducted by
Wilhelm Brückner-Rüggeberg

COLUMBIA
GUARANTEED HIGH-FIDELITY
MASTERWORKS

PAINTING: TOM ALLEN

1956
Columbia Records
America
Sleeve design by Neil Fujita
Illustration by Tom Allen

Lotte Lenya Kurt Weill's the Seven Deadly Sins

Columbia pioneered the use of illustrated artwork for 78 rpm discs
under legendary art director Alex Steinweiss. Before 1939 they came
in plain cardboard sleeves with the artist's name simply stamped on
and "looked like tombstones," as Steinweiss is quoted as saying. Neil
Fujita was employed by Steinweiss's successor and designed many of the
classic Columbia jazz sleeves of the 1950s (see p. 93). Artist Tom Allen's
exaggerated style (also seen on illustrations he did for other Columbia
releases, such as those for blues singer Jimmy Rushing) perfectly suited
the grotesque nature of Kurt Weill and Bertolt Brecht's *The Seven Deadly
Sins*. In many ways Allen's illustration is the defining image we have of the
finest interpreter of Weill's songs, his wife Lotte Lenya: the cruel brow, the
severe haircut and the prominent lips. Perhaps it was this that helped
land her the part of the evil Rosa Klebb in 1963's Bond film, *From Russia
with Love*.

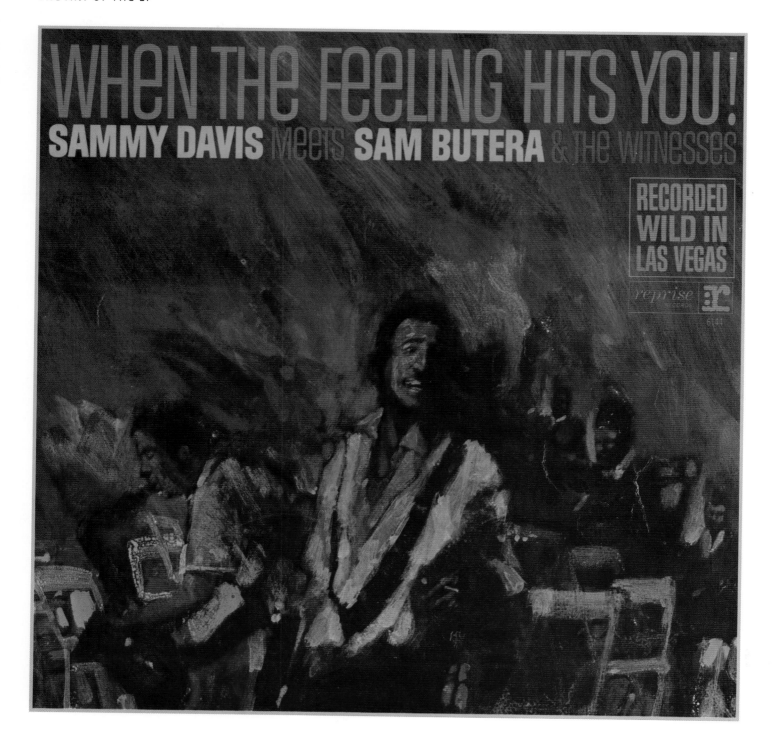

Sammy Davis Meets Sam Butera & the Witnesses When the Feeling Hits You!

1964
Reprise Records
America
Art direction by Ed Thrasher
Painting by Charles White

Warner Brothers' art director Ed Thrasher began a long association with Frank Sinatra almost by proxy when "Ol Blue Eyes's" vanity label Reprise found distribution through (and an eventual sale to) Warners in 1960. Frank had already won a Grammy for album design by then and knew what he liked on a record cover. Ed Thrasher's ideas coincided with Frank's. For this fabulous recording (not live, but "wild"), made by Davis in the wee small hours after finishing an official gig, and with backing from Louis Prima's six-piece band, Thrasher wanted something that reflected the spontaneity and vibrancy of the recording. It's a small irony that a painting rather than a photograph best represents that. The artist is Charles Wilbert White, a Chicago-born African American artist whose work hangs in the New York and Washington National Galleries, among other galleries.

1956

Verve

America

Sleeve design by Norman Granz

Photography by Phil Stern

Ella Fitzgerald & Louis Armstrong Ella and Louis

There may be no title and no name on the front cover of this album, but the faces of Ella and Louis are there at the top and any browsing purchaser in a record store would, in the mid-1950s, recognize the pair immediately. Two of the biggest names in international jazz music and popular entertainment, Ella and Louis were referred to simply by their first names at a time when Elvis was always accompanied in print by Presley. Photographer Stern was a *Life* magazine regular who learned to take photos during World War II. He is responsible for many of the covers on Norman Granz's Verve label. Most of them were in black and white, and they all had the musicians' names in them. This color photo presents the artists in their unaffected glory; not quite relaxed—note Louis' fixed grin and crossed arms—but very cool.

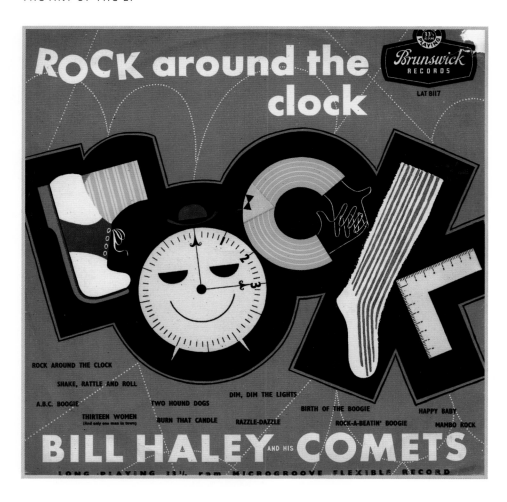

**Bill Haley and
his Comets** Rock
Around the Clock

1956

Brunswick

England

Sleeve design uncredited

Artwork uncredited

Before Elvis Presley changed
the world forever, Bill Haley
and his Comets rocked it a
little. The success of "Rock
Around the Clock" as a
single in England in 1955,
when it was featured on the
soundtrack of the movie
Blackboard Jungle, was
phenomenal. This album, not
originally released in America
at all, was an attempt to cash
in on the rock phenomenon
before it faded. Taking the
work of Jim Flora, who'd
used similar cartoon-style
graphics to great effect in
the late 1940s and early
'50s, as a starting point, the
English art department at
Decca, who owned Brunswick,
took a literal approach to
their design. And it worked.

The Ink Spots The
Original Ink Spots

1964

Allegro Records

England

Sleeve design uncredited

Artwork by David

Just because a record label
sells cheap products and
reissues, that doesn't mean
that its cover designs have
to look cheap. Allegro was
a reissue outlet for golden
oldies. When putting out this
collection they had a limited
budget for packaging, and
used the same card case
for all their products. It
came with the back printed
uniformly with a list of
the label's catalog—show
soundtracks, light opera and
classical as well as the Ink
Spots. The album tracks had
to be printed on the front,
on a separate sheet that
was stuck on with glue. This
artistic approach is striking,
simple and quite witty; check
out the For Ever Now and You
Always Hurt the One You Love
symbols.

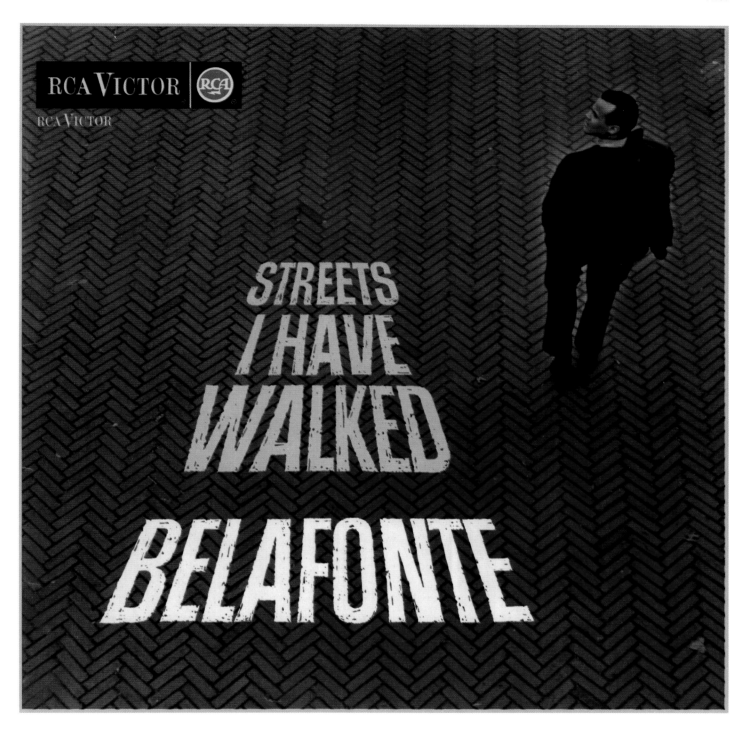

Harry Belafonte Streets I Have Walked

1963
RCA
America
Photography by Roy DeCarava

Harry Belafonte had become known around the world as a folk singer, his success in part much a result of his choosing to record international and often little-known folk tunes from countries as far apart as Australia and Mexico, Israel and France. While his early album covers were photographic depictions of the singer as a strong, proud man (see p. 334), for this album he is shown walking away from the camera. The texture of the road shows that he is obviously not on an American highway, yet he looks relaxed. Only the last name is there on the cover, which showed a huge confidence in his market—no clear photo, no "Harry." The folk boom in America was about to be replaced by Beatlemania and R&B music, but Belafonte stuck firmly to his formula of folk and protest songs. He never recorded a Lennon/McCartney song.

Jan and Dean Jan and Dean meet Batman

1966
Liberty
America
Art direction by Woody Woodward
Illustration by Bill Kane

Surfing duo Jan and Dean were second only to the Beach Boys in popularity in America before the Beatles landed. Unlike the Boys, though, they couldn't transform themselves into a new act. Which is partly why they agreed to record this album of Batman-related songs; only the Neal Hefti—composed opening theme has any relevance to the TV series. Dean Torrence went on to become an album cover designer in the years following Jan's near-fatal road crash of 1966, so may have had a hand in the final layout, working with Liberty's in-house art director Woodward. The sleeve notes on the reverse are a concise history of the Batman comic to date. Subsequent CD reissues of the album feature only the wording on a black background, suggesting that the license to use the imagery was withdrawn, or the cost became prohibitive. Bruce Robert, the writer of the back cover notes, is probably a pseudonym, being a reversal of the Scottish poet who inspired Bill Finger, collaborator to Bill Kane in creating Batman, to name Batman's alter ego Bruce Wayne.

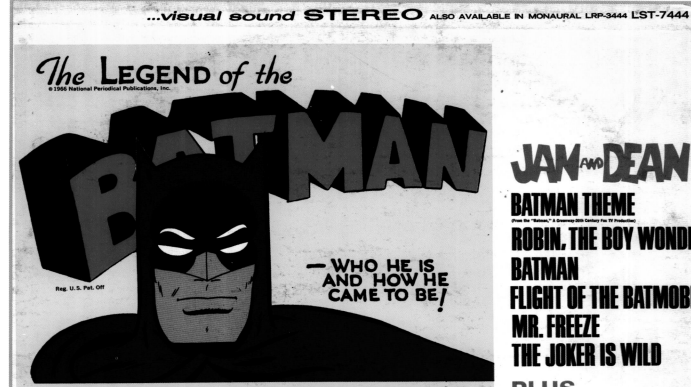

The LEGEND of the BATMAN

© 1966 National Periodical Publications, Inc.

Reg. U.S. Pat. Off

— WHO HE IS AND HOW HE CAME TO BE!

This album concerns a man of mystery. To some he is the symbol of incorruptible justice; to lawbreakers a figure of terror. He is the BATMAN. Along with his young companion, Robin, The Boy Wonder, he wages a never ending battle against crime and injustice everywhere.

BATMAN, as every comic book reader knows, is in reality Bruce Wayne, millionaire pseudo playboy. As a young boy Bruce made a solemn vow to devote his life to fighting crime because his parents lives had been needlessly and prematurely ended by a holdup man.

His father's estate provided for him. He attended the best schools, became a master scientist, and also developed himself to physical perfection. When he felt he had developed his mind and body to the fullest, he decided to wage his crusade against crime anonymously.

Knowing that criminals are a cowardly and superstitious lot, he chose the guise of a human bat. Thus was born the BATMAN.

During the early part of his career BATMAN worked alone and carried a gun to help him in his work. He was feared by both law-breakers and police because neither knew who this mysterious creature of the night was or what he was doing. Also, BATMAN used his gun when he felt it necessary to end the life of one who did not deserve to live. He later dropped this method of dealing with lawbreakers and swore never to take a human life unless absolutely necessary.

Ten issues after his initial appearance, Detective Comics, Issue number 39 introduced "The Character Find of 1940, ROBIN, THE BOY WONDER."

One evening Bruce Wayne attended a circus that had come to Gotham City. Unknown to him the circus owner was being threatened by gangsters for refusing to pay protection money. During the evening show, the gangsters made good their threat. As the trapeze artists known as the Flying Graysons were going through their triple somersault routine, minus a net, the rope broke and Mary and John Grayson fell to their deaths. On the ground their only son, Dick Grayson, witnessed the "accident." Later in the evening Bruce Wayne returned as the BATMAN and overheard the gangsters telling the circus owner that more "accidents" will happen if he doesn't pay up. BATMAN told Dick Grayson of the gang-

ster's threats and that the deaths of his parents were not accidental. Dick asked to join the BATMAN in capturing the criminals, so BATMAN took him to the Batcave hidden deep in a mountain under the Wayne mansion. There he trained Dick in the art of fighting crime. When Dick was ready he was given a costume and the name Robin, Boy Wonder. Together they captured the gangsters and saved the circus from financial ruin. Then, since Robin wanted to join with BATMAN and help him in his war against crime, Bruce Wayne became Dick Grayson's legal guardian.

In 1940 BATMAN and Robin appeared in their own magazine each month as well as in Detective Comics. They have appeared in their own magazine ever since, spanning 28 years. Also making his debut in Batman Comics #1 was one of the comic world's most infamous villians, The Joker. Along with the Joker there have been many other colorful and nefarious criminals such as the Penguin, the Riddler, Clayface, the Catwoman, Two-Face . . . the list goes on and on.

BATMAN and Robin have many crime fighting tools at their beck and call. The Batcave with its own nuclear power plant, computers, and other electronic aids used in crime detection. The nuclear powered Batmobile, capable of incredible speeds and outfitted with many anti-crime devices including a portable computer (in the trunk), is the BATMAN'S amazing means of transportation. Also, BATMAN and Robin each wear Batbelts, each belt a miniature laboratory in itself.

BATMAN and Robin have appeared in many forms since their initial appearance in Detective Comics. There have been syndicated Sunday strips in the newspapers. Two movie serials have appeared. The first, in 1943, entitled "The BATMAN" starred Lewis Wilson and Douglas Croft. The second, "The New Adventures of BATMAN and Robin," appeared in 1949. Starring as the Caped Crusaders were Robert Lowery and John Duncan.

And now BATMAN has come to television. Starring Adam West and Burt Ward as BATMAN and Robin, the series is shown twice a week, in color, on the ABC Television Network. It is to this show and its stars that Jan and Dean dedicate this album in the hope that all who hear it will come to enjoy the adventures of the Dynamic Duo as much as we do. — Bruce Roberts

PRINTED IN U.S.A.

JAN AND DEAN

BATMAN THEME
(From the "Batman," A Greenway-20th Century Fox TV Production)
ROBIN, THE BOY WONDER
BATMAN
FLIGHT OF THE BATMOBILE
MR. FREEZE
THE JOKER IS WILD

PLUS...
ON THE FLIP SIDE A SURPRISE

BAT-TACULAR!
FEATURING
JAN & DEAN'S
B.A. (BEL-AIR) BANDITS

LIBERTY
LIBERTY RECORDS INC.
LOS ANGELES 28, CALIF.

Produced by:
Jan Berry For Screen Gems, Inc.
Orchestra conducted by: Hal Blaine
Arranged by: George Tipton
Engineers: "Bones," "Lanky," Henry, Chuck, Joe, and Wally
Art Direction: Woody Woodward

Enoch Light and the Light Brigade
Pertinent Percussion Cha Cha's

1960
Command Records
America
Art by Olin

After surviving a near-fatal car crash in 1940 and then World War II, light classical violinist Enoch Light formed a dance band playing for middle-aged dancers in postwar America. He set up the record label Grand Award, which put out light orchestral and dance records, including his own, and in 1959 set up Command Records and became a star. His debut release, *Persuasive Percussion*, was one of the biggest-selling albums in pre-Beatles America. Light used Command to demonstrate the proper use of stereo and how to package records. Using Josef Albers' geometric works, he invented the idea of the gatefold sleeve for double LPs and gave a good display to the sleeve art. He also produced a lot of the Command releases, including a few with Dick Hyman, who would go on to be the next great light classical interpreter of the correct use of stereo, new instruments (see p. 316), and great cover designs. The hand-drawn geometric shapes here perfectly mirror the percussive sound of the record in classic 1950s fashion.

102

CLUB SKA '67

GUNS OF NAVARONE
GUNS FEVER COPASETIC
SKA-ING WEST
PHOENIX CITY PIED PIPER
LAWLESS STREET
SHANTY TOWN CONTACT
DANCING MOOD
STOP MAKING LOVE
BROADWAY JUNGLE
RUB UP, PUSH UP

1967
Island Records
England
Sleeve design by Guy Stevens

Various Artists Club Ska '67

Owner Chris Blackwell relocated Island Records from Jamaica to London after Kingston's new sound system labels (Duke Reid's Top Deck and Clement Coxone Dodd's Studio One) proved too much competition for him. Blackwell cleverly reinvented Island as the UK distributor for Reid and Coxone and consequently got the cream of Jamaica's rocksteady and, later, ska releases. There was no established visual lexicon for ska in the sixties, a full two decades before Two Tone reinvented it as cartoon and checkerboard. So when it came to releasing a compilation album aimed at the white audience of Mods who had embraced the sound, Island in-house producer (and future producer of *London Calling*) Guy Stevens based his design on the standard means by which this audience heard about the music—the club flyer. Except, of course, he opted for eye-catching DayGlo colors. The design and the album were so popular that the record remained in Island's catalog for decades.

The Velvet Underground The Velvet Underground

1967
MGM Records
America
Sleeve design by Andy Warhol

One of the defining examples of the genre for many reasons. It was innovative and witty: early copies had a label inviting the owner to "Peel slowly and see," and sure enough the banana skin peeled away. It is enduring. Even without the three-dimensional gimmick, the design works like all great art: immediately eye-catching yet increasingly intriguing the more you look. And it is subversive despite its simplicity. No surprise then that the Velvet Underground's then manager/producer/impresario was at the helm. Lou Reed may have later fired him as manager and he may not have contributed anything in the way of production (it was actually MGM in-house man Bob Wilson who turned the dials), but Andy Warhol certainly came up with the album design goods. The album flopped on its original release but is now, like the sleeve, rightfully regarded as a classic.

1968
RCA Victor
America
Sleeve illustration by George Bartell

Jose Feliciano Feliciano!

Blind Puerto Rican guitarist and singer Feliciano was a big star in Latin America but had little success in America until he recorded the Doors song "Light My Fire" with RCA house producer Rick Jardin (Nilsson, Jefferson Airplane) at the desk controls. It made #3 on the Billboard charts in the summer of 1968 and RCA put out this album of English language pop songs in its wake. The cover artwork is by George Bartell, an artist best known for his work with car manufacturers, in particular Shelby and Ford. The use of an artist who so instinctively puts movement and speed into his work was inspired. Feliciano's live performances were remarkably active, considering that he sat on a stool to perform; his head and fingers were never still, and the dynamism of his playing astounding. Bartell gets that across here marvelously.

1970
Columbia Records
America
Sleeve graphics by Robert Venosa
Painting by Mati Klarwein
Photography by Marian Schmidt

Santana Abraxas

Mati Klarwein's painting *Annunciation* had been around for nine years when Carlos Santana chanced upon a reproduction of it in a magazine. Since then, Klarwein's style has almost become synonymous with this album, Miles Davis's *Bitches Brew* (see opposite page), and psychedelia in general. Klarwein was born in Germany but his parents fled to Palestine to escape the Nazi persecution before settling in Paris in the fifties. Klarwein remained itinerant and his artistic style shows this, taking in Hindu iconography and Renaissance art as well as a liberal dose of pop art. Despite the almost suffocating eclecticism of the work, there is still a sense of the lascivious adolescent about the piece. Klarwein says of his twenty-eight-year-old self, "In those days I had an obsessional passion for the female body that lasted deep into my thirties." A perfect match for rock music, then.

Miles Davis Bitches Brew

Just as Carlos Santana was inspired by seeing a Mati Klarwein painting, so was Miles Davis when he saw the *Abraxas* sleeve (see facing page). Davis was in the middle of pioneering jazz fusion, having gone fully electric with 1969's *In a Silent Way* (see p. 213). But that release was housed in more traditional jazz headshot artwork. *Bitches Brew*, on the other hand, left traditional jazz behind and frequently employed rock rhythms. This is reflected not just in the inspired choice of cover art, which must have intrigued Santana and other rock fans on its release, but also by the bold statement above the title graphic: "Directions in Music by Miles Davis." The album got a mixed critical response on release but it went on to become one of Davis's best-selling releases and indeed one of the most successful jazz albums ever.

1970
Columbia
America
Painting by Mati Klarwein
Cover design by John Berg

Faces Ooh La La

1973
Warner Brothers
England
Sleeve design by Jim Ladwig
Photography by Tom Wright, Jak Kilby

It was a sign of the langor that had set in with the band. Instead of the Faces presenting their new record to Warners and setting about the design of the cover, Jim Ladwig, Warners' designer, had separately constructed a front cover on which the mouth and eyes of a character taken from an old French *fin de siècle* photograph moved when the top of the sleeve was squeezed. As Ladwig tells the story, he showed guitarist Ronnie Wood the idea and Wood said "Ohh La La." If that is so, then Wood went off and wrote the title tune with bassist Ronnie Lane in order to fit the cover concept. The inside gatefold image (right) was also originally a moving part, with the can-can dancer's leg kicking as the sleeve opened. Warners supposedly created a few that they sent out as PR copies. It was a fitting end to the recording career of the original Faces. By this time, Rod Stewart was a solo star and the Faces considered simply his backing band. Ronnie Lane quit the Faces just after this was released, though they carried on for two more years (and three singles) without him. Wood quit to join the Stones in 1975.

INSTRUMENTS (who played what)
SILICONE GROWN
Vocal: R. Stewart; Piano, I. McLagan; Bass, R. Lane;
Guitar; R. Wood; Drums, K. Jones
CINDY INCIDENTALLY
Vocal, R. Stewart; Piano, I. McLagan; Bass, R. Lane;
Guitar; R. Wood; Drums, K. Jones
FLAGS AND BANNERS
Vocal; R. Lane; Bass: Electric Guitar and Bass, R. Wood;
Electric Guitar; R. Stewart; Organ, I. McLagan; Drums, K. Jones
MY FAULT
Vocals, R. Stewart and R. Wood; Guitars, R. Wood; Piano, I. McLagan;
Drums, K. Jones; Bass, R. Lane
BORSTAL BOYS
Vocal, R. Stewart; Drums, K. Jones; Guitar and Slide, R. Wood;
Piano, I. McLagan, Bass, R. Lane
FLY IN THE OINTMENT
Guitar and Slide, R. Wood; Bass, R. Lane; Drums, K. Jones;
Organ and Wurlitzer, I. McLagan; Percussion; Neemoi; Speedy' Aguaye
IF I'M ON THE LATE SIDE
Vocal; R. Stewart; Bass and Electric Guitar, R. Wood;
Acoustic Guitar; R. Lane; Organ, I. McLagan; Drums, K. Jones
GLAD AND SORRY
Vocals, R. Lane and R. Wood; Drums, K. Jones; Piano, I. McLagan
Acoustic and Electric Guitars; R. Wood; Tambourine and Bass, R. Lane
JUST ANOTHER HONKY
Vocal, R. Stewart; Piano, I. McLagan Drums, K. Jones;
Guitar; R. Wood; Bass, R. Lane
OOH LA LA
Vocal, R. Wood; Acoustics, R. Wood and R. Lane; Drums and
Percussion, K. Jones; Piano and Harmonium, I. McLagan

1970
Atlantic Records
America
Sleeve concept by Jimmy Page
Artwork by Zacron

Led Zeppelin III

Jimmy Page, like many of his peers from the 1960s blues music scene in England, attended art college (Kingston) after leaving high school. There he met the self-mythologizing "Zacron," who left an impression on him. So much so that when Led Zep produced their third album, by which time they were international stars, Page asked Zacron if he could create a *volvelle* (a paper wheel often used for math charts) for them. Zacron, who was then creating collages, readily agreed, and using flight as his theme put together a three-layered work, which has dye-cut windows (Zeppelin would return to that idea for their *Physical Graffiti* album.) The central layer is a rotating wheel containing images of the band and airplanes and so on, which, when turned, replaces images in the various windows. In a 1998 magazine interview Page said he disliked the design, calling it "teeny-bopperish." The original design has not been possible to replicate in any working form for cassette or CD.

Syd Barrett Barrett

1970
Harvest/EMI
England
Sleeve design and illustration
uncredited

The tragedy of Syd Barrett has perhaps lost some of its power due to public over-familiarity with the story. What is less discussed is that Barrett was a gifted artist who won a scholarship to Camberwell College of Arts and returned to painting once he gave up on music. This, Barrett's second and final album, was recorded swiftly with the production help of former Pink Floyd colleagues Dave Gilmour and Rick Wright in order to avoid the lengthy recording sessions (and cost) of his debut *The Madcap Laughs*. After this album failed to chart, though, Barrett returned to Cambridge and, having nothing else to do, began painting. Unfortunately his habit of photographing his finished works and then burning them means there was little of his work left after his death in 2006. While this painting of insects does not appear to be by Barrett, it nonetheless captures the charm and appeal of his best music. It is a depiction of real life as seen through the eyes of a child.

1971

CBS Records

America

Sleeve design by Teresa Alfieri

Art by Milton Glaser

Photography by CBS Records

Photo Studio

Electric Flag The Best of the Electric Flag

The Electric Flag might not have existed for very long—eighteen months in 1967/1968—but their influence was immense. Possibly because they were an early "supergroup" comprised of renowned blues guitarist Paul Butterfield, former Dylan organist Barry Goldberg, and drummer Buddy Miles, with two of Dylan's former horn section. Their sound inspired, among others, Al Kooper to form Blood Sweat and Tears. After their debut gig at the first rock festival, Monterey Pop in 1967, the Flag scored a hit with their version of Howling Wolf's "Killing Floor." They went on to give some spectacular live shows before burning out. All of which makes the choice of Milton Glaser's electric lightbulb-lit flag for the cover of this compilation the more ingenious. Glaser, a New York—born (1929) graphic designer, came up with the I ♥ New York logo, D.C. Comics' bullet logo, and the Brooklyn Brewery logo, as well as designing *New York* magazine and winning countless design awards. Sadly, subsequent releases of Electric Flag compilations have not used Glaser's flag on their covers.

THE BEACH BOYS
SURF'S UP

Beach Boys *Surf's Up*

1971
Brother/Reprise Records
America
Art direction by Ed Thrasher
Painting uncredited, based on a
sculpture by James Earle Fraser

The song "Surf's Up" had been the centerpiece for the failed and shelved
Smile album in 1967, when the Beach Boys' popularity started to fade,
along with their leader's health. They hadn't released a hit single since
"Heroes and Villains" in July, 1967, and the album *Sunflower*, released in
1970, got to only #151 in the Billboard Top 200 chart. Within the band there
were two camps: the Wilsons fighting for musical credibility while Love,
Jardine and company wanted to be back at the top of the singles charts
again. With Wilson incapable of writing and producing everything, *Surf's Up*
came with tracks written (and sung) by pretty much every Beach Boy. The
album's jaunty and optimistic title is put into perfect relief by the painting
of the sculpture *End of the Trail* by James Earle Fraser (best known for his
Buffalo nickel design). The image might depict the warrior (i.e., Wilson) as
exhausted, but he's still seated and equipped for the fight. It perfectly
captured the mood of the band and the times, it seemed. *Surf's Up* put the
Beach Boys in the top 30 album chart for the first time in four years.

Clouds
Joni mitchell

STEREO

RSLP 6341

1969
Reprise Records
America
Sleeve design by Ed Thrasher
Painting by Joni Mitchell

❗ Joni Mitchell Clouds

No one can argue that Joni Mitchell is not a talented musician and songwriter. Few could argue that she's not an OK painter, either. At least these days one can make that argument. Unfortunately, in 1969, when she was just starting out as a singer-songwriter and artist, she was much, much better with a guitar than she was with a paintbrush. Granted that this was at a time when there was a cultural shift occurring in America away from the protesting "we generation" to the self-indulgent "me generation," but this was a step too far and too soon. Mitchell's self-portrait puts her in front of the Saskatchewan River and her hometown of Saskatoon, holding the Saskatchewan flower. Ed Thrasher clearly encouraged Mitchell in her art, and quite correctly too—even the following year's *Ladies of the Canyon* bore a much better self-portrait than this, while both *The Hissing of Summer Lawns* (1975) and *Mingus* (1979) contain paintings of some worth. Unfortunately a trend of using poorly executed self-portraits started with this release.

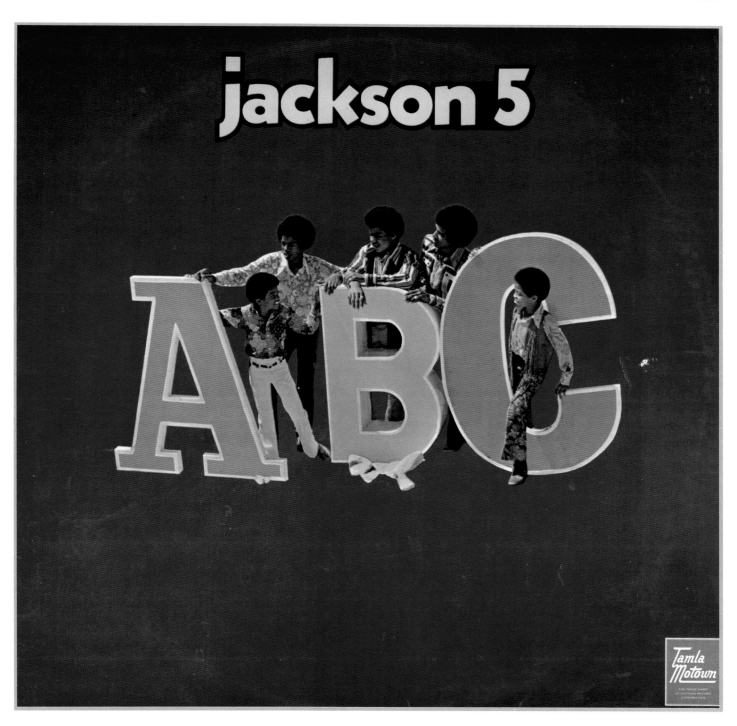

Jackson 5 ABC

1970
Tamla Motown
America
Cover display courtesy of
Ryan Outdoor Advertising
Photography by Paul Slaughter,
Joseph Hernandez

For the cover of the follow-up to their debut album, *Diana Ross Presents the Jackson 5*, Motown went for the jugular: they gave the album the same name as the recent hit single, then slapped a picture of the guys on the front with a bright background and their name emblazoned across the top. Often this brazenly commercial approach to cover design results in the most garish and lurid of sleeves. But here a shot of the band climbing through the first three letters of the alphabet against an eye-catching cerulean background is a work of art. The oversized, brightly colored letters (credited to Ryan Outdoor Advertising) reflect the innocent exuberance of the music, and the unself-conscious photograph of the brothers—almost like a holiday photo—completely captures the atmosphere of their timeless pop.

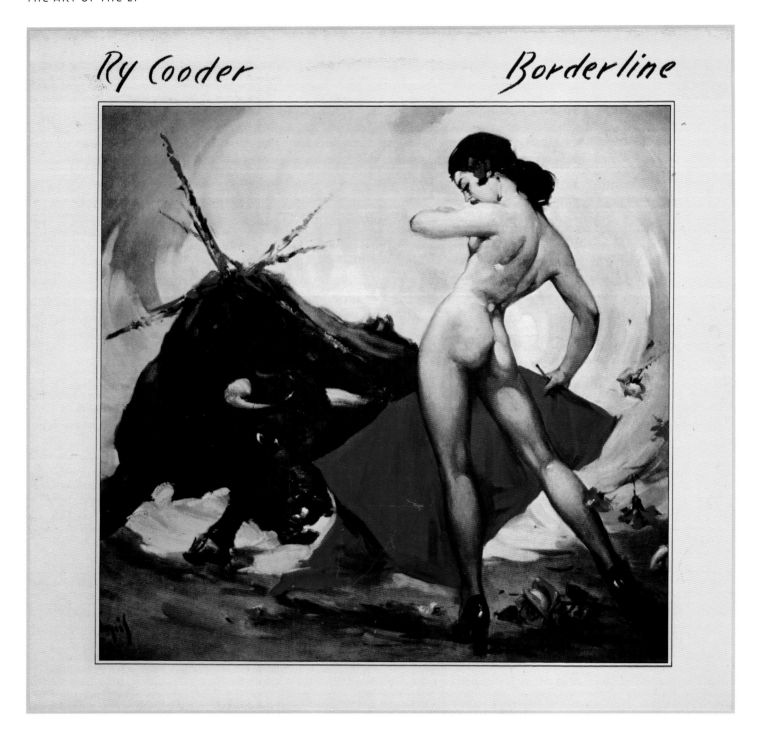

Ry Cooder *Borderline*

1980
Warner Brothers
America
Sleeve design by Kenneth Price/
Ry Cooder
Painting uncredited

Ry Cooder Borderline

Los Angeles—born guitarist Ry Cooder had started out in the business by playing slide guitar for established artists, most notably the Rolling Stones, for whom he contributed the slide parts on the soundtrack to *Performance* and then "Sister Morphine" (on *Sticky Fingers*). After releasing a series of critically acclaimed albums in the 1970s, Cooder became known for his Spanish- and Latin American—influenced music. Working with a young singer-songwriter called John Hiatt and seasoned session drummer Jim Keltner, Cooder put together a bunch of vaguely Country/Tex-Mex tunes for this album. Spending time in New Mexico in the late 1970s, he met the artist Kenneth Price, who took Cooder to the La Fonda Hotel in Taos to meet its colorful owner, a Greek named Saki Karavas—and to see some fantastic old Mexican bullfight posters. One of these hit Price and Cooder's eye, and after two-day negotiations, which saw the price rise from $750 to $1,500, Cooder bought the poster, and used the central image of the naked female bullfighter in high heels to make the evocative cover above.

ABC Beauty Stab

1983
Phonogram
England
Sleeve design by ABC with
Keith Breeden
Painting by Keith Breeden

British pop band ABC had rocketed to fame in 1982 with their massive-selling debut album *Lexicon of Love*. The follow-up was always going to be tough. No doubt Phonogram was hoping for a repeat of the lush Trevor Horn—produced pop contained on their first release, but ABC leader Martin Fry had other ideas: "None of us wanted to make *The Lexicon of Love Part 2*. We wanted to be more like a rock band." The artwork reflects this and Fry's trademark gold lamé suit is nowhere to be seen. Instead you get a matador slaying a bull, reflecting the first line of album opener (and first single) "That Was Then but This Is Now": "Why make the past your sacred cow?" The striking image is by Keith Breeden who also painted sleeves for acts such as Duran Duran and Culture Club and is now a member of the Royal Society of Portrait Painters.

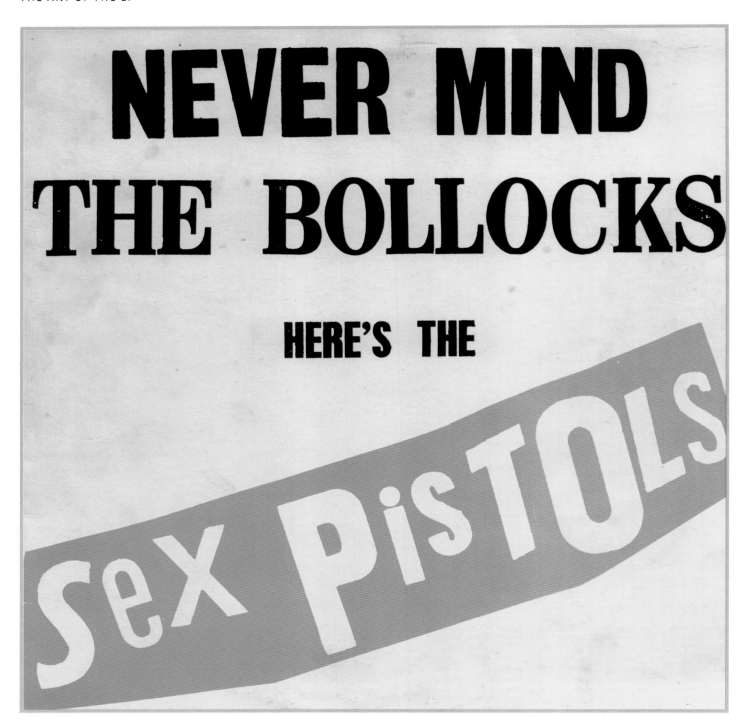

1977
Virgin Records
England
Sleeve design by Jamie Reid

Sex Pistols Never Mind the Bollocks Here's the Sex Pistols

Jamie Reid's designs for the Sex Pistols are now so iconic that it's difficult to appreciate how shocking they were in the late seventies. Growing up in London suburb Croydon in the late sixties, Reid cofounded *Suburban Press*, originally a community newspaper, which soon developed into a political magazine attempting to expose local political corruption. Radical and militant, Reid believed in many of the slogans that punk adopted, which perhaps the band and their manager Malcolm McLaren were more opportunistic about. Reid's most famous design is the one he did for the "God Save the Queen" single bag, using cut-out ransom-note lettering pasted over Cecil Beaton's portrait of Elizabeth II, which is an image that even now retains some shock value. This ransom-note idea, first used for *Suburban Press*, became the defining motif for punk. Once he was told the title of the album, Reid clearly saw no need for any extra graphics other than maximum visibility, so the offensive word could be read. Many record shops at the time insisted on a brown paper wrap to cover the word.

SRK 6063

The Ramones Road to Ruin

1978
Sire Records
America
Sleeve concept by Gus MacDonald
Art by John Holmstrom
Art direction by John Gillespie

After three blistering albums in less than two years, and despite being laden with the weight of critical acclaim, the Ramones were still scared hitless in 1978. This album was made without original drummer Tommy who had left the band, but stayed on as the producer. And possibly due to his production focus the band finally made an album that suggested pop chart potential. The artwork reflects this new readiness for the big time, softening their previous stark photographic artwork (see p. 167), giving them the bubblegum look, which their punk pop aped. It was drawn by their first artist mentor John Holmstrom, whose *Punk* magazine did much to promote them in the early days and whose brilliant comic book graphics had been seen on the back of their previous album *Rocket to Russia*. The band's other artist mentor was Arturo Vega, who designed their enduring logo, itself a recreation of the U.S. presidential seal. The logo never appeared on an original album cover, but continues to be a popular T-shirt design with kids who may never have heard a note played by the band.

Elvis Costello and The Attractions
This Year's Model

1978
Radar Records
England
Sleeve design by Barney Bubbles
Photography by Chris Grabin

Punk-era designer Barney Bubbles (né Colin Fulcher) was an ex-hippy, very much like the era's other big stylist, Jamie Reid. Yet his designs are very much contrary to the brash, bold aesthetic of the day—he was into subtlety and wit. His sleeve for Elvis Costello's second album is not only a gag in that the model is actually the photographer pointing a camera at you, but also the album and artist lettering is deliberately "off-registered," with the CMYK color bar (usually found on proofs for printer reference) visible down the right-hand side. The U.S. edition of this album was corrected by the record company, who apparently thought it was a genuine error.

Graham Parker and the Rumour
The Parkerilla

1978
Vertigo
England
Sleeve design by Barney Bubbles
Photography by Brian Griffin

Parker's final album for Vertigo (Mercury in the U.S.) was a live one so that he could quickly fulfill his contract and escape from a company he hated. Despite it not being one of the artist's best, *The Parkerilla* is blessed with great artwork. Bubbles's unique lettering is frequently at the heart of his designs and he avoided standard fonts like the plague. The gatefold sleeve opens up to reveal the lettering of the album in yellow slashes and red blood splashes like the one over the record company logo on the front (top right). Perhaps it's a visual gag, illustrating Parker's feelings toward his label. His final song for them was called "Mercury Poisoning."

Nick Lowe
Jesus of Cool

1978
Radar Records
England
Sleeve design by Barney Bubbles

Lowe's debut album was re-titled *Pure Pop for Now People* in the U.S., but the brilliant artwork was justifiably left well alone. Lowe's manager and Radar boss Jake Riviera recognized his artist's chameleon ability with musical genre (Lowe had been in country rock band Brinsley Schwartz as well as producing the Damned). On the sleeve Lowe is featured posing as rocker, country balladeer, hippy and so on. Clearly game for a laugh, he allowed Bubble to decorate his bass with flowery wallpaper and wore one of his original hippy shirts too. Always keen on including visual details which the fan had to seek out, Bubbles put tiny letters in the corner of each picture which when combined spell out the American album title.

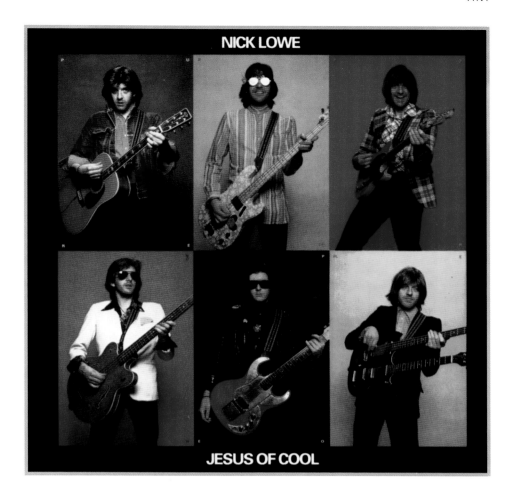

Ian Dury & the Blockheads Do It Yourself

1979
Stiff Records
England
Sleeve design by Barney Bubbles

For this follow-up to Ian Dury's massively successful *New Boots and Panties!!*, Barney Bubbles showed Stiff Records label boss Dave Robinson a book of Crown wallpaper samples, suggesting they could overprint on the actual paper for the album sleeve. The original idea was that each territory would have its own wallpaper, but that soon changed, as Robinson says in Paul Gorman's book on Bubble: "We released ten in the UK . . . it proved incredibly expensive . . . but it was worth it. As it happened the album wasn't up to *New Boots*, so maybe this is one of those cases where Barney's design was far better than the music." Also, look out for Bubbles's "Tommy the Talking Toolbox design."

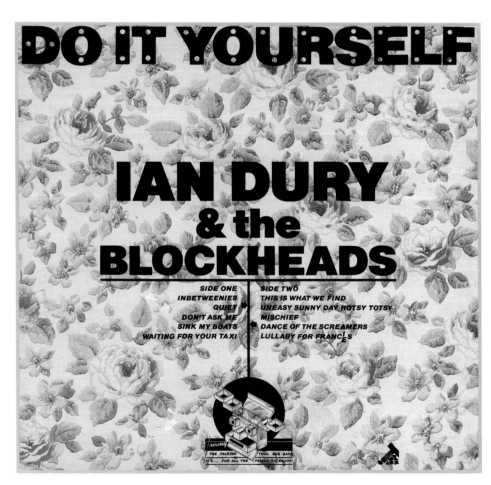

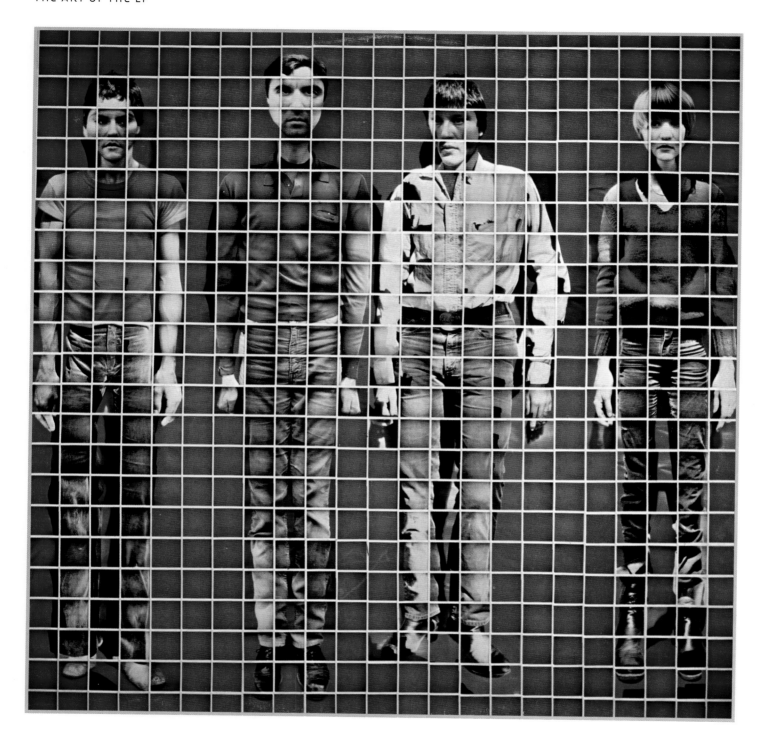

1978
Sire/Warners
America
Cover concept by David Byrne
Design by Jimmy De Sana

Talking Heads More Songs About Buildings and Food

Heads singer and songwriter David Byrne originally met drummer Chris Frantz and bassist Tina Weymouth while the three of them were studying at the Rhode Island School of Design in the mid-70s. So it's not surprising that as well as making artful soul pop with lyrical themes not generally tackled by more pedestrian bands, Talking Heads also invested a great deal in their artwork. This sleeve was put together by Byrne using 529 close-up Polaroid photographs to create a photo-mosaic. Two things are notable about the design: first the band is dressed in an astonishingly ordinary way in indistinctive faded jeans and dull shirts—but the way the faces are broken up and irregularly sized, as well as their blank stares, makes the image exceptionally striking. Second, neither band name nor album title (a joke about bands' sophomore albums usually being repeats of their debuts) feature on the cover. It was a characteristically confident and defiant move.

WIRE

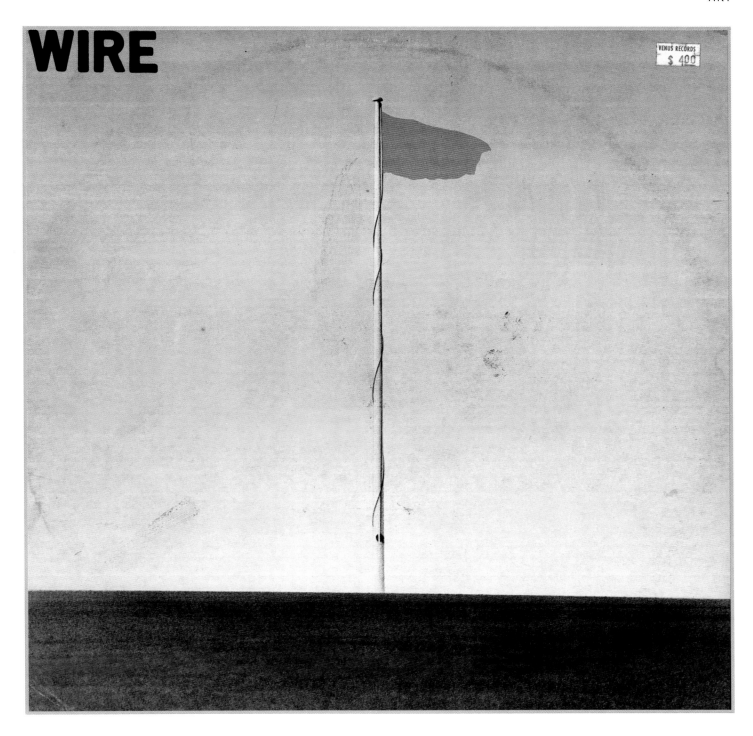

VENUS RECORDS
$ 400

1977
Harvest/EMI
England
Sleeve concept by B. C. Gilbert and
Graham Lewis
Cover photography by Annette Green
Artwork by David Dragon

Wire Pink Flag

Although regarded a part of the punk scene and certainly embodying its principal of "anyone can do it," Wire was nonetheless peripheral to London's punk elite and wanted no part of it. The cover to their debut album was shot by singer Colin Newman's future (first) wife Annette Green, who also cowrote the album track "Different to Me." It's as bold and eye-catching as the Sex Pistols' debut LP cover but a million miles away from its brash sloganeering. While on tour in 1977, Wire band members Bruce Gilbert (guitar) and Graham Lewis (bass) spotted a flagless pole on a parade ground in Plymouth Hoe, Southwest England. Entirely without the other's knowledge, each had sketched flagpoles which they subsequently agreed would make a good cover. They photographed the Plymouth flagpole and EMI's David Dragon then airbrushed the sky blue and painted the flag pink on strict instruction not to make it photo-realistic and to avoid putting the title in. The clean lines and stark pink flag stood out from the otherwise deliberate, messed-up, handmade artworks favored by the punk milieu.

Buzzcocks Another Music in a Different Kitchen

1978
United Artists
England
Sleeve design by Malcolm Garrett

Malcolm Garrett studied graphic design at Manchester Polytechnic, along with New Order designer Peter Saville (see pp. 128—29). His first commercial work was for up-and-coming local lads Buzzcocks, who had already established themselves via the seminal independent release "Spiral Scratch," a 4-track EP. Garrett's logo, with its skewed Zs, which he designed for Buzzcocks' major label debut single "Orgasm Addict," is instantly recognizable and still used by them to this day. Their debut album uses a conventional shot of the band to great effect, with a silver and orange pallet and a subtle branding in the top right-hand corner.

Magazine The Correct Use of Soap

1980
Virgin
England
Sleeve design by Malcolm Garrett

By 1980, Malcolm Garrett was much in demand and would go on to produce sleeve art for some of the biggest bands of the eighties (see opposite). His roots were, however, still very much in Manchester, and he continued to provide excellent sleeves for the now less successful Buzzcocks and the hugely underrated Magazine. The UK edition of this album was highly tactile, with a rough-side-out cardboard sleeve and thick ink that felt like a screen print. This is the U.S. edition, with the embossed soap oval beneath the band logo. Garrett went on to develop Internet design in the nineties but returned to this font and design when a reformed Magazine needed poster designs in 2009.

Duran Duran Rio

1982
EMI
England
Sleeve design by Malcolm Garrett
Illustration by Patrick Nagel

Just like Duran Duran, artist/illustrator Patrick Nagel was an eighties phenomenon. He painted from photographs—often of top models—which he would bleach out until all that remained was white skin, pastel lips and black hair, sometimes described as a combination of Japanese woodblock and art deco. His designs, often just referred to as "The Nagel Woman," frequently appeared in *Playboy* from 1976 onward and became an eighties look. The women in Robert Palmer's "Addicted to Love" video are pure Nagel, for instance. Under his design studio brand Assorted Images, Malcolm Garrett's work on the original illustration was crucial to making it effective as a sleeve. Garrett added his trademark bold lines (see opposite) and added band and album title design as well as the eye detail in the bottom right-hand corner.

ember

ben webster at ease

STEREO

1969
Ember
Denmark
Sleeve design and photography
uncredited

Ben Webster At Ease

Ben Webster was one of the great tenor saxophonists who made the successful transition from the 1940s Big Band era through the Charlie Parker—inspired Be Bop and into the Modern age. A former soloist with Duke Ellington (and many Big Bands before that), Webster became his own man in the 1950s and recorded with a range of other greats, including pianist Art Tatum, tenor player and mentor Coleman Hawkins, and Oscar Peterson. Webster wasn't a great innovator and wasn't prepared to attempt the kind of avant-garde pyrotechnics that Eric Dolphy had introduced John Coltrane to, however, and he left America for good in 1964 and moved to Denmark (ironically, the year that Dolphy died in Europe). This late recording is every inch as time-worn, laid back, and ornery as the stark photograph on the cover. The photo, like the music played on the record, is almost other-worldly. This makes sense. Webster is nearing his end in a strange land, albeit one that welcomed him warmly and thought him extremely "cool." It could be 1949 instead of 1969, and that's the point.

1980
Island Records
England
Sleeve design by Steve Averill
Photography by Hugo McGuinness

U2 Boy

The 2008 remastered edition restored this original UK sleeve which in the U.S. had been replaced by a blurred shot of the band. The label had been concerned that the band would be accused of pedophilia. The boy in the photograph is Peter Rowan, the younger brother of Bono's best friend Guggi, former member of Irish rock outfit the Virgin Prunes. Rowan went on to appear on U2's third album, *War*, as well as on the *Best Of: 1980—1990*. Photographer Hugh McGuinness took the shots of Rowan and another friend of the band—Steve Averill—designed the sleeve. Averill has been involved with pretty much every U2 release since then, reflecting the band's consistency in their choice of collaborators. They are one of the few rock bands who are still together in their original lineup thirty years after the release of this album and they have kept the same manager and same producers for most of their career. The artwork reflects the confidence of the young U2, not only in resisting a standard cover shot of themselves but, importantly, in not even displaying their name.

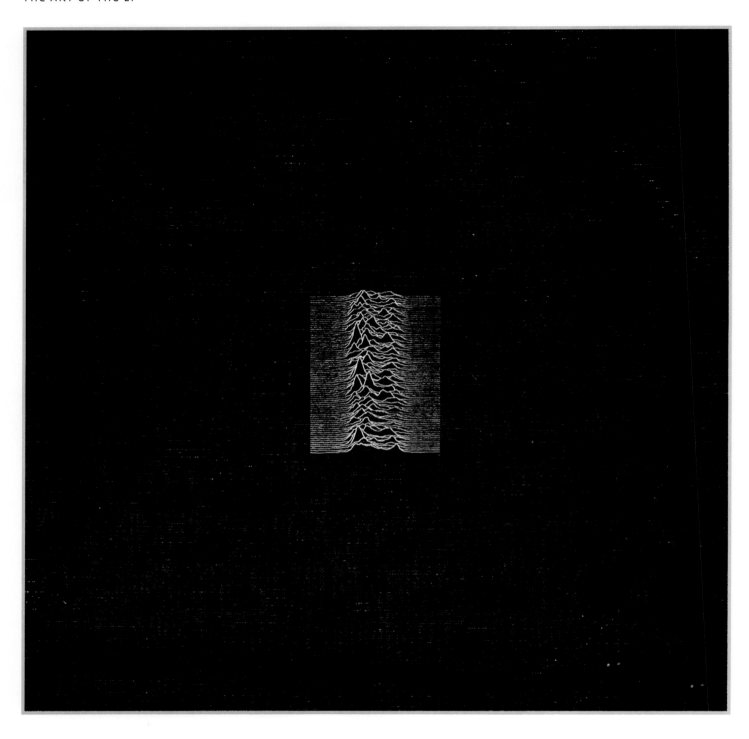

Joy Division Unknown Pleasures

1979
Factory Records
England
Sleeve design by Joy Division and
Peter Saville

Peter Saville, like fellow Manchester Polytechnic design student Malcolm Garrett (see pp. 124—25), was blessed by his locality. In the late 1970s, the Northwest of England was producing some incredible music. Influenced by his friend Garrett as well as Jan Tschichold's *The New Typography*, Saville helped found Factory Records, becoming the in-house designer for its artists and club nights. At first glance, the image on the front of Joy Division's debut album looks like a mountain range, but it is actually from the *Cambridge Encyclopedia of Astronomy*, and shows a hundred successive pulses from the first pulsar discovered. Drummer Stephen Morris suggested the image, which was originally black on a white background. Saville's reversal of the image, combined with his choice of textured cardboard and the decision to avoid giving band name, album title or track listings, results in a sleeve that does just what an album sleeve should: reflect and add gravitas to the music contained inside.

1983
Factory Records
England
Sleeve design by New Order and
Peter Saville
Painting by Henri Fantin-Latour

New Order Power, Corruption and Lies

The late, great Tony Wilson, founder of New Order's label Factory Records, recounted a conversation he had with Britain's National Gallery after they had refused to let Peter Saville use "A Basket of Roses" by French artist Henri Fantin-Latour for the sleeve of New Order's sophomore album. He asked them who owned the painting and was told that the Trust belonged to the people of Britain. "Well," Tony is claimed to have said, "the people of Britain now want it!" Whether true or not, Saville did get to use it for his design, which incorporates the French still life into an ultra modernist color-based code to represent the name of the band and the album in the top right corner. There is a decoder on the back of the album which could also be used to decode the band's next two singles, including the biggest-selling 12" of all time, "Blue Monday," the sleeve of which famously cost more to manufacture than the company made from each sale.

1980
Island Records
England
Sleeve concept and design by
Dennis Morris

Linton Kwesi Johnson LKJ in Dub

Photographer Dennis Morris had caught his first big break when he met Bob Marley in London and the Jamaican singer allowed the then sixteen-year-old Dalston-born photographer to take pictures of the Wailers. Morris became the Sex Pistols' preferred photographer and by the end of the 1970s had earned a job as in-house reggae expert, photographer and designer at Island Records (Marley's label). Morris is credited with finding and signing Linton Kwesi Johnson to the label. A Jamaican-born but London-based "dub poet," Johnson's political poems set to rock-steady reggae backings made him a post-punk star in the UK. This album, containing dub versions of tracks from LKJ's previous two Island releases, *Forces of Victory* (1979) and *Bass Culture* (1980), forms a visual accompaniment to those albums too: *Victory* is a predominantly black cover, *Bass Culture* predominantly white, neither has a photo of LKJ. The clean, spare typography that fills the margins of the sleeve make a fitting visual clue to the resounding sound of the album.

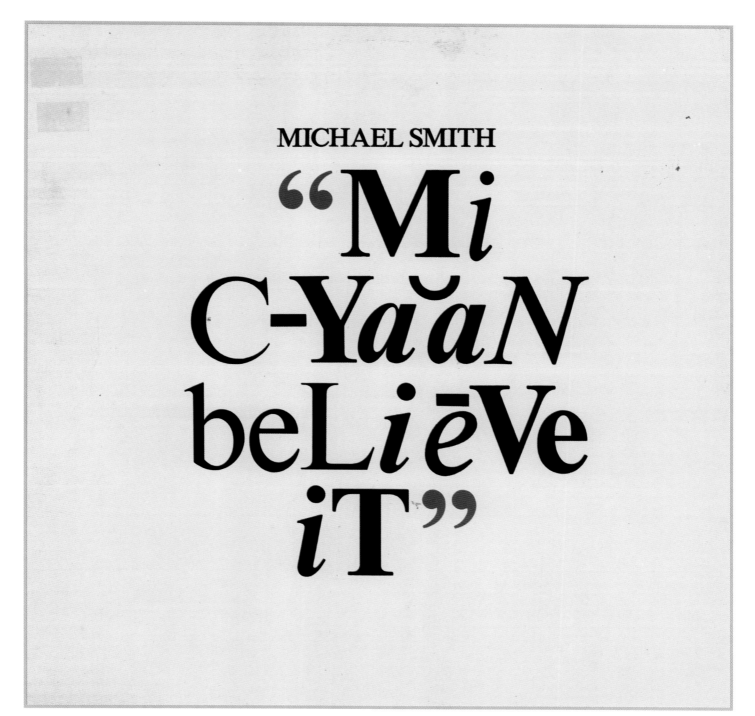

MICHAEL SMITH

"Mi C-YaaN beLieVe iT"

1982
Island Records
England
Sleeve design uncredited

Michael Smith Mi C-Yaan Believe It

Two years after the success of *In Dub*, Linton Kwesi Johnson produced fellow Jamaican dub poet Smith's debut album (along with LKJ's producer, Dennis Bovell). The ingenious idea of phonetically spelling out the title track (Smith's most famous work), leaves the uninitiated reader/listener in no doubt that here is a fierce, proud album of Jamaican protest songs. A year after the album's release Smith was stoned to death by unknown assailants at a political rally in Kingston, having heckled the Jamaican Minister for Culture during his speech. A leftist, pro-Rastafarian, Smith decried the corrupt politics of the ruling right-wing Labour Party in his public work as a poet and a social worker at Jamaica's infamous Gun Court, which operates without a jury in cases involving firearms. This spare but powerful and unsensational cover shies away from the contemporary reggae imagery of drugs and Rasta, to present a work clearly and primarily about communication.

1985
Stiff Records
England
Sleeve concept by Frank Murray
Heads by Peter Mennim/Aircraft Ltd.
Hand lettering by Lilly Lee
Original painting *Le Radeau de la
Méduse* by Théodore Géricault

The Pogues Rum, Sodomy & the Lash

The original painting upon which the Pogues based the cover art of their
second album depicted an unpleasant truth: in 1816 the French frigate
Méduse sank just outside what is now Mauritania and the ship's captain
ordered the building of rafts on which the crew lived for thirteen days,
resorting to cannibalism to stay alive. Only 15 of the original 147 survived
and the handling of the situation caused an international scandal. French
Romantic artist Théodore Géricault chose the incident because he knew
that residual public anger about the event would get his work noticed—the
Pogues' then manager Frank Murray chose the picture because he perhaps
recognized that lead singer and songwriter Shane McGowan's lyrics
depicted unpleasant truths similar to those of Gericault's painting, but
also because the sense of chaos into which the band members' faces are
added accurately reflected their public image.

Bow Wow Wow See Jungle! See Jungle! Go Join
Your Gang, Yeah. City All Over! Go Ape Crazy!

1981
RCA
England
Sleeve design by Nick Egan
Photography by Andy Earl

Legend has it that Bow Wow Wow singer Annabelle Lwin was discovered at
age fourteen, singing along to a Stevie Wonder song in the launderette
where she worked. After she joined former Sex Pistols manager Malcolm
McClaren's next project (formed with ex-members of Adam & the Ants),
there were accusations by her mother that he was exploiting a minor for
immoral purposes. This cover photograph was withdrawn, as she was only
fifteen when the shoot took place. It seems that no one thought to ask her
mother what Lwin had been doing working in a launderette at age fourteen
in the first place. Exploitation of sexuality aside, this recreation of Manet's
original 1863 painting *Le Déjeuner sur l'Herbe*—itself a subject of much
controversy in its own time—is stunning and cleverly fitted in with the New
Romantic look that was popular at the time.

1982
Mute
England
Sleeve design by Martyn Atkins
Photography by Brian Griffin

Depeche Mode A Broken Frame

Although described even by band member Martin Gore as "our worst album," Depeche Mode's second LP—their first without founder member and former main songwriter Vince Clarke—is blessed with a gorgeous sleeve. Looking to all intents and purposes like a Dutch Golden Age painting by Vermeer or Aelbert Cuyp, it is quite surprisingly a photograph. Brian Griffin, who took the shot, often worked with sleeve designer Martyn Atkins, perhaps most famously on the sleeves for Echo & the Bunnymen's albums—all of which are staged images composed in the manner of a painting. As well as continuing to design artwork, Atkins went on to direct videos. Griffin's photograph was named one of *Life* magazine's "World's Greatest Pictures 1980—1990" and was featured on the front cover of the Winter 1990 edition of the magazine.

1985
Mercury Records
America
Sleeve design by P. St. John Nettleton

Green on Red No Free Lunch

Long before the term "alt country" had been invented, Green on Red (from Tucson, Arizona, but based in Los Angeles) were creating their peculiar brand of American music. Like the Violent Femmes, GonR mixed Country, Southern rock, blues, psychedelia and dark humor in songs that were often witty, poignant and sometimes raucous. Band leader Dan Stuart had a reputation for being a heavy drinker (which he encouraged), while guitarist Chuck Prophet came across as the silent, intense type. They were both fascinated by legends of the American West and South. The cover of this mini-album is a complex mix of late 19th-century U.S. woodcut images, with a dye-cut front (the central portal) and double-printed inner sleeve, the images of which—a drunken woman with sailors on one side, a rodeo cowboy on the other—fill the portal depending on how you insert the inner sleeve. When it's out, a printed image of a trapper wrestling a grizzly bear appears in the portal. The cover was lovingly and lavishly produced, for which the band is probably still paying the record company.

Belly Star

1993
4AD
England
Sleeve design by Chris Bigg at v23
Photography by Chris Gorman

Ex-Throwing Muses member
Tanya Donnelly named her
solo project Belly because
she thought it sounded both
pretty and ugly. Regardless of
the sound of the music, being
on the 4AD label meant that
her artwork would be created
by Vaughan Oliver's v23 and
would be far from ugly. An
art director and typographer,
Oliver founded 23 Envelope
with photographer Nigel
Grierson in 1982. After they
parted in 1988, he worked
with a number of different
collaborators including,
as here, Chris Bigg. The
trademarks of v23 are
close-up, high-resolution
photography, glossy, metallic
and fur textures, and unique,
striking fonts. Here Bigg uses
Chris Gorman's shot of plastic
ballet dancers offset with a
typically stunning logo.

Throwing Muses
Red Heaven

1992
4AD
England
Cover art by Kristin Hersh and
Christine Cano
Package design by Christine Cano

With Tanya Donnelly having
left to form Belly, Kristin
Hersh continued Throwing
Muses, releasing *Red
Heaven* in 1992. Like her
ex-bandmate, she was
contracted to 4AD but
instead of using their usual
art director Vaughan Oliver
at v23, she codesigned
this with Christine Cano.
Bizarrely though, the
finished result—a collage
motif of stiletto-wearing
legs, torso and forearm
repeated on a textured
sackcloth background—is
reminiscent of Oliver's work,
and reinforces just how
distinctive v23's house
style is.

The Breeders
Last Splash

1993
4AD
England
Art direction and design by
Vaughan Oliver at v23
Photography by Jason Love

Vaughan Oliver arguably did as much to define the early direction of 4AD as the bands that label boss Ivo Watts Russell brought in. His design for the Breeders' second album is archetypal of his design style. Working with a photographer (in this case Jason Love), he creates an atmosphere of rarefied beauty which simultaneously has an air of darkness or the macabre. Here is a gorgeous, rich red heart shape, possibly a child's plastic locket, set against a lush green and pink surround. So far so pretty. But the dark liquid drops on the heart hint at something darker, as if the toy is actually the very real organ that its idealized shape represents.

Ultra Vivid Scene
Ultra Vivid Scene

1988
4AD
England
Design by Vaughan Oliver at v23

This is an earlier design of Oliver's, presumably done shortly after his original partner Nigel Grierson had left v23. It looks as if Oliver has used a stock photo here to represent Kurt Ralske's lo-fi alt-rock. What makes this cover—particularly in the original 12" format—so striking is the use of metallic ink over textured card to recreate the "gaffer" tape effect. Like many of Oliver's sleeves, it not only leaps out at you but also is almost three-dimensional in its attention to detail of card and ink. The Pixies *Minotaur* box set of 2009, "curated" by Oliver with photographer Simon Larbalestier, takes this to extremes with an enormous fur-covered book almost two feet in height.

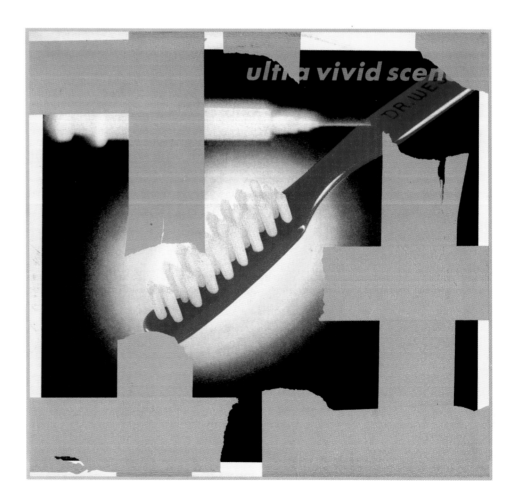

1981
Warner Brothers
America
Art direction by Richard Seireeni
Sleeve design by Pete Angelus
Painting *The Maze* by William Kurelek

Van Halen Fair Warning

Heavy metal outfit Van Halen, fronted by screaming hair-metal monster David Lee Roth, were musically far from subtle. And yet some of their album covers were subtle and witty works of art—and had surprising origins. None more so than this, their fourth album, for which they chose the best-known work of William Kurelek, a Canadian artist who was briefly hospitalized and treated for schizophrenia in England in 1952. While in the hospital he produced this painting, *The Maze*. With its echoes of Breughel and Bosch, it is almost medieval in tone and style. The manic face leering at the viewer while behind it men fight, kick, and head-butt walls could almost be a detail from one of Bosch's paintings depicting hell and sin. Kurelek went on to paint a series of religious images after converting to Catholicism, and then turning to children's books as an illustrator. He died in Toronto in 1977, at age fifty. This was the first time that Van Halen used an intriguing piece of original art as cover art, and they would go on to use other funny and surprising images (see p. 382).

Primal Scream Screamadelica

1991
Creation Records
England
Sleeve layout by ES(P)
Illustration by Paul Cannell

A hugely influential album in the UK, Primal Scream's third release captured the post–Acid House comedown and fused rock and dance music together. Band leader Bobby Gillespie knew his pop history and asked newcomer Paul Cannell for something abstract and jazzy for the sleeve of "Higher than the Sun"—clearly he wanted it to look "classic." Untrained Cannell had stumbled upon sleeve designs as a career because he wanted to be associated with cool musicians—prior to *Screamadelica* he had only created a handful of sleeves for Manic Street Preachers and Flowered Up. Unlike the 1950s-influenced multicolored abstracts Cannell created for Primal Scream's singles, though, *Screamadelica* works from a pallet of just three colors. As *NME* editor James Brown later said, "he caught the childlike wonder the recording is streaked with." The saucer eyes of the sun could also be viewed a little more cynically in the light of the band's notorious drug use. Cannell committed suicide in 2005.

The Smithereens Blow Up

New Jersey retro pop quartet the Smithereens are clearly big movie fans. One of their most well-known songs, "In a Lonely Place," takes its title and lyrics from the Nicholas Ray, Humphrey Bogart film noir of that title, and the artwork for their 1989 album *11* makes overt reference to the original *Oceans Eleven* movie. So it was hardly surprising that they turned to the granddaddy of movie poster and credit design to create an album sleeve for them. Bass had never designed a rock band sleeve before and it appears that it was his kids who pestered him to work with the Smithereens. While not his best work (see p. 94), the cover for *Blow Up* is nonetheless characteristic of Bass's unique way with lettering and simple pallet of colors. It even works with the band's logo font, although, considering Bass's legendary status, it seems a wasted opportunity for them not to have got him to knock them up a new logo.

1991
Capitol Records
America
Sleeve design by Pietro Alfieri
Artwork by Saul Bass
Art direction by the Smithereens/
Tommy Steele

Pavement Slanted and Enchanted

1991
Matador
America
Design and artwork uncredited

This is another incredibly influential album that without a doubt benefited from artwork that exactly captured the essence of the music. Pavement formed in 1989 in Stockton, California, as a recording and rehearsal studio project of Stephen Malkmus and Scott Kannberg. The disorganized nature of the band members and the music they made was very much the image that Pavement's early audience embraced, and they pretty much defined U.S. lo-fi indie music in the early nineties. Strongly influenced by UK punk band The Fall, Pavement reinforced their fractured, yelping songs with clever melodies and lyrics. The artwork to their debut album captures this: a photograph of a crescent piano keyboard (Kannberg's pseudonym was "Spiral Stairs") is scratched at and graphitized with the band's name and album title in what looks like correcting fluid. Yet, despite all the mess and apparent sloppiness, the image works. Just like the music.

scott walker · TILT

1995
Fontana/Phonogram
England
Cover photography and image
manipulation by David Scheinmann
Concept and hand by Scott Walker
Art direction and design by Stylorouge

Scott Walker Tilt

Tilt was the first Scott Walker album for eleven years and as such bore the weight of critical expectation. Musically, it's a million miles away from either Walker's mid-sixties pop or his baroque solo work from the late sixties and early seventies. This is dark, foreboding music; operatic, experimental and lyrically obscure. An image of him on the artwork must have seemed inappropriate—but what then? Photographer David Scheinmann's slick, airbrushed style can be seen in his photographs of Peter Gabriel, Enya and Cher or in his TV commercials for Canon or Suzuki. But here, he goes off the beaten track, giving free reign to his dark side. He has manipulated a photograph of Walker's hand until it looks like a lurking, feral bird of prey—are those black glinting circles actually eyes? Like the music here: whatever it is, it's not for the faint of heart.

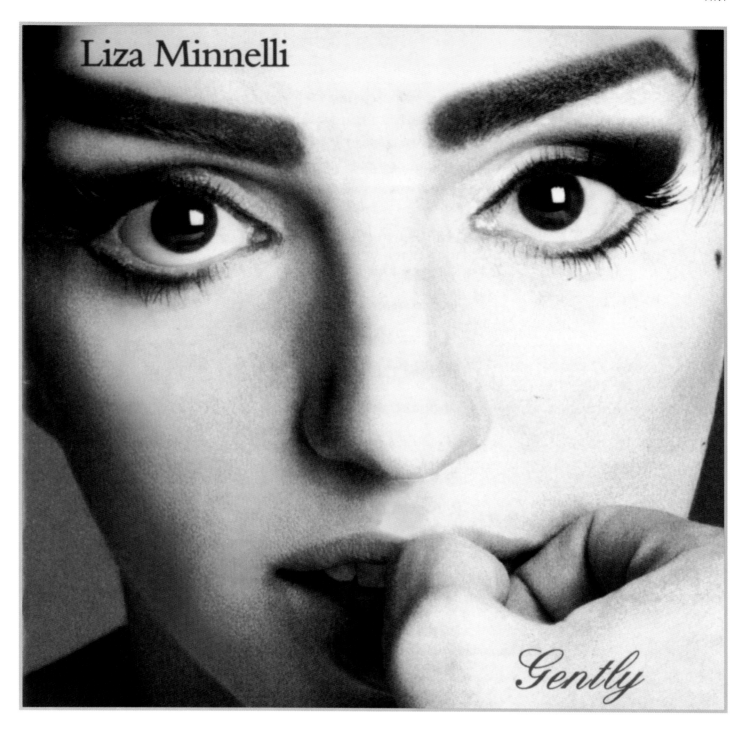

Liza Minnelli Gently

1995
Angel Records
America
Sleeve design by J. C. Squares
Photography by Steven Meisel

Liza Minnelli had just turned fifty when this was released, and yet she was still regarded in the media as an unfortunate child, forever teetering on the edge of falling badly and hurting herself. Steven Meisel's extraordinary photograph captures the child in the woman. Her eyes—big, clear and wide open—shine from a flawless face. The thumb being bitten isn't contrived—interviewers at the time commented on her perpetual gnawing on her nails as she struggled to find a way back to the answer to a question that she'd just spent minutes ambling away from. The placement of her name just above that impressive dark slash of an eyebrow is needed; few would believe that this was the same Liza Minnelli they'd seen photographed as she recovered from her hip replacement operation only eighteen months earlier. The use of the italicized title (and the very choice of the word for the title) on the thumb emphasizes not just the album's content of ballads and love songs, which ends with "In the Wee Small Hours of the Morning," but also how we should treat the singer.

1980
CBS Records
America
Painting by Tony Wright

ⓘ Bob Dylan Saved

What was he thinking? OK, so Bob had enjoyed an enlightening experience, found God, and wanted to share his faith with the world (again; he'd done it the year before with *Slow Train Coming*, another album whose cover is a contender for how not to do it). But to ask the veteran English sleeve designer Tony Wright to come up with a hand-of-God image was a mistake, at best, and an egotistical boast of the highest order at least. Is that God's hand, or is it Bob's? Do we feel flattered that the great man is reaching down to touch us, the adoring fans? Actually, no, in fact, we feel embarrassed for Bob. The record stank almost as much as the sleeve, and the cover was replaced with a painting of Bob performing (also by Wright, and originally used on the inner sleeve) pretty quickly, yet the album made #3 in the UK charts, and 29 in America. Still, it has not been a consistent seller by any means. Thank God.

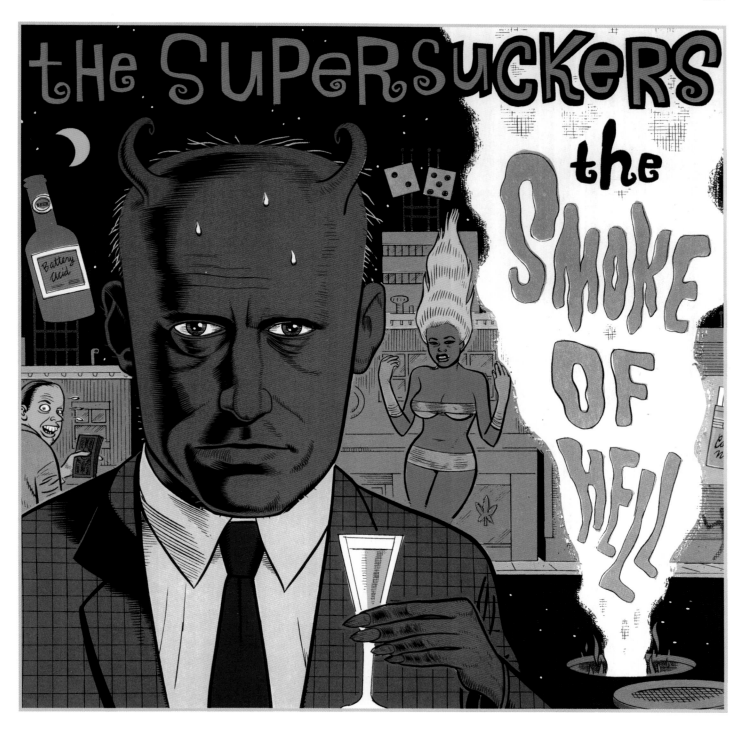

1992
Sub Pop
America
Artwork by Daniel Clowes

The Supersuckers The Smoke of Hell

Relocating to Seattle in 1989, Tucson's Supersuckers signed to the ultra-hip Sub Pop label and, in 1992, released this, their debut album. While perhaps not the most musically distinguished Sub Pop release, and pretty much ignored in favor of more grunge-friendly acts, the album was fortunate enough to have artwork designed by Daniel Clowes. Three years into his periodic *Eightball* comic book series, Clowes went on to find fame with a story first featured in *Ghost World*. *Ghost World* was published in book form in 1997, and it very much trail-blazed the way in which graphic novels would go on to be sold as literature in bookstores—although apparently Clowes still prefers the term "comic book." He later adapted it for a movie in 2001 and was nominated for an Academy Award for his screenplay. *The Smoke of Hell* is one of twenty other album and single sleeves designed by Clowes and is probably the best known. The Supersuckers continue to make music.

IDENTITY

It is key to pop music for credibility, as well as unit-shifting, to establish a recognizable visual identity. In its infancy, record sleeve design was often no more than a picture of the artists with their names displayed as prominently as possible. Similarly, record labels would insist on stamping their own identity in the top left-hand corner of every release—just think of those early Beatles albums.

In fact, despite the Fabs' absence from this chapter (although you'll be pleased to hear that you'll find them elsewhere), it was probably the Beatles who led the way in creating identity through sleeve artwork—which they had to do, because they had given up on touring in 1966. From the beginning, it was vitally important to create a unique visual selling point for an album. Central to this was designing a logo, some of which now have as much resonance as the biggest corporate brands. Consider, for example, the Monkees' guitar shape (p. 148), the "Chicago" font (p. 163), and all those heavy-metal logos that are so perfect for stitching onto your denim jacket.

Some artists were forced to establish identity through graphics due to their own anonymity, or perhaps because they wanted to remain anonymous—Boston's spaceship (p. 166) is more familiar to fans than any of the actual group members, and the same is probably true of Pink Floyd's prism (p. 156), and Iron Maiden's Eddie (p. 171). Many of the sleeves featured here were visual identities so original that they set the template for other artists to follow, while some albums were quite possibly saved commercially by the clever ID work of a graphic artist—would Brand X's demanding jazz fusion have done so well without its rock iconography? (p. 164). Would Kraftwerk's elegant electronic funk have remained so resonant without Karl Klefisch's iconic sleeve? (p. 168).

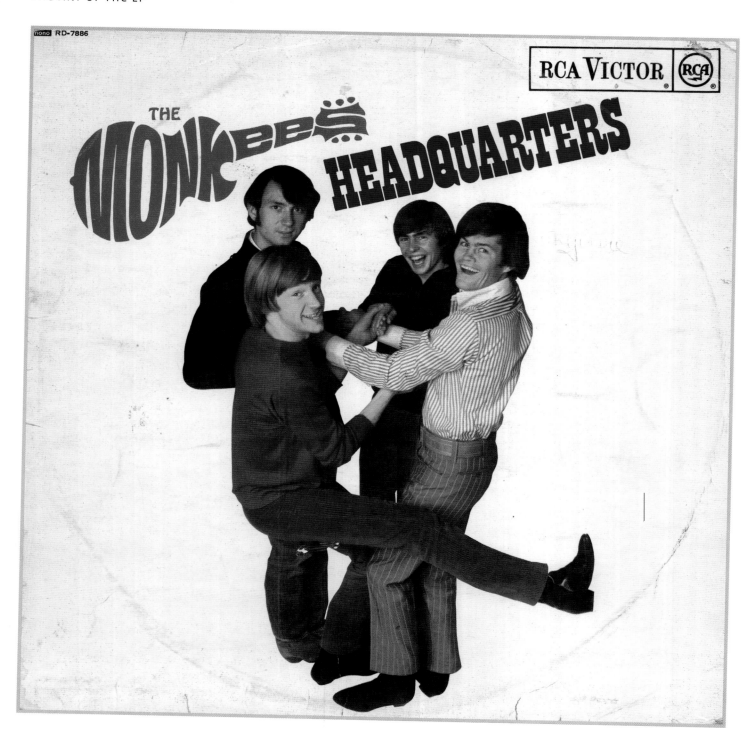

nono RD-7886

RCA VICTOR | RCA

The Monkees Headquarters

1966
Colgems
America
Sleeve design by Colgems
Monkees logo design by Nick LoBianco

The cover of their previous album, *More of the Monkees*, was a cheesy montage of the band all wearing clothing from JC Penney. It was symptomatic of the many things that prompted Mickey Dolenz to demand more creative autonomy for the band. Apparently Dolenz put his fist through a wall to make his point. It worked: later the same year, the band released this, their third album. Now, instead of just singing they also wrote most of the songs and played almost all the instruments. The cover, too, is different. The band is looking more natural and although probably just as composed, Peter Tork's goofball persona finally gets a sleeve airing. That said, they were not foolish enough to abandon the superb Monkees logo. That had been commissioned in 1966 by Screen Gems, who allegedly paid designer Nick LoBianco a mere $75 for his work. A bargain.

1968
Karma Sutra
America
Sleeve design by Acy R. Lehman
Cover art by Chrystal Starr Russell

The Lovin' Spoonful The Best of the
Lovin' Spoonful Volume Two

The first *Best of the Lovin' Spoonful* in 1967 featured a very similar
illustrated comic book—style sleeve, but with all the band members
standing, their arms outstretched. Everyone apart from singer John
Sebastian, that is, who is seated on a high stool, looking very much the
group's leader. This second volume, featuring a democratically seated
Spoonful, works much better—proof being that it is still being used by
BMG to house the current CD compilation *The Very Best*. Chrystal Starr
Russell's blobby, primary-colored artwork may be generic of the cartoon
graphics of the mid-sixties but it is a clever way of selling a band
whose varied musical styles didn't provide an instant visual identity.
Interestingly, it is the faces that Starr focused on—those are left
largely blank aside from John Sebastian's Lennon specs and an array
of sixties 'taches.

1967
Abnak Music Enterprises
America
Sleeve design by Abnak

ⓘ The Five Americans Western Union

The Five Americans are ripe for a discovery by anyone who is keen on British Invasion—influenced bands with a Byrds feel. Their Monkees-like big hit from 1966, "Western Union," was the springboard for this, their second album. But like Stevie Wonder's album of three years later (see p. 176), any semblance of cool or stylishness was thrown out of the window for the cover, which features a literal interpretation of the title track as the boys leap out of a telegram. The problem with this sleeve was illustrative of the malaise at the heart of the band's business setup. They had signed to the insurance millionaire Jon Abdor's Dallas label Abnak. It was son Jon Jr. who, after getting them to change their name from the Mutineers, subsequently pretty much controlled every aspect of the band's short-lived career.

faces.

Faces First Step

1970
Warners
England
Sleeve design by Mike McInnerney
Photography by Martin Cook

Originally entitled Small Faces in America, where Warners wanted to cash in on the small success that the Steve Marriott—led band had enjoyed, in England everyone knew that the band was made up half with ex-Small Faces and half with Jeff Beck Group members. Because Ron Wood and Rod Stewart were not small (being 5'8" and 5'9", respectively), Ronnie Lane, the bassist, suggested they drop the "Small" from the name, which they did. This, their debut album, was recorded soon after the band started playing together and in some ways the playing reflects that. The cover image, though, is a very sly takeoff of the John Mayall Bluesbreakers album from 1966. On the Mayall cover the band members sit in a row looking at the camera, all except Clapton, that is, because he's reading the comic *Beano*. Ron Wood, being the funny guy that he is, decided that he should be photographed for this cover "reading" a beginner's guitar book, from which the album takes its name. The Mickey Mouse doll adds to the childish and irreverent aspect that was always part of the band's persona.

1969
Atlantic
America
Sleeve concept by Jimmy Page
Art direction by George Hardie

Led Zeppelin Led Zeppelin

The band's name came out of a drunken conversation between Jimmy Page, Jeff Beck, John Entwistle and Keith Moon. One of them suggested that they all form a band, to which Moon replied that they'd "go down like a lead zeppelin." Page liked that idea enough not only to use the name for the band he formed with Robert Plant, John Bonham and John Paul Jones, but also to request the use of a photograph of the Hindenberg airship crashing in 1937 on the cover of their debut album release. The photograph was used, the band's reputation was set; a little old-fashioned, tasteless, vast and dangerous. There are also people who see the phallic form of the zeppelin as being relevant to the band's identity too. That may be so, but I'd guess none of the Zep thought about it at the time; this was simply a literal translation of their name, tinged with the kind of bad taste which rock music was flirting with at the time (thirty-six people died in the Hindenberg air crash in New Jersey).

T. Rex The Slider

1972
EMI Records
England
Photography by Ringo Starr

Marc Bolan's power-pop trio T. Rex was the first band in England to be compared favorably to the Beatles by the mainstream press. Not musically, but because of the hordes of screaming young girls who followed Bolan everywhere he went. After trying to make it first as a young Mod "face" in London in the late 1960s, Bolan wrote fairy-tale folk songs, wore long, flowing robes and spouted mystical garbage to a backing of purely acoustic instruments, as part of Tyrannosaurus Rex. After Bowie switched from folk to pop and discovered his wife's makeup box, Bolan decided to plug in, put stars on his eyes (glitter eye shadow) and pump out rudimentary rock & roll songs with nonsense lyrics and massive choruses. He also shortened the name of the band and they became an "overnight sensation" in 1971. A year later, former Beatle Ringo Starr directed a documentary film that followed Bolan around England as he played to screaming fans. His photo on the cover of *The Slider* perfectly captured Bolan's star appeal: hazy, sexy, a little battered. The enormous red band name projects the trio's loud sound.

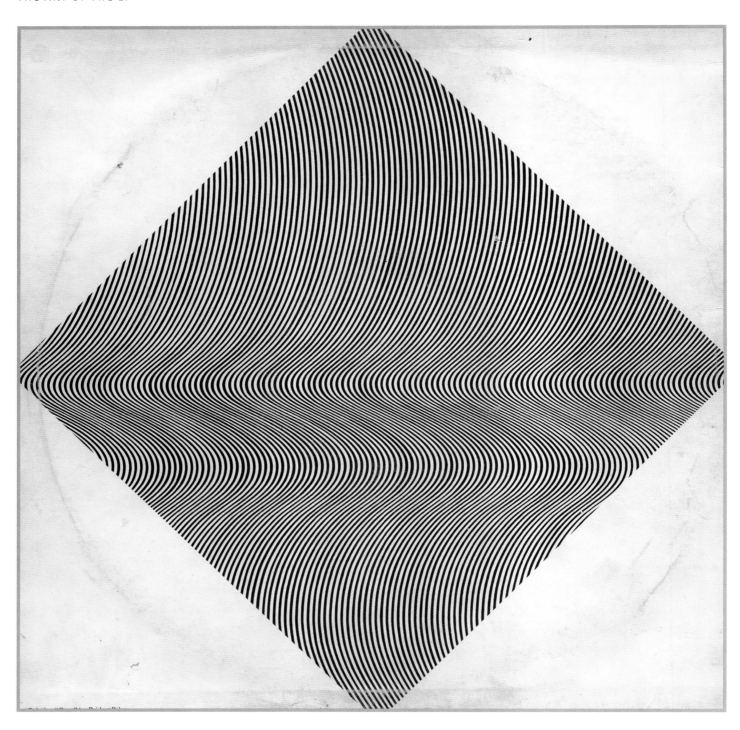

1973
Virgin Records
England
Sleeve design by Uwe Nettelbeck
Photography by Robert Horner
Painting *Crest* by Bridget Riley

Faust The Faust Tapes

Op-Art pioneer Bridget Riley's work inspired a host of artists and fashion designers in the 1960s. She was often surprised to find versions of her work adorning clothes sold in London's Carnaby Street, Canal Street in New York or Haight-Ashbury in San Francisco. Not many bands used her work as cover art, though. This work is aptly chosen since it is a diamond shape and so fits the cover well (there is no boundary on the original), and its complex monochromatic waves could almost be representational sound waves of Faust itself. German experimental rockers, the band uses a vacuum cleaner on this recording, which is made up of unedited rehearsal tapes. People tend to remember the sleeve of this more than the music it contains.

Gracious !

1970
Vertigo
England
Sleeve design by Teenburger!

The British record label Vertigo was at the vanguard of interesting prog-rock records when it launched in the late 1960s. It put out the first two Rod Stewart albums, *An Old Raincoat Won't Ever Let You Down* and *Gasoline Alley*, plus the first Black Sabbath album, for instance, all of which featured the use of arresting cover designs. This album was the tenth release on the label and the design, credited to Teenburger!, is actually by Barney Bubbles (see pp. 120—21) who was designing Hawkwind sleeves, among others, at the time. The gatefold of this album revealed a full-color pop-art montage painting resembling the work of Richard Hamilton, in complete contrast to the starkness of the outside cover. The band was a fairly mundane bunch and after one more album in 1971, they disbanded. Their cover design lasted longer in the memory of prog fans from the era, and in 1996 Gracious reformed, their debut album was rereleased in exactly the same packaging, and they recorded a whole new album of material.

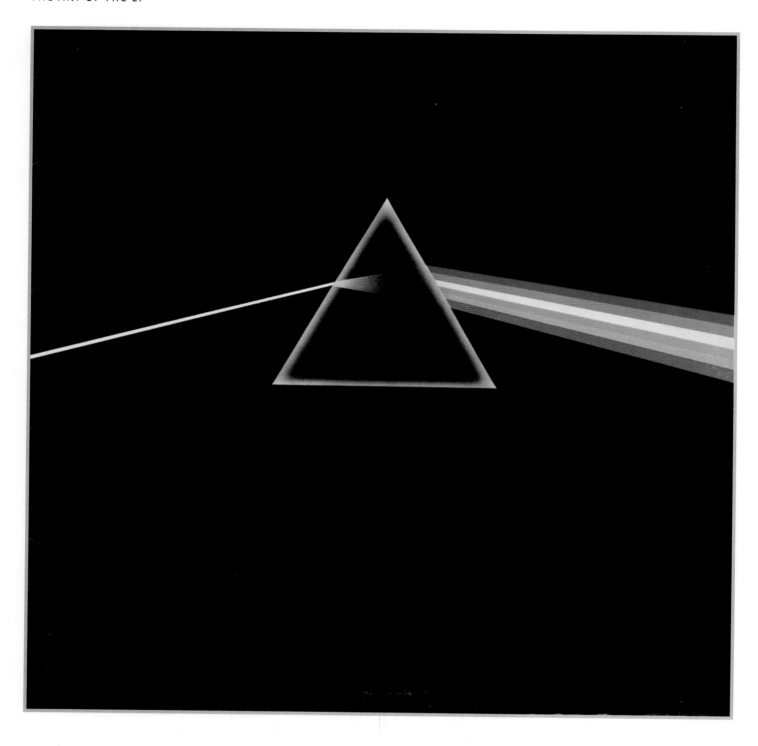

1973
Harvest/EMI
England
Sleeve design by Hipgnosis
Artwork by George Hardie
Photography by Hipgnosis

Pink Floyd Dark Side of the Moon

In spite of all the credits for the design of this cover, the idea and much of the concept came from the band members themselves. Keyboard player Rick Wright came up with the concept of the prism converting white light into a rainbow, while guitarist Dave Gilmour extended the white light line throughout the gatefold sleeve and to the reverse, where it turns back into a rainbow. Hipgnosis's Storm Thorgerson photographed the Great Pyramid at night for a poster that came with the original release, while George Hardie—renowned for his work with Led Zeppelin by this time—assembled everything to send to the printer, along with directions on how to put it all together. The album was so successful that it is this image which, for most people, immediately represents Pink Floyd. Even Floyd fans could have walked past Wright or drummer Nick Mason in the street without recognizing them, but show them the prism and they'd say: "Pink Floyd."

Steely Dan Aja

1977
MCA
America
Sleeve design by Patricia Mitsui and
Geoff Westen
Art direction by Oz Studios
Cover photography by Hideki Fujii

The shot of model Saeko Yamaguchi was taken by renowned Japanese photographer Hideki Fujii, who specialized in geisha-type imagery. Musically, aside from the title track (Aja was the Korean wife of one of their friends), there is little reference to oriental culture in the album. But the stripped-down imagery—virtually all black aside from a flash of profile, edge of fringe and a descending stripe of robe—gives this sleeve the look of a classic jazz album from the fifties or sixties. According to Brian Sweet in his book on the band, Walter Becker and Donald Fagen finally got to use an expensive photographic process called "Liquid Lamb" on Aja, which they had wanted to use on previous releases. Apparently it gave photos more depth and gloss—something to which this cover testifies. Perhaps they used it on the music as well.

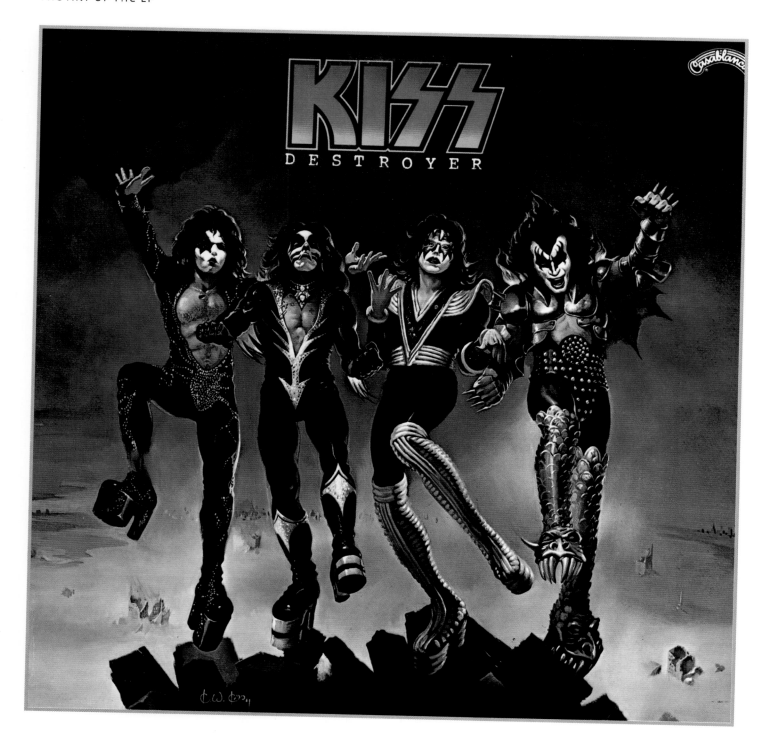

Kiss Destroyer

1976
Casablanca
America
Sleeve design by Dennis Woloch
Illustration by Ken Kelly

Designer Dennis Woloch had worked on the fourth Kiss album, a live release entitled *Alive*. He did it well enough that he was given the job of designing their fourth studio album and told that the title would be *Destroyer*. Knowing that lead singer Gene Simmons was a comic book fan, Woloch went to a local New York comic store in his lunch hour and browsed the racks until one edition of *Creepy* magazine struck him as a great cover. Woloch checked the artist's name and called him. Ken Kelly, a fantasy and comic illustrator, did a great job turning the band into superheroes, so much so that this is the cover for which they are best known. Kelly went on to draw illustrations for other metal bands, most notably Rainbow (*Rising*) and the one opposite.

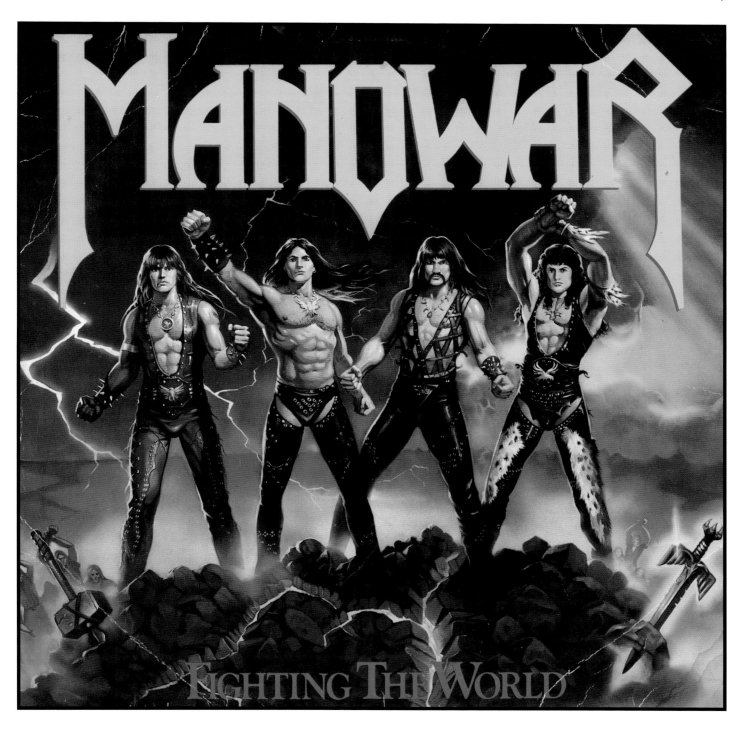

1987

Atco

America

Sleeve design by Bob Defrin

Illustration by Ken Kelly

⚠ Manowar Fighting the World

A dozen years after illustrator Ken Kelly had made Kiss into comic book superheroes he was asked to do the same for a band of fantasy and role-playing game fans who made up a fantasy and role-playing metal band named Manowar. And it certainly is the same as the Kiss one. Are they not in fact atop the same piece of rock that served as the launch pad for Kiss? After this album Kelly illustrated all of the subsequent Manowar covers, and while they're all in the same style (obviously), they are not replicas of other bands' covers. One does include a snake and naked women in a kind of homage to Whitesnake (see p. 69) but mostly they use a Thor-like figure with rippling muscles and big sword, axe or fist. Designer Bob Defrin had been nominated for three jazz album cover Grammys in the 1970s, and another for designing Foreigner's Records album cover in 1984, but he worked on some shocking metal covers in his time. Aside from this he has two other "not" covers in this book—see pages 27 and 376.

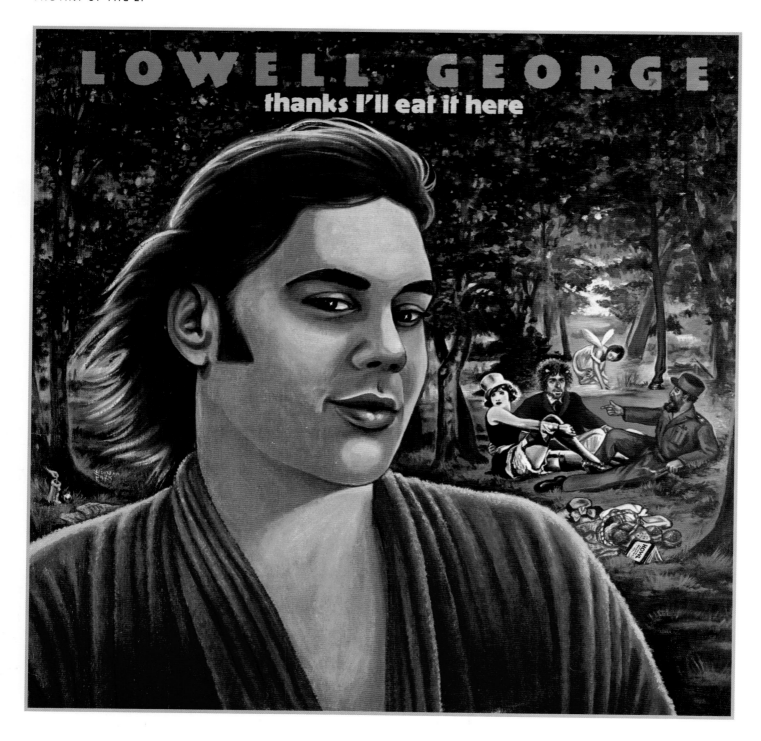

1979
Warners
America
Sleeve design by Michael Hollyfield and
Brad Kawyer
Painting by Neon Park
Creative guidance by Elizabeth George

Lowell George Thanks I'll Eat It Here

Lowell George (1945—1979), the much lamented lead singer and guitarist with Little Feat, released one solo album, and this is it. The cover art, as with most Little Feat albums, is by Neon Park (born Martin Muller, 1940—1993). Park and George met when George was a member of Frank Zappa's Mothers of Invention, and Park created the *Weasels Ripped My Flesh* cover (see p. 343). The cover is a take on Manet's *Le Déjeuner sur l'Herbe* and a wittier attempt than the one Bow Wow Wow would attempt a couple of years later (see p. 133). In Park's work Bob Dylan (with fawn's horns), Marlene Dietrich (as she appeared in *The Blue Angel*) and Cuban leader Fidel Castro enjoy the picnic and a copy of Allen Ginsberg's *Howl* lays open by the food. George, looking coy, appears to be in his bathrobe, which could be a reference to Harry Nilsson, who appears dazed and drunk in a bathrobe on the cover of his most successful album *Nilsson Schmilsson* (1971). That could be George's wife Elizabeth drawn as a fairy, bathing in the background. It's all striking and definitely Feat-like, yet uniquely George.

Little Feat
Sailin' Shoes

1972
Warners
America
Art direction by Ed Thrasher
Painting by Neon Park

Artist Neon Park had the kind of sense of humor that appealed to his clients, which is why Frank Zappa used him, and why Little Feat did, too. This was Little Feat's second album, but the first on which they used the LA-based Park. Jean-Honoré Fragonard's *The Swing* is adapted to suit the band, and particularly Lowell George's renowned sweet tooth. The original 18th-century painting was a metaphor for the loss of virginity. In Park's hands it becomes a metaphor for the loss of diet. Park's unique style became synonymous with Little Feat, and their sleeves are immediately recognizable for that.

Little Feat Down on the Farm

1979
Warners
America
Art direction and painting by Neon Park
Design by Eddy Herch

In 1979 Little Feat ceased to exist as a band. Lowell George had begun a solo career (see opposite) and the band was ready to do their own thing. This, their last album, has a cover painting based on a piece of 1940s pinup art by the only true rival to Vargas as king of the pinup sketch, Gil Elvgren. The original life-like painting was entitled *The Finishing Touch*. Elvgren died in 1980. Little Feat reformed in 1988 and went on to release several more albums, the first two of which used Neon Park paintings on the cover. Park died in 1993 but in 1996 Little Feat released a live album entitled *Live from Neon Park* as a tribute to him.

1980
CBS
England
Sleeve design by Roslav Szaybo
Photography by Photo R. Elsdalek
Retouching by Gerrard Studio

Judas Priest British Steel

Earlier Judas Priest artwork had been designed by the great John Pasche (see p. 170), but while his artwork was good, it didn't fully reflect the sort of band that Judas Priest was. The S&M dress code of singer Rob Halford, the complete absence of the blues in their rock, plus their comic book macho lyrical conceits, marked them out as a pioneering heavy metal band. And this, their sixth album, was the one that introduced them to a mainstream audience. The title and cover did much to define the look of heavy metal sleeves: it's all about the logo. This defining logo for Priest was created by CBS in-house designer Roslav Szaybo for their fourth album *Stained Class*. The "electrified" font, despite pointing downward at forty-five degrees, has proved extremely versatile but is at its most striking here on a razor blade. The resulting effect is macho, posturing and screams the band's nationality.

WT. 1.05 OZS

Chicago X

1976
Columbia
America
Sleeve design by Nick Fasciano

Back in 1969 Chicago was known as Chicago Transit Authority—before the actual CTA apparently threatened legal action. Nine albums later, in 1976, they'd discarded the experimental free-form rock that they'd specialized in and become the biggest selling pop rock band in the U.S. But importantly, they had kept the same logo that graced their debut (albeit without the other two words). Classic, American and—let's face it—Coca-Cola—inspired, the logo was originally created by Columbia in-house designer Nick Fasciano. The logo has appeared on every one of their numbered releases since. It became engraved wood on *V*, an American banknote on *VI*, the U.S. flag on *III*, and here on *X* a chocolate bar with the distinctive Hershey-style font on the wrapper beneath. A Chicago album without this logo would probably get the band sued.

1976
Charisma
America
Sleeve design by Hipgnosis

Brand X Unorthodox Behaviour

Hipgnosis founders Storm Thorgerson and Aubrey Powell were both film students and many of the sleeves they designed for rock bands throughout the seventies and early eighties reveal this. They really hit the big time with their sleeve for *Dark Side of the Moon* (see p. 156) but their highly composed photographic style was already much in demand by rock bands from the early seventies. Phil Collins's side project Brand X was a jazz fusion outfit and this was their debut release for Genesis's label Charisma. Hipgnosis's artwork, while following the album title by showing a disapproving "blinds twitcher," nonetheless gives the sleeve a rock feel that wouldn't seem out of place on one of their Pink Floyd or Genesis works. As such, like Mati Klarwein's sleeve for *Bitches Brew* (see p. 107), it probably helped sell Brand X's often demanding jazz to a rock audience.

Blondie Parallel Lines

1978
Chrysalis
America
Art direction and design by Ramey
Communications
Photography by Edo
Illustrations by Frank Duarte
Lettering by Jerry Rodriguez

There's a huge irony behind this sleeve, which was included in British magazine Q's "100 Best Record Covers of All Time": the band hated it. The core issue in the early days of Blondie was whether it was a band or whether it was all about Debbie Harry. Then manager Peter Leeds was very much in the latter camp and had apparently told the rest of the group that they were expendable. It was his idea to have all the guys grinning while Harry stares, stony faced and sexy. They claim to have agreed to a completely different sleeve, one where they would fade in and out of the lines, and the finished result was one of the things that led to Leeds's dismissal. Whatever the band thinks, it has become an icon of sleeve artwork. And at least—unlike their single sleeves—it does feature the whole band and not just Harry.

1978
Epic Records
America
Sleeve design by Paula Scher
Illustration by Roger Huyssen

Boston Boston

Boston was the studio project of one man, Tom Scholz. He'd left his previous band because he was dissatisfied with their live sound. Even after signing to major label Epic, he avoided regrouping in their lavishly offered studio and completed everything except Brad Delp's vocals alone in his basement studio. But, as the seventeen million owners (and counting) of this album know, it sounds like a big fat rock band and as such needed packaging to resemble the product of a big fat rock band. The outer-space imagery is reminiscent of Roger Dean's artwork for British prog rock band Yes, but commercial illustrator Roger Huyssen achieved such a defining identity for Boston that their sleeves were always variations of the logo in outer space. The next year ELO released *Out of the Blue* and pretty much stole Boston's logo-in-space idea wholesale. In 1979, Huyssen was commissioned to do the poster for *Star Trek: The Motion Picture*.

Ramones Ramones

1976
Sire
America
Sleeve design by Arturo Vega
Photography by Roberta Bayley

Even before she moved to New York in 1975, Roberta Bayley was in the eye of the impending punk storm. The Californian photographer had moved to London in 1972 and stayed for two years, working at Malcolm McClaren and Vivienne Westwood's store, while dating Ian Dury. On her return to the States she worked for illustrator John Holmstrom (see *Road to Ruin*, p. 119) and Legs McNeil's newly launched *PUNK* magazine, taking photos of new bands who were playing at hot club CBGB. The Ramones' now infamous iconic cover shot, originally for the magazine, was taken in a playground across the street from band designer Arturo Vega's loft (see *Road to Ruin*, p. 119). It pretty much defined the punk look. In a 2007 interview with *Stay Thirsty*, Bayley said, "They all kind of equalize their height . . . Joey's slumped down so that they don't look really awkward in their sizes, which in reality they were."

Kraftwerk The Man Machine

1978
EMI
Germany
Sleeve design by Karl Klefisch
Photography by Günther Fröhling

Kraftwerk's fourth real album (discounting the early, unrepresentative efforts *Kraftwerk 1* and *2* and *Ralf & Florian*) was the second to feature the band members on its cover, but it is with this "Robots" sleeve more than *Trans Europe Express* that the deliberately anonymous band is associated visually: restricted color palette, neat haircuts, black ties, shirts with no jackets, and white, impassive faces—this is anti-rock & roll. At the time, only thirty years since the Nazis and with the Cold War still raging, Karl Klefisch's artwork and Günther Fröhling's photograph hit some raw nerves: were the band fascists? Communists? The red shirts and lipstick suggest Berlin cabaret performers or something darker, but the inspiration for overall design is credited by Klefisch on the back cover as being Russian Constructivist and Suprematist, El Lissitzky.

HIGH FIDELITY

the B-52'S

The B-52's The B-52's

1979
Island
England
Photography by George DuBose
Direction by Sue AB Surd
Hairdos by La Vern

George DuBose was an aspiring fashion photographer when, as he describes it on Rock Pop Gallery, he "self-commissioned" the original black-and-white photograph. "I really liked the B-52's after seeing their first NYC performance at Max's Kansas City and wanted to help them with promotion . . . the photo was originally for a poster. . . They were stolen as fast as I could put them up!" *Interview* magazine published this photo with the B-52's interview and, two years later, Tony Wright (then creative director for Island Records) bought the photo to use on the band's first LP. Wright credited himself with the self-deprecating punk rock moniker of Sue AB Surd, but it was his garish coloration of the photograph that set the template for the kitsch artwork that would appear on all the band's future sleeves. They never changed the logo, either.

JUDAS PRIEST

Judas Priest Rocka Rolla

For a debut album by a heavy metal band from Birmingham in 1974, this was a very brave cover. To use no photo of the band wasn't unusual, but it invariably suggested that they weren't a bunch of "lookers." Yet Priest had a photogenic lead singer and the rest of the band looked suitably metal, with lots of hair and skinny as hell. But they opted for a deliberate pastiche of a Coca-Cola font on the lid of a bottle instead. It was inspired, in a heavy metal way. The font is immediately recognizable, the phrase "rocka rolla" sounds like "Coca-Cola," so cue attractive graphic without employing trademarked logo or bottle shape. It leaves the band appearing to be clever, and a bit mysterious. They could perhaps be another Pink Floyd.

1974
Gull Records
England
Sleeve concept by John Pasche,
Gull Graphics
Photography by Bryce Attwell

AC/DC Back in Black

1980
Atlantic
USA
Sleeve design by Atlantic

After the death of singer Bon Scott in February 1980, AC/DC considered disbanding. They can't have considered it for too long, because five months later they'd recruited brand-new singer Malcolm Young and released their sixth album, which would go on to become second only to the best-selling album of all time, Michael Jackson's *Thriller*. Unlike previous releases (see p. 27), this cover did not feature a garish picture but, as Angus Young is credited with saying, was black as a "sign of mourning" for Scott. The logo—one of rock's most immediately recognizable—is finally given space to breathe.

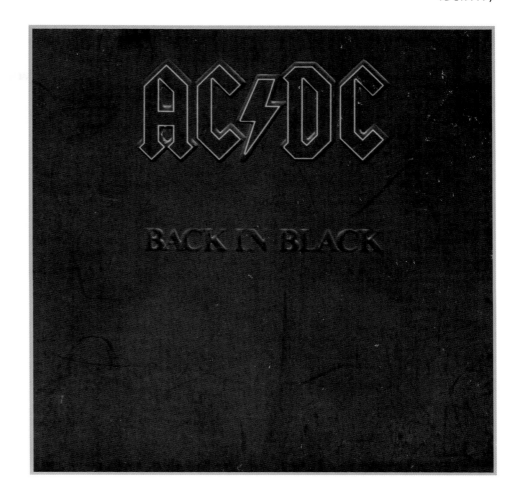

Iron Maiden
Iron Maiden

1980
EMI Records
England
Sleeve design by Cream
Illustration by Derek Riggs

Iron Maiden was at the forefront of the new wave of heavy metal and like everyone else playing the music, they needed something to make them stand out from the crowd. Enter Riggs and his creation, Eddie. The band liked Eddie enough to have an enormous puppet version of him made to use on stage. Eddie has also enjoyed a life of his own, away from the band, starring in a violent video game named Ed Hunter, and has appeared in Tony Hawkes's Pro Skater 4 game. Few apart from the band's die-hard fans would recognize members of the band in person, despite their having sold millions of records. But everyone knows Eddie.

171

Defunkt Defunkt

1980
Hannibal
England
Sleeve design by M&CO New York
Photography by Alan Lewis Kleinberg

The cover for Defunkt's debut album release is as stark, enigmatic and clever as the band was. Impossible to categorize, Defunkt played funk-punk-jazz-disco-soul-rock and was considered part of the New York No Wave movement of the late 1970s, which also conjured up the Lounge Lizards (who were much jazzier than Defunkt) and James White and the Blacks/Contortions (who were more amateurish). Led by trombone player Joe Bowie, brother of jazz trumpeter Lester, Defunkt had a fluid lineup, with members playing when and where they could. A third Bowie, Byron, played sax on this album, arranged the horns, and produced it too. Considered too avant-garde for mainstream American labels, they signed with English independent Hannibal, which was set up by American producer Joe Boyd (Pink Floyd, Nick Drake, etc.) to sign World Music acts. M&CO designed all of Hannibal's early covers, using bright colors and simple typography.

Linda Ronstadt Lush Life

1984
Elektra
America
Art direction and design by Kosh
and Ron Larson

Between 1967 and 1980 Ronstadt built a career as a multi-platinum country-rock-pop artist with several Grammys and a huge following. And then in 1983 she completely reinvented herself by recording an album of American songbook tunes with Frank Sinatra's old arranger, Nelson Riddle, entitled *What's New*. Those old songs were not hip, ironic or apparently even liked much in 1983. Except, maybe they were: it made #3 and went triple platinum. *Lush Life* was the second of three albums of American songbook recordings, and the best package of them all. The sleeve slides apart like a hatbox to reveal the vinyl. It's classy, nostalgic and cool. Ronstadt became a standards singer in the eyes of the public after this release had made #13 and gone platinum. Sadly, Riddle died while making the third album with her in 1986, the platinum-selling *For Sentimental Reasons*. Her next album release, *Canciones de Mi Padre*, saw her covering Mexican songs. It went double platinum, but subsequent album sales slipped, never to reach platinum-selling levels again.

XTC Drums and Wires

1979
Virgin
England
Scissors and Paint Brush Jill Mumford

XTC's main man Andy Partridge was always obsessive about his band's artwork and this has left the band with a legacy of great sleeves. This is their third album and revisits the band's logo as used on their 1977 debut *White Music*. Virgin Records' art director Jill Mumford (or "Scissors and Paint Brush," as she is credited) has rendered the logo into a face. A less talented artist could have made it look cheap and throwaway, but Mumford's choice of bold color and clever angling of the *C* gives the face real character. XTC's previous album, *Go 2*, had been designed by Hipgnosis, and deconstructed the album sleeve with an essay in white type on black background. It was a great idea and a good sleeve but this is better—not least because it still works thirty years later, shrunk down to thumbnail size on an iPod screen.

Toto Turn Back

1980
Columbia
America
Art direction by Tony Lane (Direction
Fitzgerald Hartley Co.)

Toto was a group of crack-session musicians who formed a band in the late seventies. They had no real image, and even after the debut album was recorded for Columbia, were still without a name. They chose Toto because it summed up their "all-encompassing" session musician abilities in Latin. The cover to their 1978 debut was very much in the rock tradition of a sci-fi illustration (see Boston, p. 166) and its follow-up, *Hydra*, was an aesthetic mess. Columbia art director Tony Lane had perhaps seen XTC's *Drums and Wires* two years earlier when he put together this rendering of the band's name for their third album. It's a great sleeve, literally giving a faceless band a face. Ironically, it was their least successful record and it wasn't until their next release, which returned to the look of their debut, that Toto became ubiquitous.

STEVIE WONDER

NEVER HAD A DREAM COME TRUE
WE CAN WORK IT OUT
SIGNED, SEALED, DELIVERED I'M YOURS
HEAVEN HELP US ALL
YOU CAN'T JUDGE A BOOK BY ITS COVER
SUGAR
AND OTHERS

SIGNED SEALED & DELIVERED

FRAGILE

HANDLE WITH CARE

FROM DETROIT WITH LOVE

DO NOT DROP

TAMLA

TS 304

1970
Tamla Motown
America
Photography by Hendin
Art direction and design by
Curtis McNair
Graphic supervision by Tom Schlesinger

! Stevie Wonder Signed, Sealed & Delivered

There are worse sleeves out there and, let's be honest, a handful of Stevie Wonder's other records are in some of them. But this one is particularly offensive: A smiling "Little Stevie"—an identity thrust upon him by Motown when he launched his career—popping out of a box? It's tempting to make a joke about how the art director wouldn't have gotten away with it if Wonder had been sighted. The album was actually Stevie's twelfth for Motown and it's interesting to think that his classic period, which began with *Where I'm Coming From*, was only just over a year away. Can you imagine him popping out of a box with a big grin on his face on the sleeve of *Music of My Mind*? But perhaps the main offense of this sleeve is not so much the patronizing treatment of Wonder's serious talent but the aesthetic composition—the chief offender being the large "seal" with the album title. Shocking!

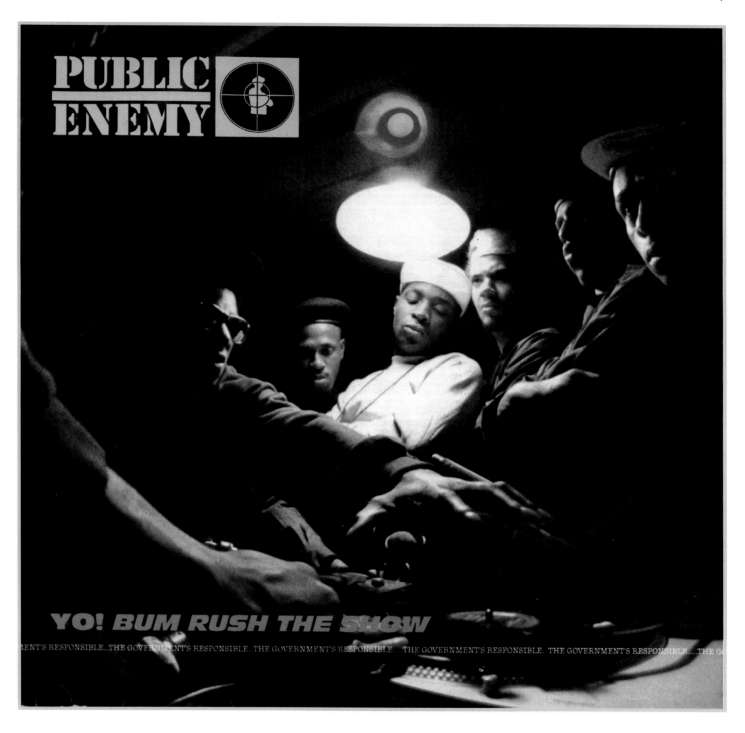

Public Enemy Yo! Bum Rush the Show

While they didn't inspire a whole load of copycat righteous hip-hop artists in their wake, Public Enemy did set the tone for the rap group look. When Def Jam label boss Rick Rubin saw photographer Glen E. Friedman's shots of the Beastie Boys, he hired him to take photos for Def Jam. Friedman had been photographing the emergent skate culture that was developing hand-in-hand with hardcore and rap and would help shape the aesthetics of late eighties hip-hop. At first glance the photo puts one in mind of a heist being planned; the subterranean lightning, the quasi-military berets, and gang members leaning over a plan. But then you notice main man Chuck D. illuminated in white, and Terminator X leaning over nothing more sinister than a DJ turntable. The definitive marksman logo appeared on all their subsequent releases.

1986
Def Jam
America
Sleeve design by Glen E. Friedman

DRUGS

Once the business of rock & roll had become sufficiently established and the music business understood there would be no immediate end to things, the creatives who worked at major labels began to experiment. Once the Beatles had made it mainstream to reference drugs (first with *Revolver* and then *Sgt. Pepper's Lonely Hearts Club Band*), then everyone could. Art departments at record companies were employing people as designers, photographers and illustrators who were part of the market to which the company was trying to sell their product—by any means necessary.

Not all drugs are illegal substances, of course, and cigarettes and alcohol had been a part of cover design at jazz labels since the 1950s, the blue smoke and reflective glasses of a club adding to the atmosphere of a sultry jazz recording. But the creep of marijuana and then LSD–influenced art onto album covers came swiftly and in an enormous wave after 1966. Psychedelic art was everywhere for the latter half of the decade, and some of the best examples are to be found in the following pages.

Also here are later examples of subtle drug references, as well as crass promotion of the clichéd idea that rock & roll "rebels" had to be heavy drinkers and smokers. There are also examples of cultural drug references, which demand an understanding of the context in which they are used.

And then there are the dumb, ill-advised takes on how "drug culture" should be presented. Not everyone who worked at a record company understood what "the kids" were into, but some tried to pretend they did. Sometimes with hilarious results.

PR 7350

ERIC DOLPHY IN EUROPE, VOL. 2

PRESTIGE

1965
Prestige
America
Sleeve design by Don Schlitten
Photography by Burt Goldblatt

Eric Dolphy In Europe, Vol. 2

Eric Dolphy's drug of choice was music. An inspired avant-garde virtuoso sax, flute and oboe player, Dolphy was the band leader of one of the two ensembles that played simultaneously on Ornette Coleman's ground-breaking *Free Jazz* album (1960). He also wrote the sheets for John Coltrane's *Africa/Brass* sessions and introduced Coltrane to the idea of "free" playing, contributing to *Olé* and a score of legendary live Coltrane quintet performances of 1962—3. Dolphy was an inspirational member of the Mingus band of the early sixties, with whom he made his final, fateful trip to Europe in 1964. When Mingus left the Continent Dolphy stayed behind and played a series of gigs in Germany and Scandinavia with various pickup bands. Mingus was worried about Dolphy's health; the horn player wasn't eating and was spending every waking hour practicing his playing. As Goldblatt's inspired photograph shows, Eric smoked a pipe—the shape here echoing his horn, the smoke billowing from either the horn or the pipe. Dolphy died in June 1964 of causes aggravated by undiagnosed diabetes.

1965
Columbia Records
America
Photography by W. Eugene Smith

Thelonious Monk Monk

Thelonious Monk was one of the most inspired and revolutionary jazz pianists of the 20th century. He was obsessed with his music, not quite to the exclusion of all else as Dolphy was, but almost. Having grown up with the heroin culture of the Bop players such as Charlie Parker and Fats Navarro, Monk had dabbled in it, but preferred alcohol and cigarettes. This cover, shot by a former war photographer and *Life* magazine contributor, is a tribute to the atmosphere of smoke-infused rooms where jazz was made. Smith lived in a New York loft in the garment district, where every night there would be scores of jazz musicians gathered after hours to jam. Smith let everyone use the space on the understanding that he could photograph and record them all. No one minded the photographs, a huge pile of which stood at the entrance to the loft, and which Smith would sell when possible for a dollar each. Today they'd be worth a lot more. The recordings remain mostly unreleased, although they are being collated and notated for possible future release.

The Beatles Rubber Soul

The cover to this iconic sleeve was taken in the garden of Kenwood, a house in Surrey where Lennon lived with his first wife Cynthia. Photographer Robert Freeman later said, "The distorted effect in the photo was a reflection of the changing shape of their lives," but the original picture was a standard shot, taken without any special lens. In the *Anthology* film, Paul McCartney tells the story of how Freeman showed them the photos using an overhead projector and the screen slipped backward by mistake, distorting the image. "Can we have that one?!" they all shouted. The band had met dope-smoking Bob Dylan in the Delmonico Hotel in New York the year before and everything about this sleeve suggests the discovery of mind-expanding substances. The lettering, which set the template for so many psychedelic fonts, was done by a young advertising executive friend of Freeman's called Charles Front. Note that the word "Beatles" doesn't even need to appear on the sleeve.

1966
Parlophone
England
Art direction and photography by
Robert Freeman
Lettering by Charles Front

The Beatles Sgt. **Pepper's Lonely Hearts Club Band**

1967
Parlophone
England
Sleeve concept by Paul McCartney
Design and art by Peter Blake and
Jann Haworth

It's easy to read drug references into the exuberance of much of 1960s pop—for example, "Mr. Tambourine Man," frequently taken as a metaphor for a dope dealer, is about Dylan's tambourine player Bruce Langhorne. And McCartney himself has said, "It's easy to overestimate the influence of drugs on the Beatles' music." And so it could be with Peter Blake's much-honored sleeve for the Fabs' 1967 ground-breaker. But while urban myths like the flower guitar containing cannabis plants are untrue, it is undeniable that without the influence of marijuana, McCartney's new-identity-for-Beatles idea would never have happened.

Monkees Head

1968
Colgems
America
Sleeve design uncredited

By 1968 the Monkees had ceased to be purely a teenage pop sensation. Or so they thought. The TV show that made them in every sense came to an end in March of that year (the last two episodes saw appearances by Frank Zappa and Tim Buckley), but they were working on their first and only movie with director Bob Rafaelson and writer Jack Nicholson, who went on make *Five Easy Pieces* together. A drug-influenced mess of a movie, *Head* bombed. The soundtrack fared little better, and the foil cover, designed so that buyers could see themselves branded as a "head" in their reflection (slang for dope or acid head), apparently wrecked the pressing plant. *Head* contained no singles and Peter Tork left the band after its release.

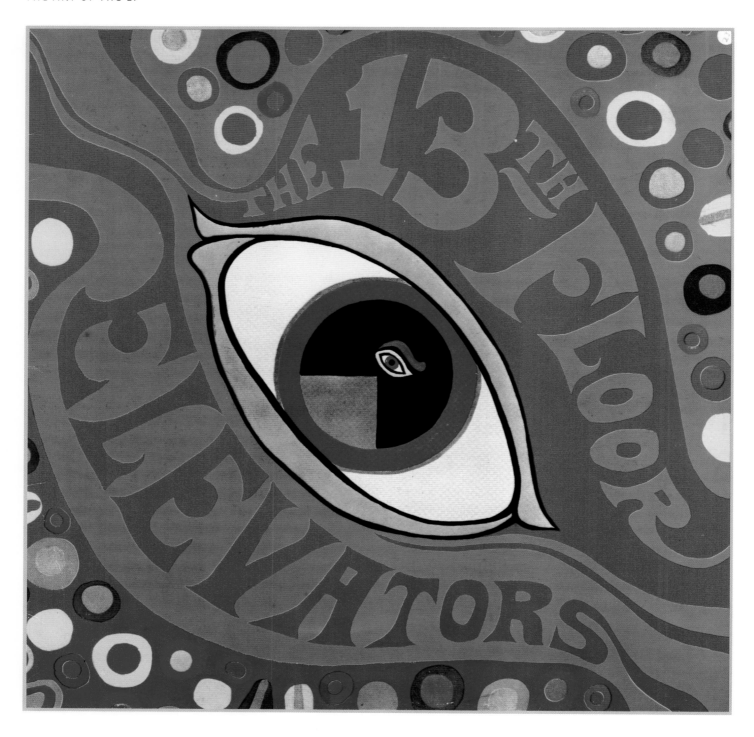

1966
International Artists
America
Sleeve design by John Cleveland

The 13th Floor Elevators The Psychedelic Sounds of

Roky Erickson, leader of Austin, Texas's 13th Floor Elevators, was the Syd Barrett of American psychedelia. A voracious LSD consumer, he wrote songs under the influence of the hallucinogenic, and played under the effects, too. Like Barrett, Erickson suffered from mental fragility and the effects of LSD contributed to the deterioration of his health to the point that in 1968 he was hospitalized after being diagnosed as a paranoid schizophrenic and was given electric shock therapy. A year later he pleaded guilty to possession of a marijuana joint on the grounds of insanity and was incarcerated until 1972 in the state mental institution. Unlike Barrett's, Roky's ex-bandmates didn't go on to become international superstars. The cover of their first album was painted by an Austin native who painted oils for live shows onto lights. The clashing greens and reds combined with the all-seeing eye in the center have become clichés of psychedelic imagery. After two decades of instability, Erickson was finally properly medicated, rehabilitated, and returned to making music.

Cream Disraeli Gears

1967
Atco
America
Sleeve design by Martin Sharp

Eric Clapton, Ginger Baker and Jack Bruce became an immediate success from the moment of Cream's inception. In 1967 Clapton was persuaded by then Graham Bond Organization drummer Baker to leave John Mayall's Bluesbreakers for a second time and form a trio with him and bassist Jack Bruce (also in the GBO). Clapton has said that Baker asked him to join during a return drive to London in the drummer's Rover automobile. "I was very impressed with his car and driving," Clapton said. Five months later their debut album, *Fresh Cream*, was released and became a UK Top Ten album. The following year they released *Disraeli Gears* with a strong, psychedelic cover created by Australian Martin Sharp. He put together the collage in black and white using various Victorian "found" images, and photos of the band obtained from the record company (they were PR shots), and then hand-painted it all. At the time psychedelia was only just entering the mass public consciousness and so was considered very hip. *Disraeli Gears* made Cream credible and successful in the U.S., where it had been recorded.

Chuck Berry Live at Fillmore Auditorium

1967
Mercury
America
Photography by Erik Weber

Of the original wave of rock & rollers to make it big internationally, only Bo Diddley and Chuck Berry were ever revered by successive generations of blues-influenced musicians. Mostly because both men were guitarists and inspired many of the 1960s-era rockers. This 1967 recording was made at the famous Fillmore West, opened and run by promoter Bill Graham, a man not known for his overgenerosity toward acts (the sleeve gives "thanks to Bill Graham for half his stage and all his hot water"). Berry's backing band was the Steve Miller Band (though before Boz Scaggs had joined them), and they supply a suitably semi-psychedelic blues feel to Chuck's trademark reelin' and rocking. Chuck wears an attractive two-tone suit on stage for the gig, and it almost clashes with the psychedelic oil light show going on behind and above him. The artwork is a deliberate attempt to sell the old rocker to the generation of kids then listening to music with the aid of certain illegal substances, and it's a very good representation of hippy poster art of that time.

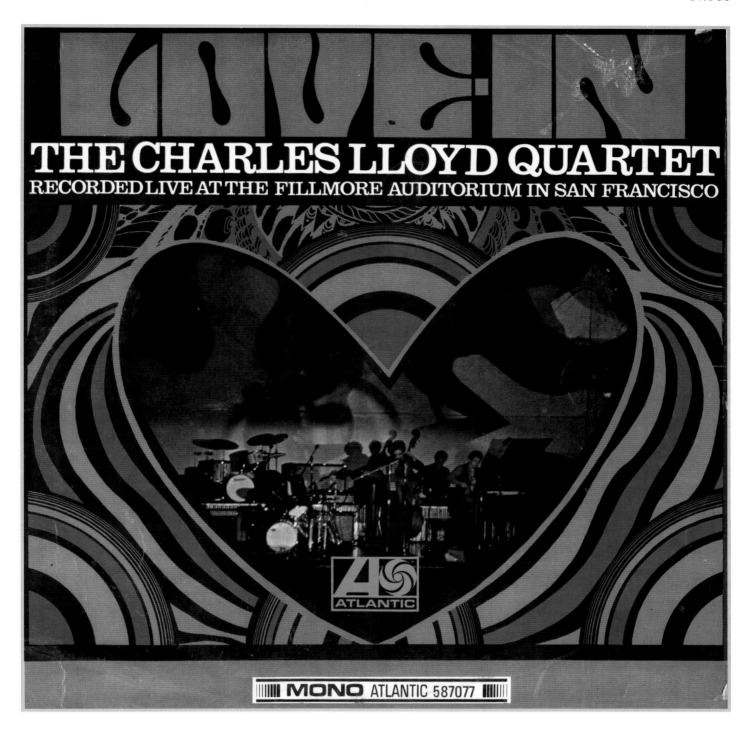

LIVE IN
THE CHARLES LLOYD QUARTET
RECORDED LIVE AT THE FILLMORE AUDITORIUM IN SAN FRANCISCO

MONO ATLANTIC 587077

The Charles Lloyd Quartet Love-In

1967
Atlantic
America
Sleeve design by Stanislaw Zagorski
Photography by Jim Marshall

Like the Chuck Berry album opposite, this album was recorded live at the Fillmore Auditorium, and also like that record, it has a psychedelically designed cover that was typical of the time. The difference with Chuck Berry's album, though, is that this is a psychedelic record. Charles Lloyd's quartet included pianist Keith Jarrett, drummer Jack DeJohnette and bassist Ron McClure: two white guys, two black. The set recorded here features four numbers written by Lloyd (including the title track), two by Jarrett, and the Lennon—McCartney song "Here, There and Everywhere." The Quartet began playing the venue regularly after an unannounced gig on a Sunday afternoon proved to be a hit. They kept coming back and Chet Helms, founder of the arch-hippy Avalon Ballroom, soon called them "the first psychedelic jazz group." They may have been the only one. Lloyd enjoyed playing to the audience of stoned kids enough to write pieces for them, and the success of his 1966 album *Forest Flower*, along with this, the first live album to be recorded at the Fillmore, proved that the kids appreciated it.

Iron Butterfly In-A-Gadda-Da-Vida

1968
Atlantic
America
Sleeve design by Loring Eutemey
Photography by Stephen Paley

"IRON—symbolic of something "heavy" as in sound. BUTTERFLY—light, appealing and versatile . . . an object that can be used freely in the imagination." The opening sentences of the liner notes to this, the second album by Iron Butterfly, sum up exactly the confused, pretentious state of the psychedelic overground in 1968. The Butterfly was from San Diego, not Frisco, and were not among the original vanguard of psychedelic innovators. The whole of side two of this album (all seventeen minutes) is taken up with the title track, a lumpen, Farfisa organ—driven dirge with nonsense lyrics and a riff that sounds like Cream's "Sunshine of Your Love" (1967). The "heavy" reference is considered by some people to be among the first used in reference to rock music and contributed to the invention of the term heavy metal. The cover, displaying in full Iron Butterfly's enormous oil-cell light display, suggests that this could be a live recording (it's not), and captures the essence of a typical live psychedelic show, then all the rage from San Francisco to Boston, and all points in between.

RCA

VICTOR

JOYRIDE
FRIEND SOUND

1969
RCA Victor
America
Illustration by Edna O'Dowd

Friendsound Joyride

This is a true psychedelic oddity. There are no pop songs on here; neither is there any traditional form of rock song. The record starts mid-track, with words spoken into an echo chamber apparently at random while a bass guitar plays the melody, and a flute joins in now and then, as does a heavily distorted and echo-laden guitar. Throughout the album sounds come and go, tracks begin and end seemingly on a whim. One track is an ambient recording made at a children's playground. Friendsound appear to be an experimental musical collective of esoteric artists. In fact, they're ex-members of Paul Revere and the Raiders, apparently on one long, strange trip. Stereo separation is used to full effect and the album is mixed for hearing that has been heightened by psychedelics. The cover art is an incredibly intricate painting by Edna O'Dowd, of whom nothing is known. It's as intriguing as the album it covers.

ROLLING STONES LET IT BLEED

DECCA

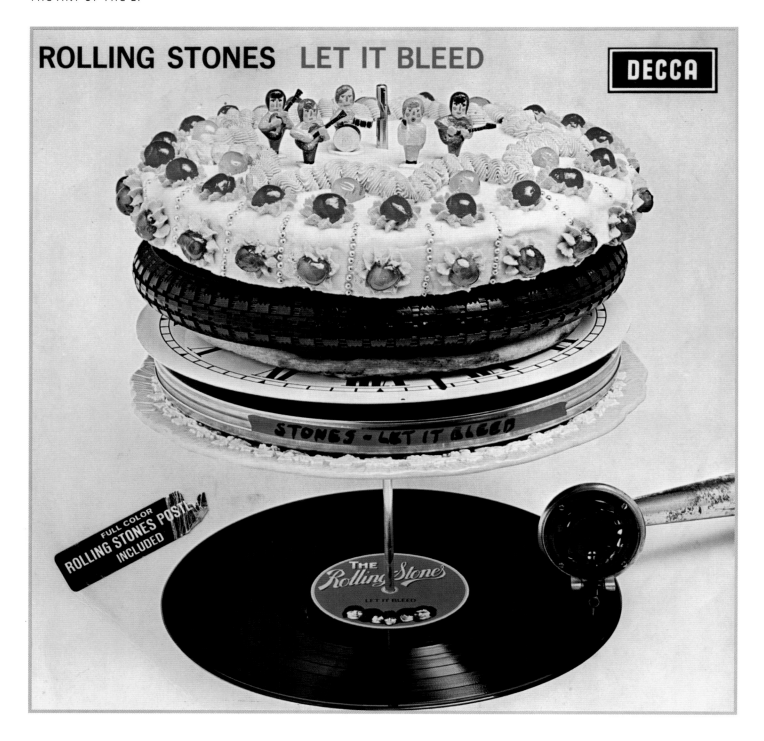

Rolling Stones Let It Bleed

1969
Decca
England
Sleeve design by Robert Brownjohn
Photography by Don McAllester

It's hard to believe now, but this 1969 career high, made during the height of the Stones' hedonistic, drug-fueled reign, has a cake on its cover baked by future TV chef Delia Smith. Originally the album title was going to be *Automatic Changer*, which would have made the cover image of an auto-change record player seem slightly less psychedelic and more prosaic. Whatever the title, Smith's cake-baking brief by designer Brownjohn was to make something as gaudy and over the top as possible. The sleeve budget was a psychedelic £1,000, so she must have gone through a good number of glacé cherries. The effect is at once cutesy and sickly and simultaneously foreboding—rather like heroin. It would be nice to think that some sixties hipsters sat around after the session and ate the cake, but the item had a different destiny, as the back cover shows it with slices taken out, the record broken and pieces falling off, and the Stones figures all askew.

STEREO   LYC 1144

1969
Fantasy/Liberty Records
America
Cover by Basul Parik

Creedence Clearwater Revival Bayou Country

Czech photographer Basul Parik's family escaped from Prague in 1949, his father Arno—also a photographer—eventually settling in San Francisco where he opened the Professional Color Laboratory. Basul grew up taking photos and developing them too. Unusually for the time, he developed and played around with color shots (professionals usually worked only in black-and-white darkrooms.) Basul got a job working with Fantasy Records and began photographing bands. In 1968 he shot Creedence, a hard-driving southern blues band with a psychedelic edge. With a new technique he had developed using a zoom, Parik managed to capture the incredible energy and movement of the band, and in the process created a wholly psychedelic image for this, the cover of their second album. In 1969 he photographed the band standing in a wooded glade for the cover of *Green River*, their third album, and using the natural pattern of light through the trees managed to convey a sense of lustrous, almost unnatural, color.

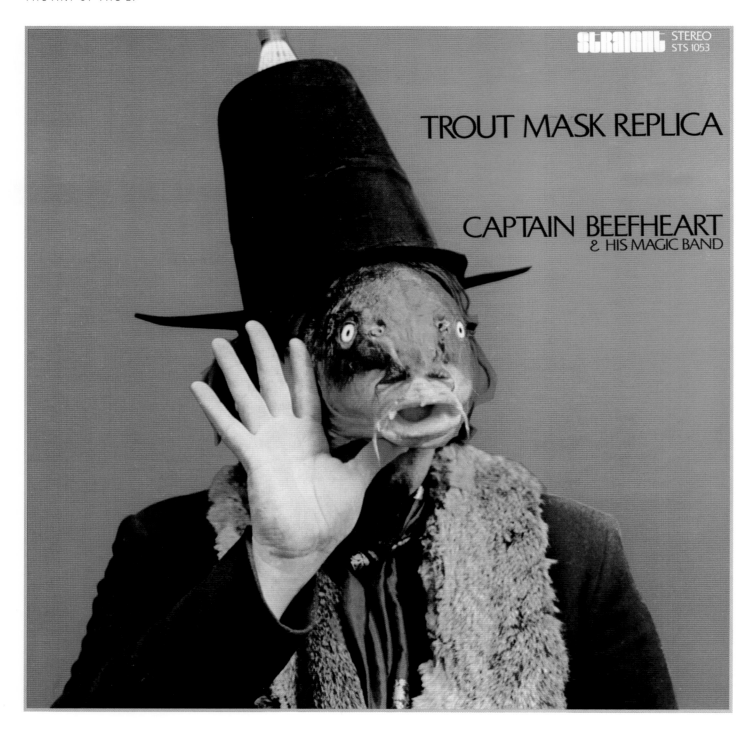

STRAIGHT STEREO
STS 1053

TROUT MASK REPLICA

CAPTAIN BEEFHEART
& HIS MAGIC BAND

1970
Straight Records
America
Sleeve design by Cal Schenkel
Photography by Ed Caraeff

Captain Beefheart & His Magic Band **Trout Mask Replica**

Those familiar with this album will either love it or hate it and its sleeve
inspires a similar polarization. The fractured, discordant free-jazz-meets-
psychedelia of the music, complete with lyrics about the "mascara snake"
and "fast and bulbous," could never have been housed in anything less
hallucinatory than this. Cal Schenkel, who was Beefheart's in-house
designer, said of it, "Someone, I guess that was me, decided, 'Well, why
don't we get a real life fish head?' So we went to the farmer's market and
got this actual fish head, a real fish." Beefheart (Don Van Vliet) wore the
mask and a quite splendid British racing green fur-collared jacket, which
sits comfortably against the lurid pink background. The addition of a
stovepipe hat topped with a shuttlecock adds to what teenagers would
describe as "the randomness." The sober lettering only adds to the feeling
of disorientation.

1974
RCA
America
Cover concept by John Lennon and
Harry Nilsson
Art direction by Acy R. Lehman

Harry Nilsson Pussy Cats

It's not very often that a record's producer gets his name on the front cover. But then, John Lennon didn't produce many records, and he did play, sing, and inspire so much of this album that it might as well be a Lennon/Nilsson release. The record was made, produced, mixed and released during Lennon's eighteen-month holiday from the Dakota and Mama Yoko between 1972 and 1974. In the same period he wrote and recorded his only solo album to make the #1 position on the album charts, *Walls and Bridges* (which also contained his only solo #1 hit single, "Whatever Gets You Thru the Night"). Away from Yoko, Lennon was on a creative roll. The cover of this record, made when the men were sharing a house and large quantities of their drug of choice at the time, alcohol, with Ringo Starr and Keith Moon, is as much fun as the album sounds. The cover concept is based on an old postcard they found, according to May Pang, who was there at the time. To read the blocks (D and S) as Nilsson intended, put the object in the picture between them into a word, and read.

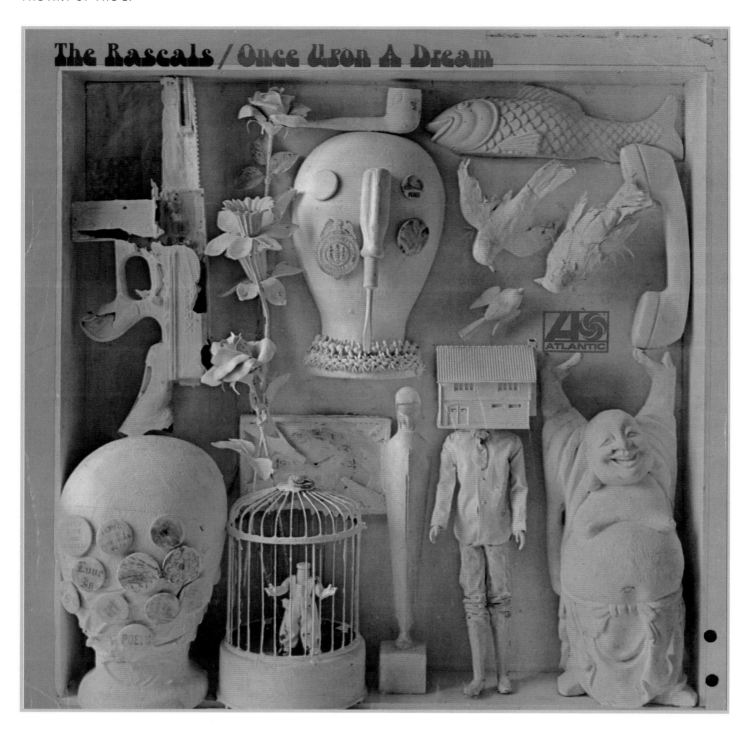

1968
Atlantic
America
Sculpture and design by Dino Danelli
Photography by Russell Beal

The Rascals *Once Upon a Dream*

The world was a rapidly changing place in 1968. There were riots in major American cities to protest civil rights issues, the war in Vietnam and global capitalism. Recreational drug use was rife among the young of America, with most smoking marijuana as a rite of passage, and many also dropping LSD and experimenting with other legal and illegal highs. The rock & roll world reflected the changes taking place. The Monkees released *Head* (see p. 183) and the Rascals dropped the "Young" part of their name and let the drummer design their album cover. Actually he did a great job in creating the art and then placing the type. Anyone listening to the album while stoned could spend the twenty minutes each side played for seeing meaning in the sculptures. The album's pretty good too: it was a departure from their R&B-flavored past and a progression from the soulful swing of *Groovin'*. There are weird, distorted voices, sounds and squeaks among the songs, most of which are pretty catchy. Prior to this drummer Danelli was best known for his uncanny likeness to Paul McCartney.

UNDERGROUND
THELONIOUS MONK

1968

Columbia

America

Sleeve design by John Berg,
Dick Mantel

Photography by Horn/Griner

Thelonious Monk Underground

Steve Horn and Norm Griner were very successful Madison Avenue ad
photographers who both knew the Columbia head of art John Berg
separately, and he introduced them to each other in 1959. They worked
together until 1974 when Horn concentrated on TV work and Griner went
into partnership with another photographer, Mike Cuesta. They must have
had great fun with this cover, in which Monk pretends to be a World War II
resistance fighter. The title may well have been Monk's dismissive take on
the then current fad for calling hippy counter-culture "the underground,"
but it doesn't come across as any sort of satire; rather as a crazy
endorsement. Monk looks angry in the photo, and as usual he's smoking.
He also looks as if he's on something—it may have been anti-psychotic
drugs, which were possibly wrongly prescribed. It's alleged that Monk
took LSD and peyote, that he drank and did all kinds of weird things as he
approached the end of his life (he died in 1982). His last tour was in 1971,
and throughout it he did not speak a word to anyone.

SING IT AGAIN ROD

mercury

PRINTED IN U.S.A.

Rod Stewart Sing It Again Rod

1972

Mercury

America

Sleeve design by Shakey Pete Corriston
Photography by Cosima Scianna, Sam
Emerson Loew and Steve Azzara

It was a sign of Rod's success in America that this compilation album, rushed out to capitalize on his success post-"Maggie May," is not a cheap and shoddy package at all. The sleeve is cut and shaped as a whisky tumbler. The inner sleeve, when slid out from the top of the jacket (not the side), depicts the same whisky glass as on the front, but without liquor and ice. Turn the outer sleeve over and the glass is empty but photographed closer in, the photo of Rod behind it distorted, as if seen through a drunken haze. Rod looks suitably drunk in the photo, which is in all three incarnations of the tumbler. The flip side of the inner sleeve shows Rod on stage—alone, with no Faces in view, to ensure people knew that Rod was a solo star, not the front man of a band. The glass helped cement the idea of Rod as a hard-drinking Scot, despite the fact that he was born and raised in north London.

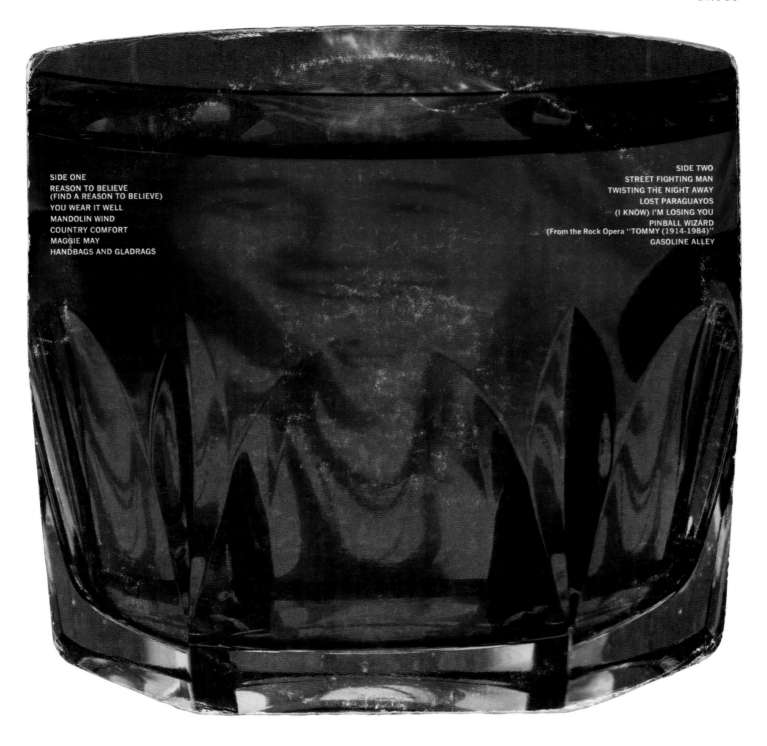

SIDE ONE
REASON TO BELIEVE
(FIND A REASON TO BELIEVE)
YOU WEAR IT WELL
MANDOLIN WIND
COUNTRY COMFORT
MAGGIE MAY
HANDBAGS AND GLADRAGS

SIDE TWO
STREET FIGHTING MAN
TWISTING THE NIGHT AWAY
LOST PARAGUAYOS
(I KNOW) I'M LOSING YOU
PINBALL WIZARD
(From the Rock Opera "TOMMY (1914-1984)")
GASOLINE ALLEY

U-Roy Dread in a Babylon

1975
Virgin
England
Sleeve design by Ken Dolman
Photography by Eric Tello

By the mid-1970s reggae music in its rawer, dub-infused form was breaking out into other countries. Jamaicans living in England imported original Jamaican records from King Tubby, Lee Scratch Perry and Coxone Dodds's studios, and the sounds of Jamaican Rastas such as Big Youth, Junior Murvin and U-Roy were discovered by early punks like the Clash's Paul Simonon and Sex Pistol John Lydon. It wasn't only the beats and tunes that appealed; there was also the cult of the rebel rocker and the Rasta's insistence that cannabis was an important part of his religion. When Virgin rereleased U-Roy's *Dread in a Babylon* they used this photo of the toaster very definitely inhaling the sacred herb smoke, taken by fellow Jamaican musician Eric Tello. To those in the know, the cover was a signifier to similarly minded souls: if you didn't "get" it then you weren't with them. "Babylon," to a Rasta (or Dread), signified the rest of the world—in other words those who didn't follow their righteous path. It became synonymous with England among the ex-pat Jamaican musicians who settled there in the 1970s.

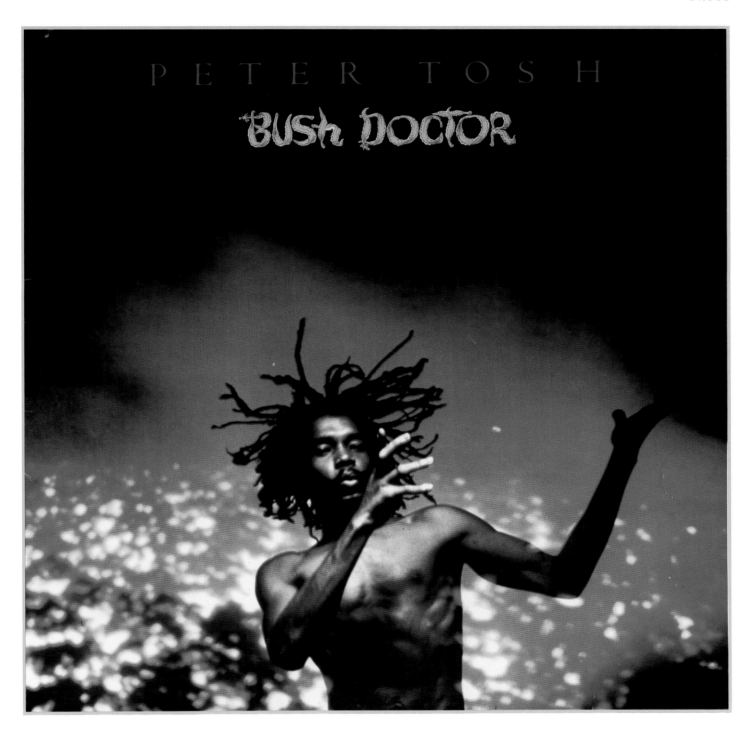

Peter Tosh Bush Doctor

1978
Rolling Stones Records
England
Photography by Ara Gallant

Jagger, Richards and the rest of the Stones had first visited Jamaica in 1972 when they recorded part of *Exile on Main Street* there. Enchanted by the ambience of drugs, guns and music, when they got their own label it was natural that they'd sign a Rasta reggae musician. Thankfully the Stones rarely attempted to play it, "Cherry Baby" on *Black and Blue* being just about passable white reggae. Peter Tosh, a former Wailer with Bob Marley, had a more mystical, spiritual approach to life than Bob, although his lyrics were tinged with sarcasm. The bush that he "doctors" is of course cannabis, but it's also the lush wooded mountains of his homeland where tribes of Rastas dwell in remote communities, living the righteous life. Photographer Gallant was also a hairdresser and worked for some years as a stylist primarily in the fashion industry and with Richard Avedon, before becoming a commercial photographer full time. This was undoubtedly his greatest photo. He died in 1990 in LA. Peter Tosh died during a robbery at his Jamaican home in 1987.

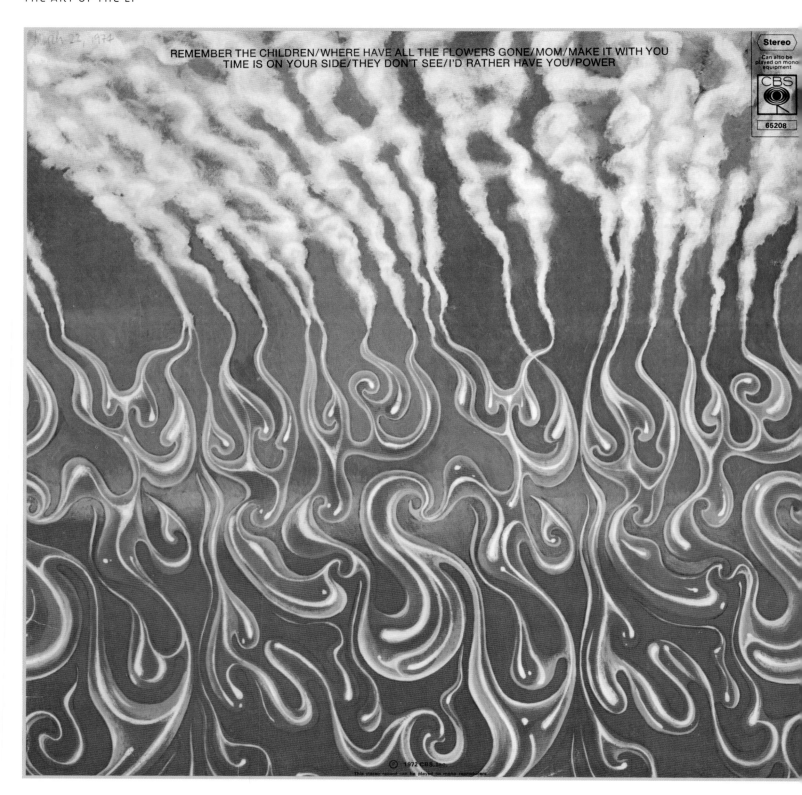

REMEMBER THE CHILDREN/WHERE HAVE ALL THE FLOWERS GONE/MOM/MAKE IT WITH YOU
TIME IS ON YOUR SIDE/THEY DON'T SEE/I'D RATHER HAVE YOU/POWER

Stereo
Can also be
played on mono
equipment

CBS

65208

© 1972 CBS, Inc.
This stereo record can be played on mono reproducers.

1972
CBS Records
America
Sleeve artwork by Mati Klarwein

Earth, Wind & Fire Last Days and Time

Earth, Wind and Fire were signed to CBS by the label's then boss, Clive Davis, after he'd seen them perform. Being the MD's band, they were given the CBS top cover illustrator to work with. This cover is unusual for Klarwein at the time; his Greg Allman *Laid Back* art ('71) and Buddy Miles's *Message to the People* ('71) both feature the artist's head. Unlike *Abraxas*, *Bitches Brew* or *Live Evil*, this album doesn't feature a large African nude, either. Instead, it has what could be the seven-piece band walking a street with a naked woman whose head is exuding lightning. The "rain" is like mercury, band leader Maurice White's head is exuding wondrous things. Klarwein did do LSD, but apparently said he didn't "need it" for his work.

Doctor Feelgood
Private Practice

1978
United Artists
England
Art direction and design by
Paul Henry
Photography by Keith Morris

Having been at the forefront of the UK's "pub rock" scene, Dr. Feelgood was doing its best, like so many pre-1977 artists, not to be swept away by the tsunami of punk rock. On this album, "Milk & Alcohol," a song referencing their drug of choice, got them into the charts. Paul Henry had designed the band's previous three albums, but this one—perhaps because it doesn't feature the band—is his most effective. The band's logo is a maniacally grinning "doctor" wearing shades who featured in most of their artwork. This sleeve cleverly references it via the photograph.

Peter Gabriel 3 [Melt]

1980
Charisma Records
England
Sleeve design and photography
by Hipgnosis

Between 1977 and 1982, ex-Genesis vocalist Peter Gabriel released four eponymous solo albums, each of which is now known by its cover: *Car* (see p. 310), *Scratch*, *Melt* and *Security*. This one, like all of them designed by Storm Thorgerson's company Hipgnosis, is perhaps the most recognizable of the three as well as being the one that contains his two massive hits "Games Without Frontiers" and "Biko." Thorgerson took the photograph himself with a Polaroid SX-70 instant camera. Interestingly, he cannot remember whether it was him or Gabriel who manipulated the image but it must have been done soon after the picture was taken, as the manipulation process is only possible when the Polaroid ink is still damp.

The Pretty Things Savage Eye

1975
Swan Song
America
Sleeve design by Hipgnosis

Sometimes being literal in a design works. This is a striking gatefold sleeve with the same image of the eye and finger on both sides, and because it's much larger than lifesize, while still looking lifelike, the result is unsettling. Which the Pretty Things, who at the time were consuming too many Class A drugs, with excessive amounts of drink and debauchery, would have liked. The band personified the punk attitude before Rotten was out of diapers and they reveled in making "straight" people uncomfortable. The red fingernail is reminiscent of the razor blade that slashes an eyeball in the Buñuel surrealist film *L'Âge d'Or*. The album failed to sell as well as its predecessor, the band left Swan Song and then didn't release anything for five years.

1969
CBS Records
England
Sleeve design uncredited

Fleetwood Mac The Pious Bird of Good Omen

This compilation album of early Fleetwood Mac singles was released (entitled *English Rose* in the U.S.) to cash in on the surprise success of the single "Albatross," which made #1 in the UK singles charts. The cover, of a pregnant nun standing on a beach holding an albatross, is either a deliberately clumsy joke that is so bad it's good, or a desperate attempt at being edgy and "underground" by the people at CBS records. The U.S. cover uses a close-up of a grotesquely made-up man in drag wearing a red feather boa. Why? Exactly.

Spiritualized Lazer Guided Melodies

1992
Dedicated Records
England
Sleeve design by Andrew Sutton
for Blue Source
Original artwork by Mr. Ugly
Logo by Albert Tupelo
Model by Gavin Lindsay
Photography by Pete Gardner

Singer and guitarist Jason Pierce, aka J. Spaceman, has made a career out of heightened states of consciousness gained from copious drug use—even to the point of punning references in album titles like *Complete Works and Songs in A&E*. This, his first release as Spiritualized after disbanding Spacemen 3, appears to show the shapes and figures you might see if you were to stare at a lava lamp for a long time. For Pierce, this is a pretty conventional sleeve; after this he would go on to have many no doubt chemically assisted sleeve concepts—for a glow-in-the-dark box (*Pure Phase*, 1995), the CD in a blister pack contained in a pill box (*Ladies & Gentlemen We Are Floating in Space*, 1997) and a concave sculpture box (*Let It Come Down*, 2001). The fact that this sleeve works within the confines of two-dimensionality recommends it over the others.

EGO

The title to Sandie Shaw's second album, the first sleeve to feature in this chapter (p. 208), says it all.

Also in this section you will find bands who specialize in ego massage, and who generally are dominated by one particular member—usually the singer—who inevitably believes that it's all about them. John Lydon, for example, appeared solo on the front of PiL's debut album release, then packaged his band's next release onto three discs housed in a specially made metal film canister with no image at all, just the band's logo: after all, everyone knew that PiL was him (p. 238).

This ego—and, let's face it, without it pop musicians would not exist—frequently produces amazing results: Miles Davis's immaculately posed thousand-yard stare on the cover of *In a Silent Way* (p. 213) articulates precisely the nature of the sound inside; Brian Eno's careful scattering of his own personal effects must have turned thousands of fans into private detectives looking for clues and meaning as they listened to his beguiling debut album (p. 222).

Eno's old friend David Bowie is arguably the daddy of ego artwork. Regardless of cultural reference points or nomenclature (Ziggy, Aladdin Sane—p. 226—the Thin White Duke . . .) Bowie's sleeves always feature, and are always about, him.

Rap is a rich source of ego, not least because the music itself originates from the bragging of improvised rap on street corners. The sleeves featured here all depict strength either through sexual prowess or just plain machismo.

And then, there are those who go too far . . .

Sandie Shaw Me

1965
Pye Records
England
Photography by Michael Williams

Her first album was called simply *Sandie*. This, Ms. Shaw's second long player, naturally had to be called *Me*, because what else could it be? Everyone—so the photo and title proclaim—knows who "Me" is. Don't they? If the title had been left off this would be a beautiful and striking cover. With the inclusion of the title it becomes beautiful and striking but for the wrong reason—that of monstrous ego. Sandie's not to blame, though; she was nineteen and had become an enormous star in England and France in the space of a year, under the tutelage of her dominant and smart manager Eve Taylor. The decision to use this cover must have been that of Eve and the bosses at Pye, and it was released on the back of three successive Top Ten singles (none of which are on here), suggesting that they knew what they were doing. Unfortunately the album flopped. Perhaps it should have been entitled *Hubris*.

I Haven't Got Anything Better To Do/Astrud Gilberto

1969
Verve
America
Sleeve design by David E. Kreiger
Photography by Joel Brodsky

Astrud Gilberto I Haven't Got Anything Better to Do

Look hard and you'll see the artist's name at the top left of the cover. That's if you can pull your gaze away from the beautiful face and those big brown eyes filled with tears. It was an enormously egotistical statement to put the face of João Gilberto's wife on the cover with no strong identifying text. At the time of this release, Astrud was still only known for being the voice of the "Girl from Ipanema," a hit in 1964, and hardly a recognizable face anywhere but her native Brazil. Yet the design works and you can't help but be intrigued by the photo, taken by the man who also shot the Doors' *Strange Days,* among other album covers. Why is she crying? Verve was still known as being a jazz label in 1969, and there was a long tradition going back to the mid-1950s of using the artist's face blown up on jazz LP covers, although often that was a political statement as much as an artistic one. This seems to be a wholly commercial statement, designed to attract male record buyers without exposing too much flesh. Astrud was gorgeous and confident enough to do it.

HI-FI
RECORDING

KRUPA and RICH

CLEF RECORDS

SUPERVISED BY NORMAN GRANZ

1955
Clef Records
America
Sleeve design by Norman Granz
Photography by Herman Leonard

Gene Krupa and Buddy Rich Krupa and Rich

Obviously Krupa and Rich are drummers. They're playing monogrammed drum kits. They're so well known that they don't need to print their first names on the cover, so it's just Krupa and Rich. The photo, by legendary jazz photographer Herman Leonard, is superbly constructed, the colors of their clothes cutting a swathe through the image, the rhythm of their playing stilled perfectly in a frame. They share the cover and the title, and the record has some drum solos played by both men. It also contains the talents of, among others, Dizzy Gillespie, Oscar Peterson, Ray Brown, Illinois Jacquet, Roy Eldridge, and Ben Webster, but you need to look hard on the back of the sleeve to find their names. This is all about Krupa and Rich, just like it says on the front.

Frank Sinatra No One Cares

1959
Capitol Records
America
Art direction by Frank Sinatra

Four years after the release of his first Capitol album and the beginning of a second career as America's number one male vocalist, Sinatra was settling into a new, self-mythologizing image. As he had done with *Come Fly with Me*, Sinatra commissioned Sammy Cahn and Jimmy Van Heusen to write him a title song, and then chose other numbers to record, which fitted the album's mood. Uniquely, the cover photo shows an unsmiling Sinatra, in a setting that could almost be from a movie (note the man to his left; he looks remarkably like arranger Nelson Riddle). This is the third of his songs for losers "blues" albums, and where *Only the Lonely* (1958) used a drawing of the singer with a tear on his cheek and *Where Are You* (1957) similarly used an illustration of Sinatra, for this we see Frank in person with a scotch, Trilby, trench coat and cigarette, looking like he's alone amid a crowd of couples. Sinatra designed the set, had the extras employed, and stars in his own mini-movie. It was probably the most expensive cover he ever had for an album.

211

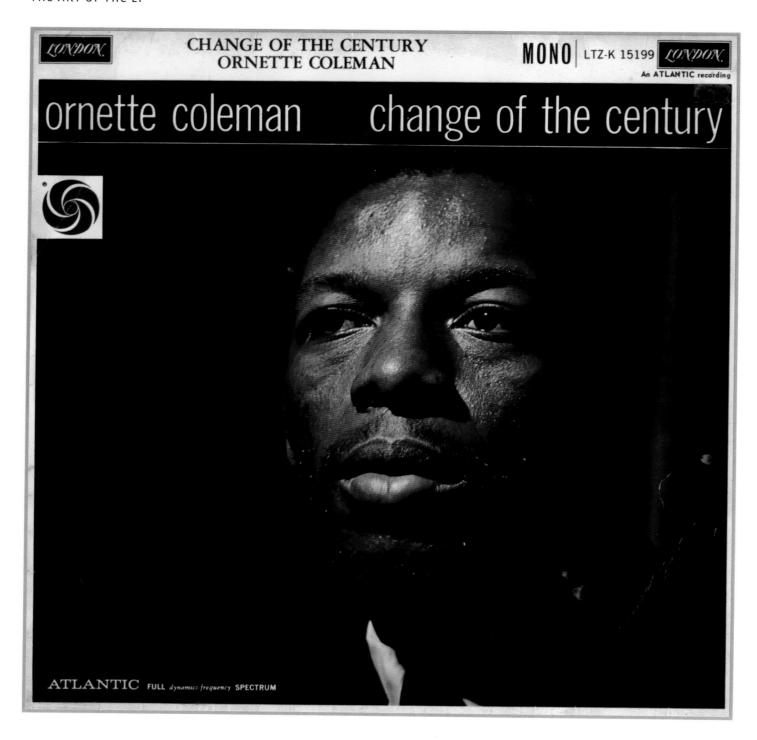

Ornette Coleman Change of the Century

1959

Atlantic Records

America

Photography by Lee Friedlander

Lee Friedlander was the in-house photographer at Atlantic Records in the 1950s, and while he's now known for his street photography, his portraiture skills were honed by working with a range of great jazz and blues artists. The image is clearly untouched, and Coleman's every pore is visible, his forehead shining and eyes far from sparkling. Despite that, the title suggests that here is a man more than happy to have his ego on full display. The fact that Coleman is claiming to be the "change of the century" is audacious, of course. Somehow the lack of capital letters makes the statement more audacious still. Recorded in just two days in California, the album saw Coleman use his then steady team of Don Cherry (trumpet), Charlie Haden (bass), and Billy Higgins (drums), but refuses to acknowledge anyone on the front (there's no "Quartet" credit). The previous album was entitled *The Shape of Jazz to Come*, and the subsequent release would be *This Is Our Music*. Coleman was never shy of making grandiose statements about himself or his work.

Miles Davis In a Silent Way

Miles Davis didn't always appear on his album sleeves, but if he did it was invariably in a broodingly intense shot (the only exception being the uncharacteristic cover shot for 1966's *Miles Smiles*). Here, jazz photographer Lee Friedlander (see opposite page) captures Davis on exceptionally melancholy form. His eyes suggest that he is thinking rather than looking, which is perfect for the album title. This is the album that began Davis's move toward jazz fusion, a move that continued to *Bitches Brew* the following year. It features future Mahavishnu Orchestra leader/ guitarist John McLaughlin and producer Teo Macero's pioneering tape-editing collages. But, despite the modern sound, the artwork shares a look and feel with Davis's earlier work, particularly the then decade-old *Kind of Blue*, with its deep blues behind luminescent black skin. This is classic Davis and a far cry from the headlong dive into sixties rock culture that was the *Bitches Brew* sleeve (see p. 107).

1969
Columbia
America
Sleeve design by Columbia
Photography by Lee Friedlander

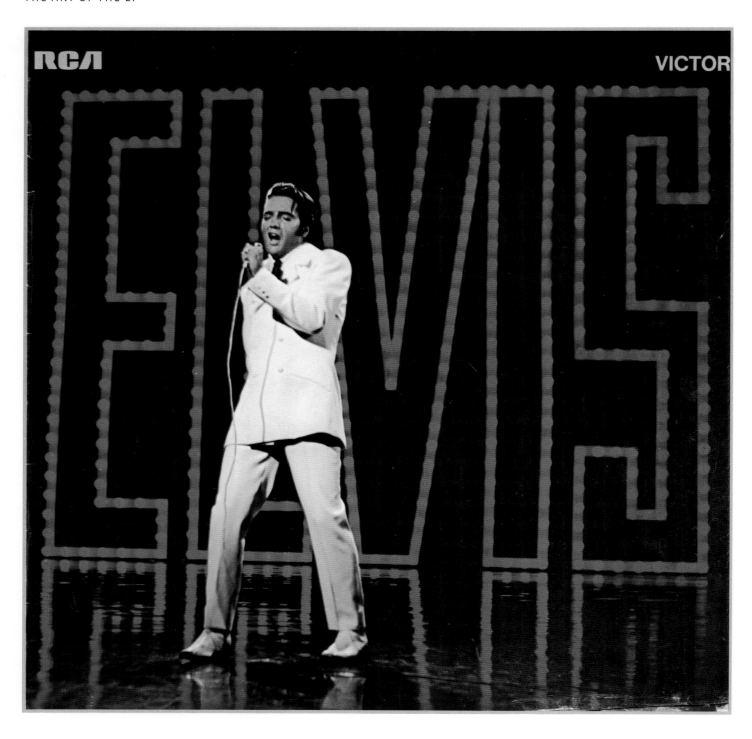

RCA   VICTOR

1968
RCA
America
Art direction by Gene McAvoy

Elvis Presley NBC TV Special

This is the soundtrack to what is now known as the '68 Comeback Special. It was issued without the title on the front cover, which was a good thing because the prosaic album title would not have done the King any favors. The word "comeback" is now used because Elvis, who had been treading water musically for much of the sixties, turned his career around (if only briefly) with his performance, reminding people what they had liked about him in the first place. Before he took the stage he said to the show's executive producer Bob Finkel: "I want everyone to know what I can *really* do." The singer in white suit/name in red lights combination has an undeniable romance to it, but few stars aside from Elvis could justify such rampant egotism. Former Smiths frontman Morrissey spelled out his own name in the same lettering on a 2009 tour with characteristic irony.

EGO

JUDIE·TZUKE
Sportscar

1980
Rocket Records
England
Photography by Chalkie Davis

⚠ Judie Tzuke Sportscar

Singer-songwriter Tzuke scored a huge hit in the UK in 1979 with "Stay with me Till Dawn," and her debut album, *Welcome to the Cruise*, which contained the hit, went to #14 on the album chart. For the cover of her debut the rather attractive 23-year-old was photographed facing away from the camera by arch sleeve designers Hipgnosis. A year later, the theme of "mystery" attempted on that cover was carried over to this, possibly the most pointless and clumsy solo album cover portrait of the decade. Forget the literality of the title implied by the toy sportscar in the frame, and note that a successful, young, attractive pop star has disguised herself on the front cover of a commercially promoted record. The jumpsuit hides her figure, the pose her face. Perhaps it's not actually Tzuke in the photo? Despite the cover, the album made #7 in the UK charts, but after her "boss" Elton John, co-owner of Rocket Records, canceled half his U.S. tour and with it her support slot that year, it failed to make any impression on the U.S. charts. Subsequent Tzuke album releases all have her facing front.

215

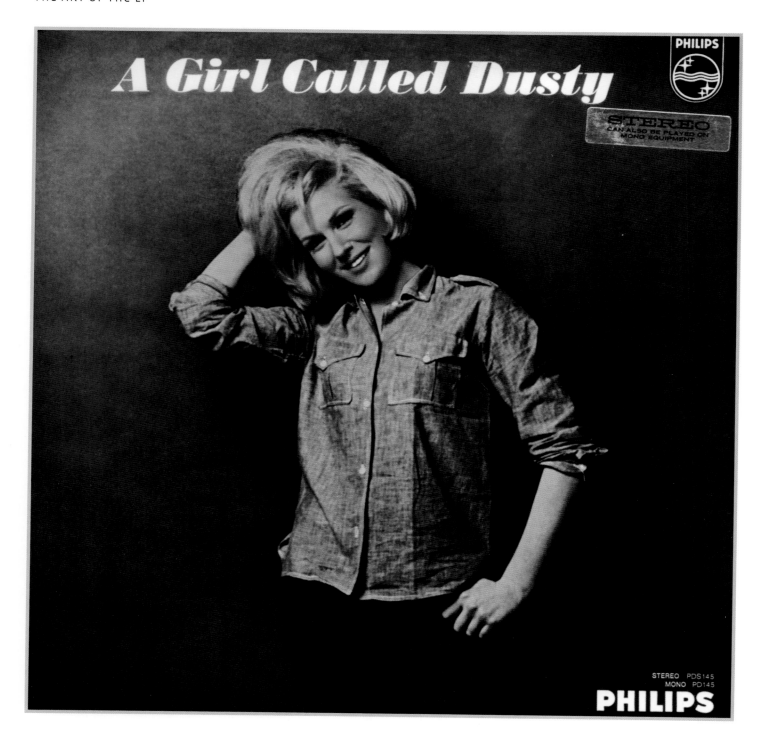

Dusty Springfield A Girl Called Dusty

1964
Phillips
England
Sleeve design by Dusty Springfield
Photography uncredited

Born into an Irish family in west London, Mary O'Brien was a tomboy as a child and thereby earned the name she used for the rest of her life. Despite the trademark beehive hairdo she sported throughout the early days, Dusty's tomboy look is very obvious on the cover to this, her debut album. The artwork is strangely timeless; her loose-fitting, untucked denim shirt along with trousers are echoed in the blue of the wall behind her and the eye is drawn to the smile and the hair. And despite not opting for a miniskirt and big earrings like most of her contemporaries, she still manages to look glamorous. Jerry Wexler, who produced her later album *Dusty in Memphis*, described her as having a "gigantic inferiority complex," which isn't backed up by the evidence provided here: she designed the sleeve, and didn't have to put herself front and center, but chose to anyway.

Delaney & Bonnie & Friends To Bonnie from Delaney

1970
Atco (Atlantic)
America
Sleeve design and photography by
Barry Feinstein and Tom Wilkes for
Camouflage Productions

Singer Bonnie O'Farrell had been a teenage Ikette, the first white backing singer for Ike and Tina Turner. She was an in-demand session singer when she met husband and session guitarist Delaney Bramlett. He and close friend Leon Russell had played together and with various musicians who went on to make up the Joe Cocker backing band for the infamous Mad Dogs and Englishmen tour of America in 1970. Delaney & Bonnie & Friends, a changing mix of musicians who shared the couple's love of American blues and roots music, played support to supergroup Blind Faith on tour in 1969. After that tour, Eric Clapton joined Delaney & Bonnie for a tour that was recorded and released (see p. 306). This, their fourth album (and second that year), featured Duane Allman on lead guitar, and was produced and packaged with all the care that Atlantic Records could muster for rock royalty—it's a gatefold single album. Note that the "throne" on which they're seated is ripped and worn through; the message is that Delaney & Bonnie were hippies and didn't care about material things.

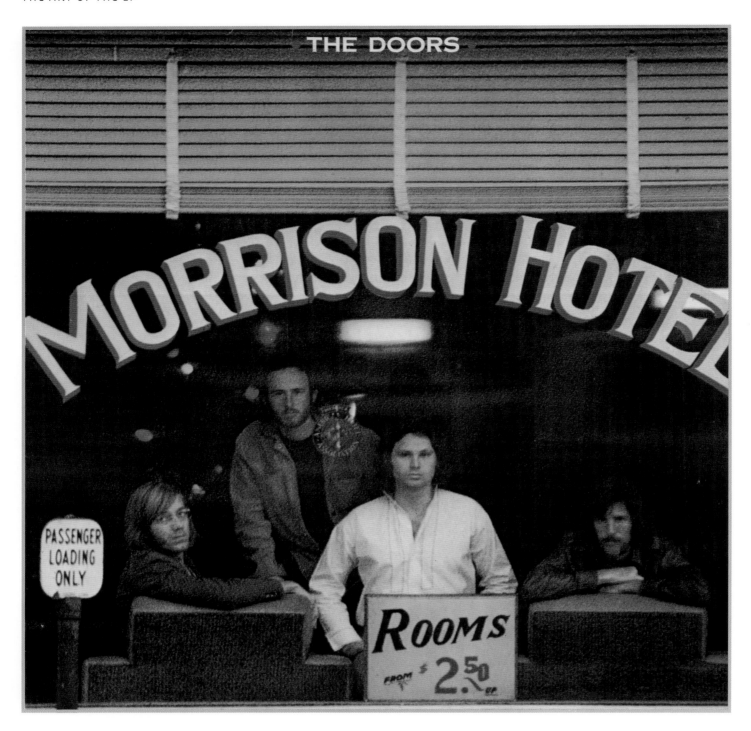

THE DOORS

MORRISON HOTEL

PASSENGER LOADING ONLY

ROOMS FROM $2.50 EP.

1970
Elektra Records
America
Sleeve design by Gary Burden
Photography by Henry Diltz

The Doors Morrison Hotel

No, the hotel didn't belong to singer Jim Morrison, nor was it named after him. In fact the hotel at 1246 South Hope Street in Los Angeles refused permission for the band to be photographed against its facade. But photographer Henry Diltz, a former musician and member of the Modern Folk Quartet who became the official photographer at the Woodstock Festival, sent the band into the hotel, where they lined up in the window and he shot them from across the street, without the hotel manager knowing. All that in-house designer Buden (who worked on a number of famous Atlantic album covers) had to do was place the band name. Look hard; it's at the top. By this point, Doors singer Jim Morrison was supposedly disillusioned with being seen as little more than a sex symbol and with the Doors being regarded as nothing more than his backing band. Which makes you wonder why he'd agree to pose for such a cover shot and call the album *Morrison Hotel* (although side one of the record does have "Hard Rock Cafe" printed on it). Diltz now runs a photo gallery called Morrison Hotel.

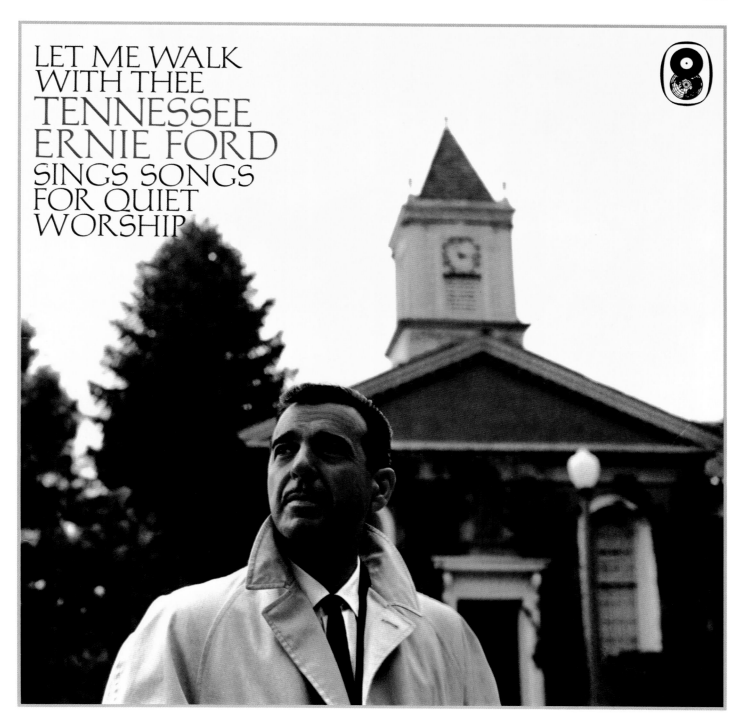

LET ME WALK
WITH THEE
TENNESSEE
ERNIE FORD
SINGS SONGS
FOR QUIET
WORSHIP

1965
Capitol/World Record Club
America
Sleeve design by Ed Thrasher

Tennessee Ernie Ford Let Me Walk with Thee

Although best known for his worldwide hit single "16 Tons" (1955) and "The Ballad of Davy Crockett" the same year, Ford earned three stars on the Hollywood Walk of Fame, for records, radio and TV. While enjoying success as a pop singer (though Country-tinged), he hosted the *NBC Ford Variety Show*, named for the automobile manufacturer sponsor rather than the host, and after it was canceled in 1961 hosted his own talk show out of San Francisco (1962–1965). In 1964 Ford won a Grammy Award for *Great Gospel Songs*, and so naturally followed it with another gospel album. Here he is, in front of a church, in his Sunday best, looking cool and sophisticated, gazing reverentially toward Heaven. The angle of the shot, taken from below, makes Ernie look almost heroic and keeps the eye line direct to the steeple behind him. Because of the way the type is arranged, it can be read as if we are asking to walk with Ernie, which must have been coincidental. He died in 1991, at age seventy-two, of liver failure, after leaving a White House dinner hosted by then President George H. W. Bush.

1967
Track/Polydor
England
Sleeve design by Ed Thrasher
Photography by Bruce Fleming

The Jimi Hendrix Experience Are You Experienced

For such an influential cover, Hendrix's debut had really gone through the mill. This was largely because it was released by independent label Track in the UK who then licenced it out to various foreign affiliates. The original cover does not have Hendrix's name above the album title, which was added by Polydor in Germany, Italy, and Spain. In each of those countries a different color was used (green, red and yellow respectively). France even added correct punctuation to the album title—it's a question, correct? Whatever tweaks were made, this is a great sleeve for two main reasons. First, photographer Bruce Fleming captures the band's mercurial spirit perfectly, and second, Ed Thrasher's font is great. So good they printed it twice. During '67 and '68 Fleming was Jimi's "personal photographer"—now *that's* ego.

David Bowie Hunky Dory

1971
RCA
England
Art direction by George Underwood at
Main Artory
Photography by Brian Ward
Colorization by Terry Pastor

In the credits on Bowie's fourth album it states that producer Ken Scott is assisted by "The Actor." It was the singer's conceit at the time to describe himself as such and this theatrical mindset has remained very much evident in his approach to cover art. On the sleeve to previous album *The Man Who Sold the World*, photographer Brian Ward shot Bowie reclining on a chaise longue in a dress. This shot looks as if it was from the same photoshoot, but the close-up is more ambiguous, bisexual and effective. Bowie's friend from art school, George Underwood, designed the sleeve but it was Terry Pastor who colorized the shot; as he told *Record Collector* in 2009, "David asked George if he could color up Brian's photograph but he didn't do that kind of work. Being an airbrush artist, I could do that sort of thing and George asked me . . . I was given a black and white matte photographic print, which was about the same size as the LP cover." The image is so powerful that no artist name or album title is needed.

Eno Here Come the Warm Jets

1973
Island
England
Design supervision by Carol McNicoll
Photography by Lorenz Zatecky

It's interesting that on a sleeve that features a large number of unique and interesting objects one of the standouts, possibly because it is next to Brian Eno's reflected face, is a boring old English teapot. Why? Well, the design for Eno's post-Roxy Music debut album was by Carol McNicoll, who is now a well-respected ceramicist who specializes in bizarrely shaped teapots. Back in the early seventies she was Eno's girlfriend and designed his Roxy Music—era "feather collar" costume, which is now in the Victoria and Albert Museum in London. Eno allowed his ego free reign on this sleeve, not only getting his girlfriend to design it but doing the shoot in his own apartment on Grantully Road, Maida Vale, in London. There is a lot of his personal clutter and, importantly, at least two pictures of him. Could that be him again in the reflection on the teapot?

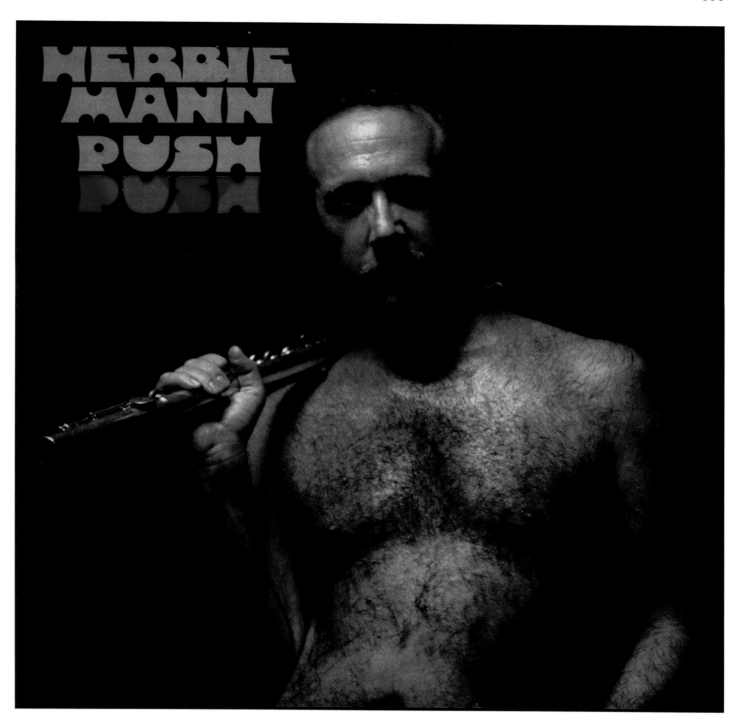

● Herbie Mann Push Push

1971
Embryo/Atlantic
America
Sleeve design by Paula Bisacca
Photography by Joel Brodsky

No No! It was the very early 1970s and Herbie was forty-one years old. "Swinging" had spread from the suburbs of John Updike's New England villages (as depicted in *Couples*, 1968) to middle America and sex was regularly used to sell everything from cars to razor blades. Although Herbie clearly wasn't into razor blades, or any kind of depilatory methods, as you can see. This release on Herbie's own label had an enormously expensive sleeve; it's a gatefold, the bright orange inner part of which contains a felt flock image of a couple making love, the lower "Push" on the cover is die-cut for no apparent reason, and the information contained on the cover could easily fit onto the back or inner sleeve—even the statement from Herbie that "Marvin Gaye's album *What's Going On* is the best album of the year!!" Sleeve designer Bisacca also worked on the Ohio Player's *Pain* album the same year, on which a bald female model poses wearing a studded bikini, and carrying a whip. There must have been something in the air that year.

Robert Fripp Exposure

1979
Polydor
England
Sleeve design by Chris Stein
Photography by Chris Stein
Colorization by Steve Sprouse
VTR images by Amos Poe

The commonly held view is that prog and rock are at opposite ends of the rock & roll spectrum. But in the late seventies, ex-King Crimson main man Fripp was living in New York's Bowery, hanging out and jamming with bands at CBGB, as well as producing albums. The sleeve to Fripp's solo album was designed and photographed by none other than Blondie guitarist Chris Stein. Originally showcasing Darryl Hall's voice on most tracks, the album ultimately featured an array of guest musicians from UK punks XTC to Phil Collins. It's not clear whether New Yorker Stein was inspired by Paul Morrissey's *Chelsea Girl* (see opposite page) but the close-up/longshot combination and color palette are strikingly similar; the main difference is that the close-up is a still from a video by Stein. It was a big ego massage for Fripp who, let's face it, doesn't make as good a cover star as Nico. Fripp didn't repeat the design device again, suggesting that he knows that his face doesn't offer a prime selling tool.

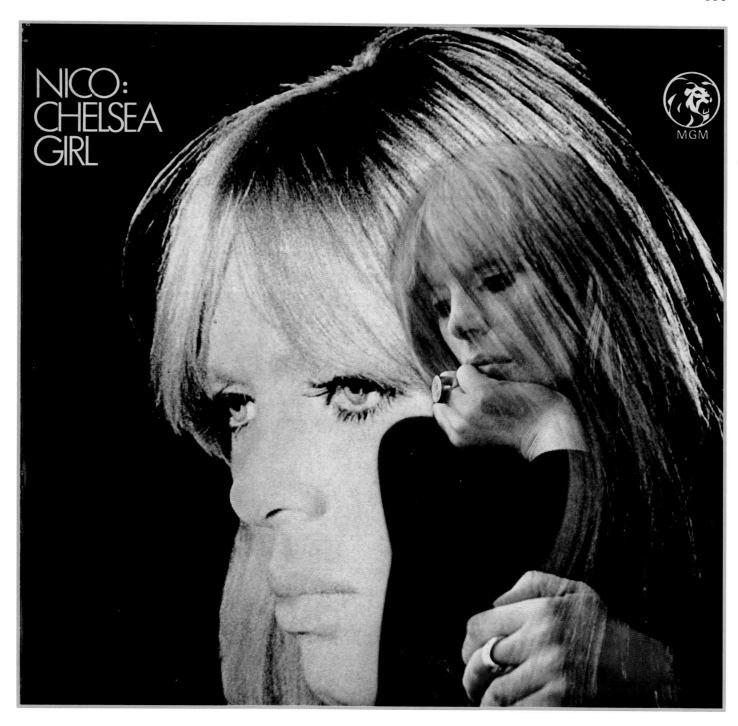

1967
MGM Records
America
Photography by Paul Morrissey

Nico Chelsea Girl

How remarkable that there are not one, but two images of Nico on the cover of her debut album release. Factory filmmaker Paul Morrissey had made the film *Chelsea Girls*, starring Nico among other Factory "stars," in 1966. He and producer Andy Warhol made it as two films to be shown concurrently, one black-and-white, one in color. While the 210-minute movie is patchy and the music on this album is frequently hard to love, the sleeve design is wonderful. It is not a soundtrack, by the way, but Nico's first studio album, featuring songs from Lou Reed as well as Dylan and Tim Hardin. German model Nico's fine cheekbones and blond hair provided Morrissey with a great subject, and using the original film idea, he juxtaposes the black-and-white close-up with the color long shot. The hair from the close-up follows the line of the color shot and the viewer gets a dynamic and dramatic effect from shifting his or her gaze between the eyes in each shot.

David Bowie *Aladdin Sane*

1973
RCA
England
Sleeve design by Duffy and Celia Philo
for Duffy Design Concepts
Photography by Brian Duffy
Makeup by Pierre La Roche
Album produced by Ken Scott

Although another one of "The Actor's" (see *Hunky Dory*, p. 221) creations, the sleeve to *Aladdin Sane* is clearly Ziggy Stardust part two. Bowie's punning title (a lad insane, geddit?) was possibly derived from his schizophrenic older brother who had a profound influence on him. Fashion photographer Brian Duffy was hired to shoot Bowie, who had been made up by Pierre La Roche from the Elizabeth Arden Salon. Bowie's personal stylist at the time, La Roche went on to do the makeup for *The Rocky Horror Picture Show*. Duffy used a seven-color photographic process which necessitated the album sleeve to be printed in Switzerland. The zigzag on Bowie's face was Bowie's idea: "The flash . . . was taken from the 'High Voltage' sign that was on any box containing dangerous amounts of electricity. I was not a little peeved when Kiss purloined it. Purloining, after all, was my job." Artist Celia Philo worked on the finished picture to give it its distinctive hyper-realist look. Underneath it all, of course, is David Bowie, as everyone was very aware.

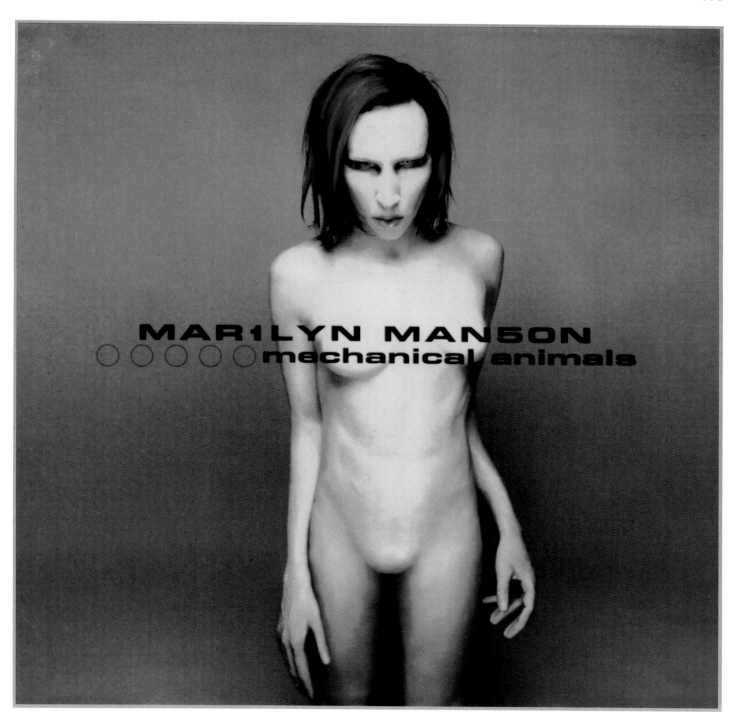

Marilyn Manson **Mechanical Animals**

Massively inspired by David Bowie and Alice Cooper, Marilyn Manson took the Ziggy/Alice alternative persona idea and continues to run with it. This, his third album, was probably his creative and commercial high point. The character on the sleeve is called Omega (although few but MM's hardcore fans know that; it's really all about MM being "extreme"), and makes the creation of the *Aladdin Sane* sleeve look like child's play. For the cover shoot, Manson's designer Brown worked with George Lucas's Industrial Light and Magic makeup artists to create a latex suit complete with nipple-less prosthetic breasts and a sixth finger on each hand. No Photoshop was used, apparently. Like Chris Cunningham's later blood-chilling creations for Aphex Twin, Joseph Cultice's photograph is striking because even though you know it can't exist it still looks real. Walmart refused to stock the album and it was banned in Japan; not for the fact that it featured a naked, busty alien but because they objected to the six fingers. Weird.

1988
Nothing/Interscope
America
Sleeve design by Paul Brown
Photography by Joseph Cultice

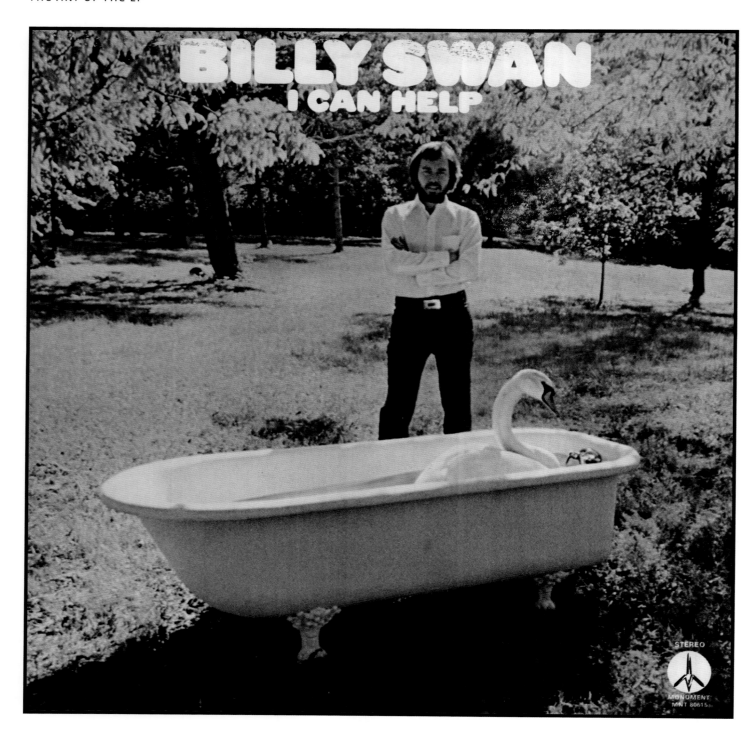

Billy Swan I Can Help

1974
Monument Records
America
Sleeve design by Bill Barnes and
Julie Holiner
Photography by Ken Kim

Nashville-based singer, songwriter and bass player for Kris Kristofferson, Billy Swan recorded the song "I Can Help" in just two takes. It was a worldwide hit and made #1 on the Billboard Hot 100—the first time since the early 1960s that Monument, who released Roy Orbison's early singles, including "Only the Lonely," had hit the top spot. A well-regarded session musician and producer, Swan was an Elvis fan, but the closest he got to the King was to produce Tony Joe White's (original) version of "Polk Salad Annie" in 1969. Billy was unable to recapture the success of his "I Can Help" single and album (the LP made #1 on the U.S. country charts and #21 on the Hot 100 pop chart). The very obvious choice of cover image can't have helped; it does make Billy look lacking in original ideas and just a bit desperate. It must have taken a lot of work to get the bath into the garden and fill it with water, and then get the swan in there for long enough to get a good enough shot. The flip side of the cover shows the swan escaping, wings flapping. The symbolism seems somehow poignant.

Roy Harper Flat Baroque and Berserk

1970
Harvest
America
Sleeve design by Lon Goddard
Photography uncredited

Despite not enjoying enormous popular success, English folk singer-
songwriter Roy Harper influenced and worked with a lot of famous people,
including Led Zeppelin (for whom he photographed the cover of *Physical
Grafitti*) and Pink Floyd—it's Harper's voice you hear on the "Have a Cigar"
track of *Wish You Were Here*. After the release of this, Harper's fourth
album but his first for Harvest (an EMI subsidiary), he went on his debut
American tour. Renowned for his long and winding electric folk-blues
freakouts (members of the Nice played on a track here called "Hell's
Angels"), Harper was unwilling to pander to record company pressure in
any way. Which partly explains the strange portrait used for the cover of
this album. Sleeve design is credited to ex-pat American Lon Goddard, who
moved to London in 1966 and became a staff writer for music mag *Record
Mirror*. In 1973 he became head of press at CBS records in London. Sadly,
the sleeve doesn't credit the photographer, but whoever it was deserves
applause for creating a fine mix of textures and color balance.

Johnny Winter *Second Winter*

1969
CBS Records
America
Sleeve design by Tony Lane
Photography by Richard Avedon

Although packaged as a double album, which allows the fantastic full use of the sleeve for the action image, there are only three sides of recorded music on this album, with the fourth being all run-out groove. It's not Johnny Winter's second album, either, it's the third—although it is the second to carry the words "Johnny Winter" in the title (he'd released *Johnny Winter* the previous year). The title and the sleeve can almost be regarded as enabling the use of fashion photographer Richard Avedon's solarized shot of the albino guitarist in movement. While Johnny had an albino brother, Edgar, who played keyboards on the album, both the images on the cover are of Johnny.

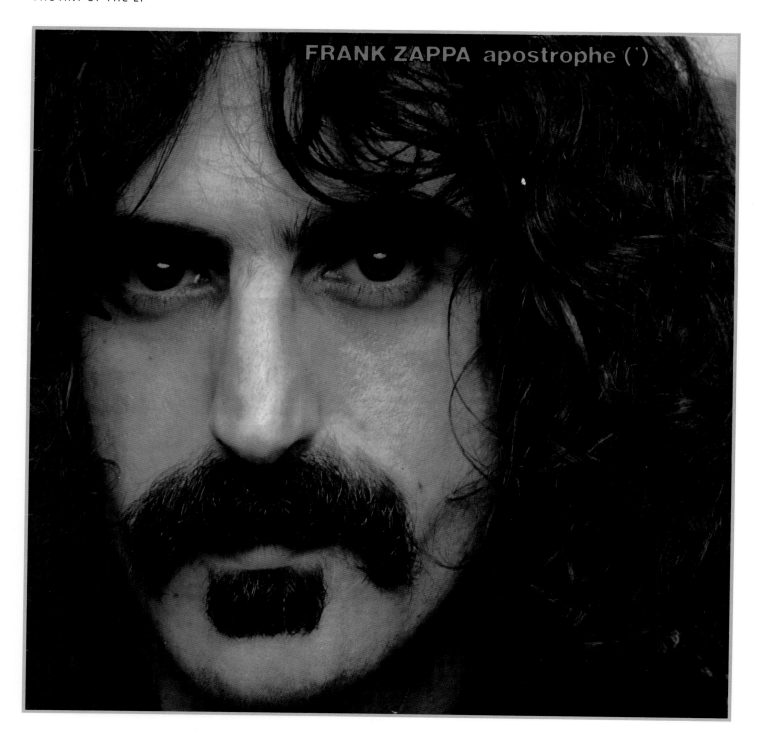

1974
Disc-reet Records/Warners
America
Graphic design by Cal Schenkel
Photography by Sam Emerson Loew

Frank Zappa Apostrophe (')

This was arguably the most shocking cover that Zappa had so far produced. Whereas previously he had either used graphics, illustrations (see p. 374) or group photos (including the Sgt. Pepper "tribute" *Only in It For The Money*) for the sleeves of his albums, this time the singer-songwriter-guitarist-producer used just his plain, unadorned portrait in an obvious, full-out manner. Five years later he would almost repeat the pose for *Sheik Yerbooti*, wearing only a headdress. Funnily enough, this proved to be the most successful album of Zappa's long and varied recording career—it was his seventeenth release and there would be at least forty more before his untimely death in 1993. Long-time sleeve designer Cal Schenkel put the (') onto the great photo by surprisingly little-used cover photographer Sam Emerson Loew.

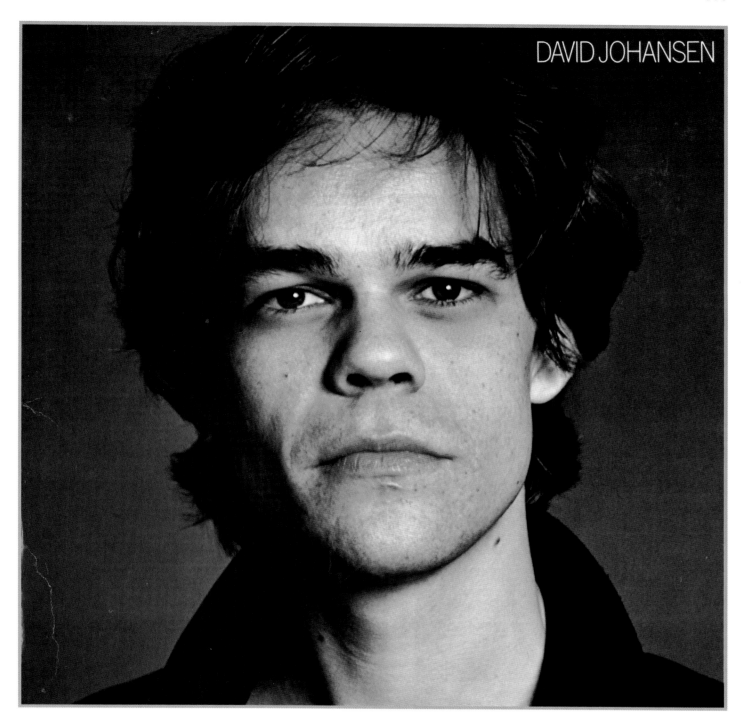

DAVID JOHANSEN

1978
Blue Sky/CBS Records
America
Sleeve design by Elena Pavlov
Photography by Benno Friedman

David Johansen David Johansen

Singer Johansen had been the front man for the wild, debauched and raucous New York Dolls, and when performing with them he'd worn exaggerated makeup—lipstick, false eyelashes and rouge—and with his hair in a back-combed bouffant mess. Which makes this cover for his debut, self-titled album somewhat shocking. Clear-eyed, clean-skinned, he looks almost boyish (he was twenty-eight at the time). Originally (and still) from the Boston area, Benno Friedman worked as a commercial photographer at magazines such as *Harper's Bazaar* and for record companies as a means of financing his artistic work. He manipulated his photographs—which have appeared at the Whitney and at MoMA—in the darkroom, and in the seventies helped to push boundaries about what was considered acceptable for art photography. His record cover portraiture (see also Cheap Trick's *In Color*, p. 36) is relatively straightforward, though the sense of confrontation Johansen exhibits here is as strong as that of his ego.

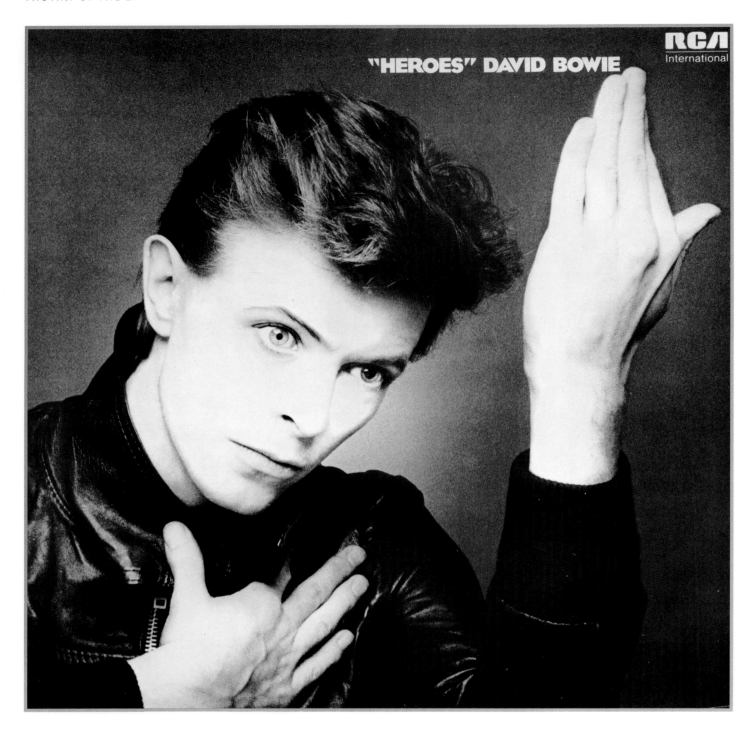

"HEROES" DAVID BOWIE

RCA International

1977
RCA
England
Photography by Masayoshi Sukita

David Bowie Heroes

"There's Old Wave. There's New Wave. And there's David Bowie." So ran the RCA advertising slogan for *Heroes* toward the end of 1977. His two previous albums, *Station to Station* and *Low*, had cheated and used imagery from Nic Roeg's startling 1976 film *The Man Who Fell to Earth*, even though the finished sleeves looked great. Now in the wake of punk, Bowie came out fighting. Returning to the photographer of the *Ziggy Stardust* sleeve, Masayoshi Sukita, he chose a stripped-down, black-and-white, leather jacket look. But no, this was no new wave cover: being Bowie, it had to have a backstory. It was inspired by Brücke artist Erich Heckel's print called "Roquairol." Iggy Pop's pose on the cover of *The Idiot*—produced by Bowie the same year—references a Heckel painting with the same name. Note that Bowie is hiding the floppy seventies collar of the jacket, which adds to the timelessness of this picture.

1969
Astor Records
Australia
Sleeve design uncredited
Photography uncredited

Marty Feldman Marty

Comedian, writer and actor Marty Feldman was one of the biggest names in British entertainment in the late 1960s and 1970s. Having begun his career as a trumpeter in small clubs and pubs of London, his bug-eyed appearance and quick wit soon won him admirers at the BBC, and he cowrote some enormously successful radio shows for them. In 1967 he made his TV debut appearance in *At Last the 1948 Show*, which he cowrote with John Cleese and Graham Chapman (who went on to form Monty Python's Flying Circus with another Feldman collaborator, Michael Palin). *At Last* was a hit, Feldman became a star and in 1968 he was given his own show, *Marty*, from which the sketches on this spoken word release are largely taken. The cover is simply astounding. The scotch and cigarette are not simply props. The suit and hat are Feldman's own. Within five years he had begun a working relationship with Mel Brooks and starred in *Young Frankenstein* with Gene Wilder and Peter Boyle. Sadly, after six more movies, Feldman died in 1983 from a heart attack.

1977
Warner Bros
America
Cover concept by Fleetwood Mac
Sleeve design by Desmond Strobel
Photography by Herbert Worthington
Hand lettering by Larry Vigon

❗ Fleetwood Mac **Rumours**

Herbert Worthington's cover photograph for *Rumours* is on such a ubiquitous album that it's easy not to see beyond the cover's beige background and ornate lettering. But if you look closely you'll see Mac singer Stevie Nicks posing in a chiffon dress and dancing slippers, arms stretched out behind her like a child pretending to be on an airplane. Next to her is the usually preternaturally scruffy Mick Fleetwood done up like a flamenco dancer. His slippered foot rests on a footstool and his raised knee supports Nicks's outstretched leg as she holds his left hand. Right hand on hip, he looks imperiously down as if to say: "What the hell am I doing here?! How come I give my name to one of the most credible blues rock groups to end up dressed like a fool with this ethereal fairy queen leaning on my leg? Plus, whose idea was it to give me these wooden testicles? Still, if we're going to sell forty million, who's complaining?"

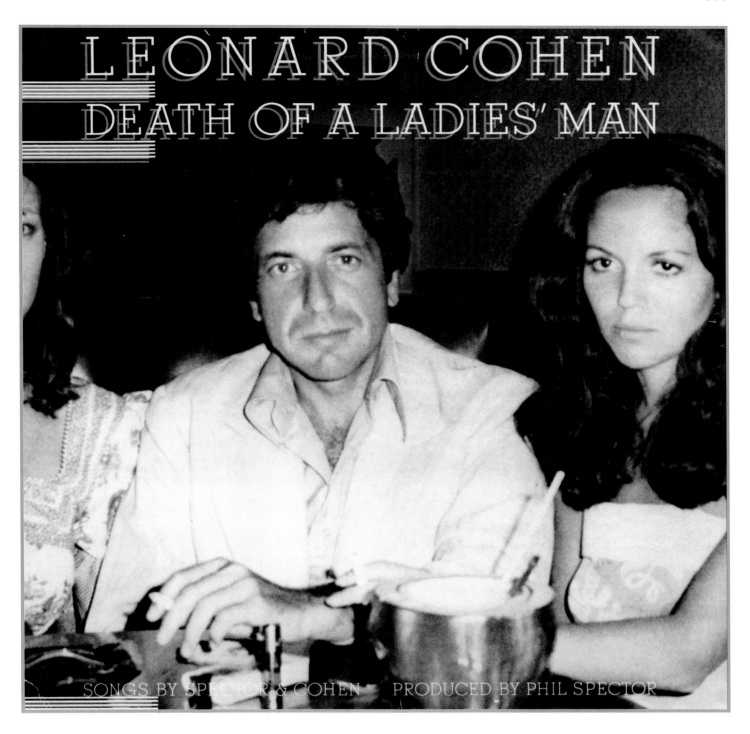

Leonard Cohen *Death of a Ladies' Man*

1977
Columbia Records
America
Art direction by John Cabalka
Sleeve design by Ron Coro, Bill Naegels/
Gribbitti
Photography by an anonymous roaming
photographer

Leonard Cohen had taken something of a break from music in 1974, and
his return was eagerly anticipated, especially since he was working with
legendary producer Phil Spector. As was often the case with Spector's work
in the 1970s, though, the process was painful for the artist and involved
Spector working alone on the final mix. The album was not well received.
Possibly its only saving grace is the cover. To Cohen's left is a Canadian
friend (now filmmaker), Eva La Pierre, and to his right is Suzanne Elrod,
the mother of his two children. Cohen gazes directly at the camera with
a louche half smile, showing chest hair and cigarette. As Eva recalls, the
"roaming photographer" was a "lovely young woman in a short skirt. She had
a Polaroid with a *huge* flash. Leonard paid her and tipped her for the photos.
Later, when Leonard asked if he could use the photo and I said 'yes,' he cut
it up so that Suzanne was on it twice and there was a seam down the middle
of my face. He said he had to do that to please her, which I found hilarious!
I still have an original photo—a very sweet yellowed little snapshot."

Public Image Limited Metal Box

1979
Virgin
England
Sleeve concept by John Lydon
Art direction by Charles Dimont

Former Sex Pistol John Lydon (né Rotten) had given Virgin a Top Ten single ("Public Image") and Top Thirty album (*First Issue*) in 1978, and he was still considered the man most likely to become an international star to emerge from the wreckage of the Pistols. Being the contrarian he is, Lydon asked for his band—whom he referred to as a "corporation," hence the name—to have their second album released in either a sardine-type can, which needed a key to peel back the cover, or a sandpaper outer sleeve (which Durutti Column would do the following year), in order to ruin any album either side of it on a shelf. Instead Virgin allowed PiL to release three 12" singles in a film canister specially made for the purpose. The band's logo was embossed in the lid and a sticker bearing the serial number METAL1 was stuck on the back. There were no photos or title; that shows either an immense ego at work or an enormous self-destructive streak. Given that after the initial 60,000 pressing sold out the album was rereleased as a double package, entitled *Second Issue* in America, the former seems more likely.

1988
Blast First!
America
Sleeve design by Sonic Youth
Xerox by Todd's Copy Shop, NY

Ciccone Youth The Whitey Album

This is not a Sonic Youth album. It features key Sonic members Kim Gordon, Thurston Moore, Lee Ranaldo, and Steve Shelley, but it also features Mike Watt, former Minutemen and fiREHOSE founder. Six months after *The Whitey Album* was released—which includes tracks released as a maxi-single in 1986—Sonic Youth released their seminal double album *Daydream Nation*. *The Whitey Album* includes sampled and reinvented Madonna songs "Burnin' Up" and "Into The Groove(y)" as well as a version of Robert Palmer's "Addicted To Love" and several ironic, satirical "pop" tunes by Ciccone Youth. The xeroxed photo of Madonna's mole in close-up at once parodies the objectification of the pop star and rejects the materialism being projected by her at the time. The members of Ciccone Youth all rejected the traditional music business approach to making pop, and regarded their music as examples of their art, which contains meaning and protest. The title is both an ironic play on the Beatles' *White Album* and a reference to the exploitation of black dance music by white pop stars such as Madonna.

Side One   *OVER AND OVER   SECOND HAND STORE   INDIAN SUMMER   AT THE STATION*
Side Two   *TOMORROW   INNER TUBE   THEME FROM BOAT WEIRDOS   LIFE'S BEEN GOOD*

Joe Walsh "But Seriously, Folks . . . "

Guitarist Walsh joined the Eagles in 1976 to replace Bernie Leadon and recorded *Hotel California*. His cowritten "Life in the Fast Lane" became the third single taken from it (making #11 on the Hot 100). Between *Hotel California* and the next Eagles album, *The Long Run*, Eagles members guest-starred on this, Walsh's fifth solo album. His satirical take on being a rock star, "Life's Been Good," taken from this album was an international hit, as was the album. Walsh is a funny man, and the title, a line used by stand-up comedians of old, is a self-satirizing reflection of that. The swimming pool was considered to be a rock star's major signifier of self-importance and wealth. He's a funny guy.

1978

Elektra/Asylum

America

Sleeve design and photography by Jimmy Wachtel, aquatically assisted by Mark Foltz

BIG DADDY KANE

It's a Big Daddy Thing

1989
Cold Chillin'/Reprise Records
America
Photography and design by
George DuBose
Styling by Dorian Lipman
Hair and makeup by Sam

Big Daddy Kane It's a Big Daddy Thing

Photographer George DuBose was pretty hip to the New York scene in the eighties, capturing the shot of the B52s which two years later became the cover to their debut (see p. 169). By the end of the decade he was a regular contributor to Andy Warhol's *Interview* magazine and specialized in shooting over-the-top, bizarrely dressed musical personalities such as Klaus Nomi and Afrika Bambaataa. This was boastful rapper Kane's second album and his most successful. His appearance anticipates the bling look which rap would soon adopt (see opposite): plenty of gold, some joints in a case and champagne on ice, but with added "booty." While this is a fine rap record, it's not for those who are easily offended. The artwork was a step up from Kane's debut which, despite featuring him as a Roman emperor surrounded by fawning women, was not quite as salacious. Big Daddy Kane achieved the ultimate ego high when he was asked to appear alongside Madonna in her 1990 *Sex* book.

L.L. Cool J

Mama Said Knock You Out

1990
Def Jam
America
Sleeve design by the Drawing Board
Photography by Michel Comte

LL Cool J Mama Said Knock You Out

Swiss-born fashion photographer Comte also took photos of boxer Mike Tyson in 1990 and this could almost be one from a session with the former world heavyweight champion. Which is exactly what the rapper LL Cool J wanted; in the span of five years he'd gone from being an original old-skool rapper (see *Radio*, 1985, p. 45) to a rap-pop crossover success with *Bigger and Deffer* (1987) and *Walk with a Panther* (1989). However, by the time of this release, West Coast rap had come to dominate the scene, with gangsta rap enjoying particular popularity. A former choirboy and Boy Scout from Queens, Ladies Love Cool James had some hard work to do in order to keep fresh and happening. So he worked out, beefed up, donned gold chains, rings and bling and posed bare-chested and sweating for the cover of what would become a three million-selling release. It was the beginning of a long career in which he'd become a fearsome character on his musical releases and in TV roles such as a death row inmate in *House* in 2005 and DJ Ridiculous in *30 Rock* in 2007.

Stetsasonic In Full Gear

1988
Tommy Boy
America
Sleeve design and layout by
Steven Migilio
Photography by Janette Beckman
Art direction by Monica Lynch

Originally the Stetsons, then the Stetson Brothers and finally Stetsasonic, these guys were one of the very best old skool hip-hop outfits. They employ rap and turntables as well as live instrumentation, and band members Prince Paul and Daddy O went on to become hugely respected producers. It was this, their sophomore album, which gained them the initial critical and commercial success they craved (and deserved). Their look is exemplary of the "rap posse" dress code of the late eighties, which was almost a variation of the tuxedos and two-tone suits of sixties vocal groups, except in Stetsasonic's case it was white leisure suits, often with piping down the arms and legs. The pronounced angling of the photograph was a common trick among rappers (NWA's *Straight Outta Compton* from the same year and Public Enemy's *Yo! Bum Rush the Show* [p. 177] being two examples). Don't they look mean and magnificent, like a real-in-the-movies street gang, though?

Deee-Lite World Clique

1990
Elektra
America
Sleeve design by Nick Egan and Tom
Bouman (VIVID-ID)
Art direction by Nick Egan and Daisy
Photography by Michael Holsband

Cartoon versions of bands had been done before—obvious examples
being the Beatles' *Yellow Submarine* movie and the Jackson 5ive cartoon
series. But Deee-Lite came out of New York with a very defined comic book
image—starting from the names up. Fronted by Lady Miss Kier and flanked
by Super DJ Dimitri and Towa Tei, the band rocketed to fame off the back
of single "Groove is in the Heart," which featured a old skool larger-than-
life performer, Bootsy Collins from Funkadelic. The music was anything but
two-dimensional, though, using clever samples from old jazz records and
featuring guest artists of quality and integrity like Q-Tip from Tribe Called
Quest and Fred Wesley and Maceo Parker from James Brown's band the JBs.
The art director responsible for making all this happen on the cover, Nick
Egan, was originally part of the Malcolm McClaren and Vivienne Westwood
set in London and had designed sleeves for Bow Wow Wow (see p. 133) as
well as INXS's *Kick*. He is now a video director in LA. Despite Deee-Lite's
claim of world domination, they disappeared pretty soon after this.

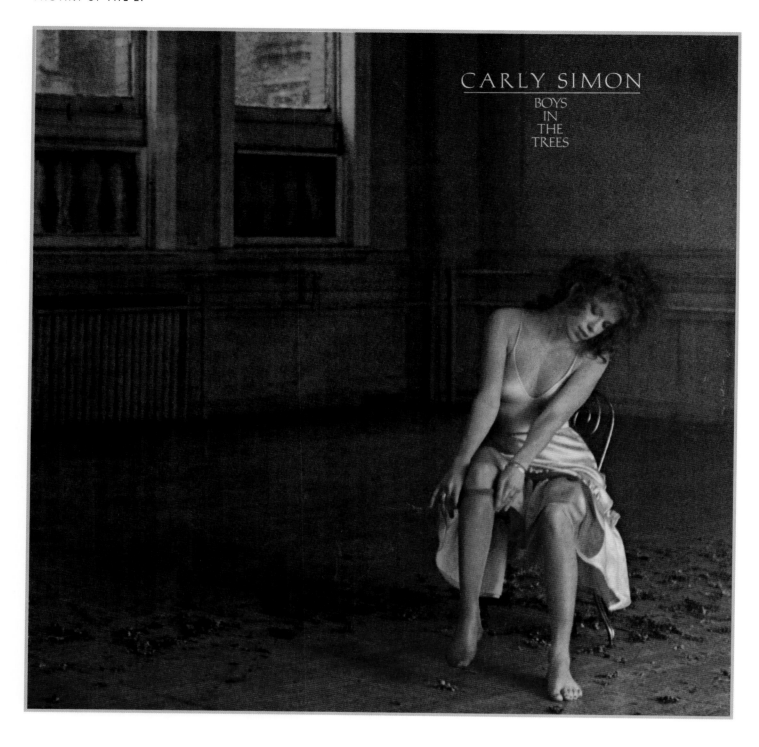

CARLY SIMON
BOYS
IN
THE
TREES

Carly Simon Boys in the Trees

Carly Simon is best known for two things: her 1972 song "You're So Vain"—
which might be about Warren Beatty. Or Mick Jagger. Or Ryan O'Neal. And
the cover art of her 1975 album *Playing Possum*, which was shot by Norman
Seef and in which Carly wears little except boots and a teddy suit. That
cover was more about Seef than anything else. This cover, however, is all
about Carly. And it won the 1979 Grammy Award for Best Packaging for
Johnny B. Lee and Tony Lane. The daughter of one of the founders of the
publishing house Simon & Schuster, Carly Simon was not averse to using her
physical attributes to sell her records—her second LP, *Anticipation*, has
her photographed in a diaphanous dress, legs apart, holding open some
wrought-iron gates, for instance. After the Top Ten success of the *Possum*
album, the cover of the follow-up, *Another Passenger*, used a head shot of
the singer and it only made #29 on the Hot 100. Being photographed in her
underwear for this album pushed the record to #10. The following release,
Spy, also used a head shot—and made #49.

1978
Elektra
America
Art direction by Johnny B. Lee and
Tony Lane
Photography by Tony Lane

246

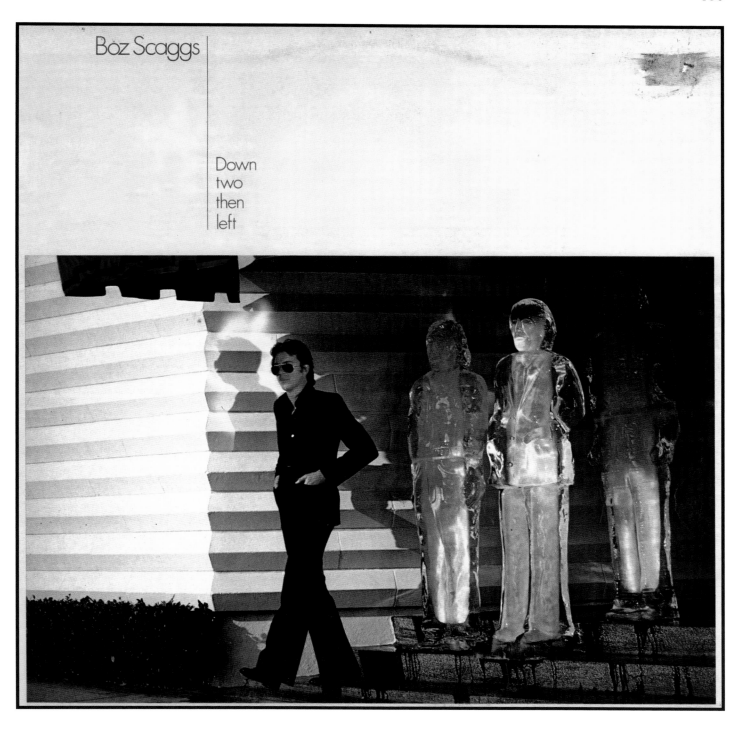

Boz Scaggs

Down
two
then
left

Boz Scaggs Down Two Then Left

1977
CBS Records
America
Sleeve design by Nancy Donald
Photography by Guy Bourdin

Scaggs's eighth solo album followed a year after the enormously successful and award-winning *Silk Degrees* (see p. 74). While it made #11 on the Billboard Hot 100 charts, it didn't match its predecessor in sales or reviews. The choice of cover image is not as successful, either. Nancy Donald had designed *Silk Degrees* (and worked on a large number of great covers while at CBS), yet she possibly didn't have much input on this. French fashion photographer Guy Bourdin (1928—1991) was famously difficult to work with and apparently treated his fashion models as if they were props. He developed a style of creating narratives for his fashion shoots in the late 1960s and clearly something along narrative lines is being attempted here. What exactly, is far from clear. Those ice sculptures are of Scaggs, and this is in LA, so of course they're melting. The cost clearly doesn't matter. At least Scaggs has his clothes on; on one version of the cover of *Slow Dancer* he is photographed in speedo-style trunks walking toward the camera on a beach. As for the title's relevance, maybe Bourdin knew?

Björk **Debut**

1993
One Little Indian
England
Photography by Jean Baptiste Mondino
Styling by Judy Blame

Despite being a naturally kooky and stylish person, Björk didn't take any risks on this, her debut solo album after leaving the Sugarcubes. Not only was she styled by London's then number-one stylist Judy Blame, but she also used the coolest fashion photographer and video director, Jean Baptiste Mondino. The production credits, including Massive Attack's Nellee Hooper, are likewise a Who's Who of early nineties hipsters. Björk was at that point in her career when she really could not get any more fashionable, and this album became a coffee table and dinner party favorite among Britain's "chattering classes." Not only did Mondino shoot the sleeve but he also directed the video to "Violently Happy," which features Björk and others in a padded cell acting as if they are crazy. Perhaps it was because her ego was so stuffed after this project that Björk shifted progressively more left field with every subsequent release. It's quite a statement of intent to make with your first solo album after leaving a wholly unsuccessful alternative rock band from Iceland, though.

Pet Shop Boys, actually.

1987
EMI Records
Country
Sleeve design by Mark Farrow at (3) and
Pet Shop Boys
Photography by Cindy Palmano

The Pet Shop Boys Actually

The cover to the Pet Shop Boys' second full album is perhaps their most well known—which is quite some achievement, given their history of unique and striking artwork (1993's *Very* came in a custom-designed Lego-style jewel case; 2002's *Release* in a custom-made white case with an embossed foil slip case). The photograph by Cindy Palmano (who went on to capture Tori Amos for her first three album sleeves) shows Neil Tennant yawning while Chris Lowe stares impassively into the camera lens. Both men are dressed in tuxedos. Given Tennant's absolute grasp of pop's aesthetic—he had been editor at the UK's most popular pop magazine, *Smash Hits*—it is unlikely that this shot is a genuine yawn. The cover nails the deep, postmodern irony of the Pet Shop Boys' music, seen in Tennant's voice which, while melodic and clear, is strangely distant and unemotional, as if he is commenting on pop music while simultaneously being a pop star. They would later record a song called "Being Boring." Ironically, of course.

1988
Paisley Park/Warners
America
Photography by Jean Baptiste Mondino

ⓘ **Prince** Lovesexy

With *Sign O' the Times* (see p. 41) Prince had confirmed his reputation as the biggest, most credible pop star in the world. *Sign* had been his third Top Ten album in a row and had certified seven times platinum sales. Yet he was also cool; he wrote songs for other artists who benefitted greatly from his patronage. His live shows were thrilling and high-energy entertainments with props, but a band that could play. And then he went and did this. The cover was originally banned in certain U.S. states, because of that flower, supposedly, although it could have been on grounds of ego-suppression. Fashion photographer and pop video director Mondino was the darling of the day and had worked with Madonna, Bowie and Bryan Ferry before getting the call from Prince. There's probably a very good reason for Prince being nude, for having his hand on his heart, and peering enigmatically into the middle distance in the photo. However, there can be no good reason for why his chest hair runs wild while his legs look waxed. One word comes to mind when you see this cover, and that flower is it.

Annie Lennox
DIVA

Annie Lennox Diva

This was Lennox's first album since leaving the confines of her former employ as half of the Eurythmics. At the time, the common consensus fuelled by the inherent sexism of the music business was that her ex-partner Dave Stewart (they had been lovers years before) had been the real creative force behind the band and that Lennox was just the singer. This was driven by Stewart's prodigious side project activity even while he was in the Eurythmics. So Lennox needed a strong ego to prove everyone wrong. It must have helped that her manager is Simon Fuller, who went on to manage the Spice Girls as well as to produce Simon Cowell's TV talent shows. Calling your album *Diva* is tempting fate, even if it is meant ironically, and dressing up in a feather-bedecked crown could have only made matters worse. Fortunately, not only is Satoshi Saikusa's photograph a beautiful composition, but the album was a Grammy Award winner too.

1992
RCA/Arista Records
England
Sleeve design by Laurence Stevens
Photography by Satoshi Saikusa

R**E**AL WORLD

When you've had your likeness put on one
album sleeve, what else can you do? Many
keep resorting to photos of their aging
selves on the front of subsequent releases,
but most get bored with the idea (as well
as not wishing to remind fans that they're
aging). Some artists commission original
works of art, or paint, or photograph
something themselves.

Most artists get someone else to create
cover art for them, of course, and ask
that it be based either on their recording's
"concept" or something inspired by it. They
look to the real world for inspiration too.
As with great visual artists, musicians are
inspired by the trees, flowers, buildings
and fabric of the world that surrounds
them. Naturally, they may want that to
be reflected in the packaging of their
recording.

Cover artists can take—and often have—
a brief for a job which, while it might
not make much sense, becomes their
understanding of what they think the client
wants, often with spectacular results.
Those results—intentional, accidental or
monstrous—are shown over the following
pages.

There are cows, trees, beaches, roads,
floors, shoes, bridges and street scenes.
The majority of them show actual objects
in photographic form, though some
are illustrations. Many offer inspired
perspectives on the object depicted, while
others question the validity of their usage.

Welcome to the real world.

Pink Floyd Atom Heart Mother

1970
Harvest/EMI
England
Sleeve concept by Pink Floyd
Design and photography by Hipgnosis

The sleeve for Pink Floyd's fourth album is more a reaction than anything else. The band was exhausted with the increasingly predictable, psychedelic look of other bands' sleeves, with their fold-outs, pop-ups, inserts and complex graphics. So Floyd requested "something plain" on the sleeve from Storm Thorgerson, who duly went in search of a simple image. A former roommate of Syd Barrett, Thorgerson and his company Hipgnosis had been designing sleeves for the band since their second album *Saucerful of Secrets*. Apparently, he drove to the London suburb Potters Bar and, inspired by Andy Warhol's cow wallpaper, photographed the first bovine animal he saw. According to the cow's owner, she was a Holstein called Lulubelle III. After the success of this sleeve Hipgnosis was given a lot of room to experiment on Floyd's subsequent album covers and, while their ideas were not always accepted, the partnership continues to this day.

1965
Blue Note
America
Sleeve design by Reid Miles
Photography by Francis Wolff

The Ornette Coleman Trio At the "Golden Circle" Stockholm Volume Two

The composition of this sleeve is almost perfect. The position of the trio, with Coleman in the center, the text in different shades of color set against the snows of Sweden, and the bare, stark trees, which look as if they have recently been razed by shell fire, combine to create a wholly attractive image. The combined effect of the snow and the uneven ground on which the trio stands is that they appear to be floating, away from the ground but tied together toward the tops of their bodies. It's a perfect visual metaphor of the music the sleeve contains—free-floating, separate, but joined if not in melody then in time and tempo. This was bassist David Izenson's (left) greatest recording and it's telling how of the three he appears most grounded, his right foot almost buried in the snow. The real world here—while it provides a setting no studio could ever approach—also looks slightly unreal.

1964

Capitol Records

America

Photography by Capitol Photo Studio /
George Jerman

George Shearing Quintet Out of the Woods

In-house photographer at Capitol Records George Jerman was a big jazz
fan and worked as a sound engineer in the studios when not out taking
photos. Clearly, George liked the natural outdoors: he snapped the Beach
Boys with llamas for the cover of *Pet Sounds*. He also liked to incorporate
some element of the album title in his work, it would appear, if with a witty
take on it. Llamas were not many people's idea of a pet in 1967, and this
enormous, ancient, giant redwood tree and its surroundings wouldn't be
what many called "the woods," either. The gorgeously attired model is
almost lost in the tree trunk and would clearly need help getting out of
those woods. The album is something of a rarity in that all the tracks were
composed by vibraphonist Gary Burton, who wrote very few numbers for
himself in a long and successful jazz career. The sounds are as light and
breezy as you'd expect from a Shearing album, though, and the air that
surrounds the model is all that the record has in common with the photo:
there are no huge slabs of wood to be heard, just light vibraphone keys.

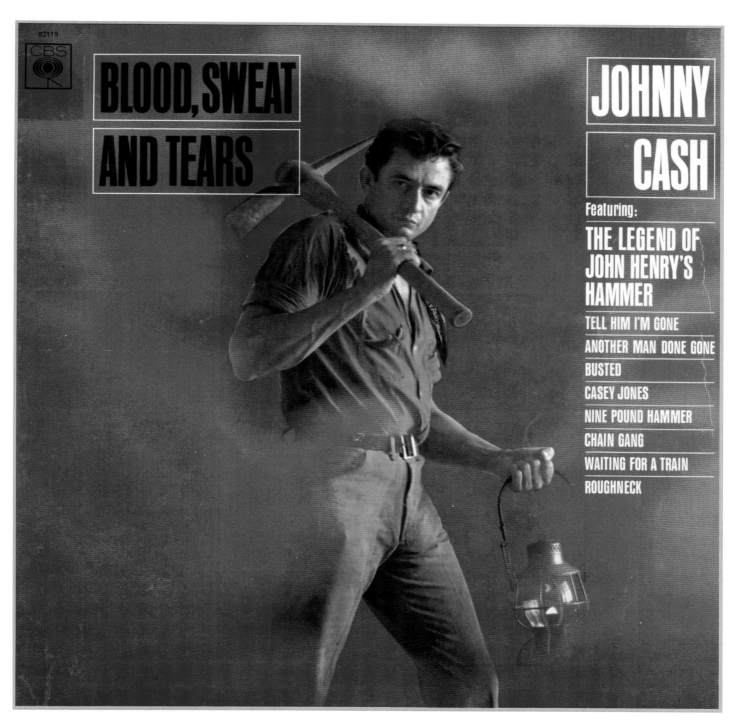

Johnny Cash Blood, Sweat and Tears

1962
Columbia
America
Sleeve design uncredited

Johnny Cash was always a master of his own mythology. He was never a miner and, in truth, not much of a working man either—although he did sell vacuum cleaners door-to-door before becoming a singer. However, his family were dirt-poor cotton farmers and Cash understood working-class America. Not that he's attempting to exploit them here; rather, he's promoting them as a cultural icon, the way Jimmie Rodgers did the railway workers in the 1920s. The red smoke suggests he's emerging from Hell— which is what many miners said it was like down in the mines—or from some oppressive mist that engulfs the underrepresented working poor. Certainly the Cold War was red hot in 1962, and the world narrowly avoided a nuclear disaster when neither Kennedy nor Krushchev pressed their respective buttons over the Cuban missile crisis. But it was close. Although the sleeve may have been unpremeditated, the Soviets *had* been making the workers subjects of iconic, heroic art and sculpture since the 1930s when Stalin ordered the deification of workers, something echoed in Cash's look here.

K47507
(CP 0111)
STEREO

⊚ CAPRICORN recording distributed by WEA RECORDS LTD., ® & © 1973

The Allman Brothers Band Brothers and Sisters

1973
Capricorn Records
America
Layout and design by Barry Feinstein
and Vicki Hodgett for Camouflage
Photography by Dan Hudson Jr. and
Bo Meriwether
Graphic concept by Judi Reeve

This evocative image of a young, blond boy amid the dead leaves of fall perfectly sums up the mood of the Allman's fifth and most successful release. The boy is emblematic of the deceased Duane Allman (killed in a motorcycle accident). The girl is representative of the healing power of love: the Brothers found solace in one another, their lovers, friends and musicians. The inner portrait of the whole "family" grouped together could have been taken after Duane's wake. The band also lost bassist Berry Oakley long before they finished the recording. He was killed in a separate motorcycle accident a year after Duane. This first whole album made after Duane's death made #1 on the Billboard album chart.

RCA **VICTOR**

Synanthesia

1969
RCA Victor
England
Sleeve design and photography by
Terence Ibbott

Synanthesia Synanthesia

Toward the end of the 1960s, there was a kind of folk music revival in
England, which saw several young bands adapting ancient folk songs into
pscyhedelic forms. Some were hugely successful—the Incredible String
Band and Fairport Convention, particularly—while others made only a few
albums before being consigned to the folk club circuit. Synanthesia—the
name, a bastardization of "synesthesia," which is the ability to see music
as colors, was taken from a Cannonball Adderley track of that name—made
one album only. It's actually very good. It was recorded acoustically in
two days by producer Sandy Roberton without a record deal, when it was
picked up by RCA who then put no money into its promotion; it flopped,
and the band split up. The ancient, gnarled tree trunk provides a perfect
and natural prop for the cover image. Its age and appearance could easily
be the inspiration for a couple of the gentle, folky/fairy-tale songs on
the record. The flip side of the sleeve has the band spread out against an
enormous 16th-century manor house. Very English whimsy.

Fat Mattress Fat Mattress

1969
Polydor Records
England
Sleeve design by Paragon Publicity
Photography by Gered Mankowitz

Fed up with simply being the bass player behind Jimi Hendrix, Noel Redding formed Fat Mattress with an old Folkstone pal, Neil Landon, in 1968. Redding got to play lead guitar and sing with Fat Mattress on songs that flirted with then vogueish folk-tinged psychedelia. Their first single was entitled "Magic Forest," and so photographer Mankowitz—famous for his portraits of the Rolling Stones taken in Primrose Hill Park, London, for the cover of *Between the Buttons*—sought out a suitably magical forest for the cover image. The tree under which the band sits is enormous, almost equal to the faith that Polydor clearly had in the band, as the sleeve folds out into a copious sheet, of which the front cover is just one corner: the rest of the image is the tree and a bit of sky (it measures twenty-four inches by twenty-four inches). The album made #134 on the Billboard chart but wasn't successful enough. A second album (*Fat Mattress II*) appeared in 1970 with a much cheaper and bizarre cover featuring a cartoon of an old woman. That flopped and the band split up.

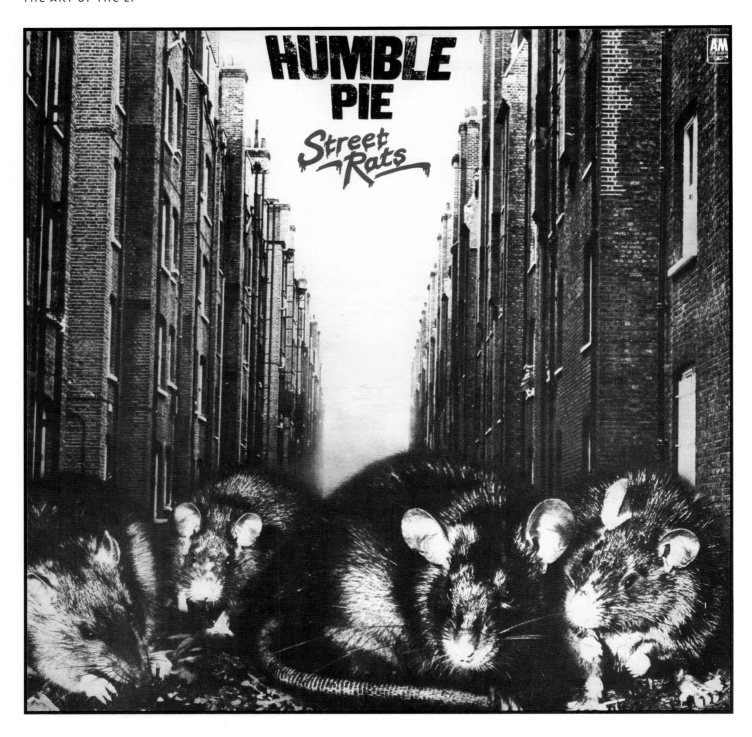

1975
A&M Records
America
Art direction by Fabio Nicoli
Design by Michael Ross

ⓘ **Humble Pie** Street Rats

There's a real street. There are real rats. What else would there be on the cover of an album entitled *Street Rats*? Peter Frampton was long gone, and Humble Pie had been a metal band and an R&B act complete with ex-Ikettes as backing singers, but after spending fours years doing twenty-one tours of America, Steve Marriott called it a day with Humble Pie and returned to England. There he began writing and recording a solo album. Unfortunately, he still contractually owed A&M a Humble Pie album and so the label "confiscated" his sixteen-track tapes, had ex-Immediate label-owner Andrew Loog Oldham (who'd released the first two Humble Pie albums) remix and edit them, and put out this mess. The extraordinarily unattractive cover is appropriately devoid of inspiration, invention and creativity. Which is somewhat surprising given that art director Nicoli had worked on Supertramp's *Crime of the Century* and *Crisis, What Crisis?*, among others. The reverse of the sleeve has the four Pie members replacing the rats. Clever, it isn't?

1972
Atco (Atlantic)
America
Cover photography and design by
Barry Feinstein and Tom Wilkes for
Camouflage Productions

Dr. John Dr. John's Gumbo

New Orleans legend Dr. John was just thirty-two when he made *Dr. John's Gumbo*, but he looked at least fifteen years older in the image on the cover: the stick and bent posture, beard and dark glasses adding years to his life. After spending the early and mid-sixties working as a pianist for the likes of Sonny and Cher, Dr. John became the Night Tripper and mixed New Orleans boogie with psychedelia, voodoo and carnival-influenced costumes. With the release of his debut album, *Gris-Gris*, he became a cult figure. After three more albums, none of which had the same impact on sales, the Dr. turned to his musical and spiritual influences for this next album. Losing the costumes and voodoo schtick, Mac Rebbenack (real name) showcased songs written by fellow New Orleans–born musicians. Photographer Feinstein—now best known for his work with Bob Dylan—shot over five hundred album covers in his time. This is one of his best: the juxtaposition of the surreal mural with Dr. John perfectly encapsulates the strange and timeless quality of the music on the record inside.

263

SHVL 795
(IE 064 o 04917)
stereo

Pink Floyd Meddle

1971
Harvest/EMI
England
Sleeve design by Pink Floyd
Photography by Bob Dowling

While Hipgnosis, and in particular Storm Thorgerson, are most commonly credited as the sleeve designers for Pink Floyd albums of the late 1960s and early 1970s, many of them in fact originated from a brief that was given by the band. The Floyd album preceding this, *Atom Heart Mother*, had used only photographs of cows with no other identifying matter, which was as the band had requested (though they had said it should be "plain"). With *Meddle*, they were much more specific, however, and requested a close-up of an ear under water. The circular water drops are a perfect visual representation of the blips of sound that open the album. The fact that so many Floyd covers appear in collections of great album covers has been determined by the band's involvement in the artistic process. As proof of this, we have the various Hipgnosis designs for the Scorpions in this book, none of which had input from the band, as they later claimed. Photographer Dowling became a much in-demand commercial photographer. He also shot the cover for Floyd's *Momentary Lapse of Reason*.

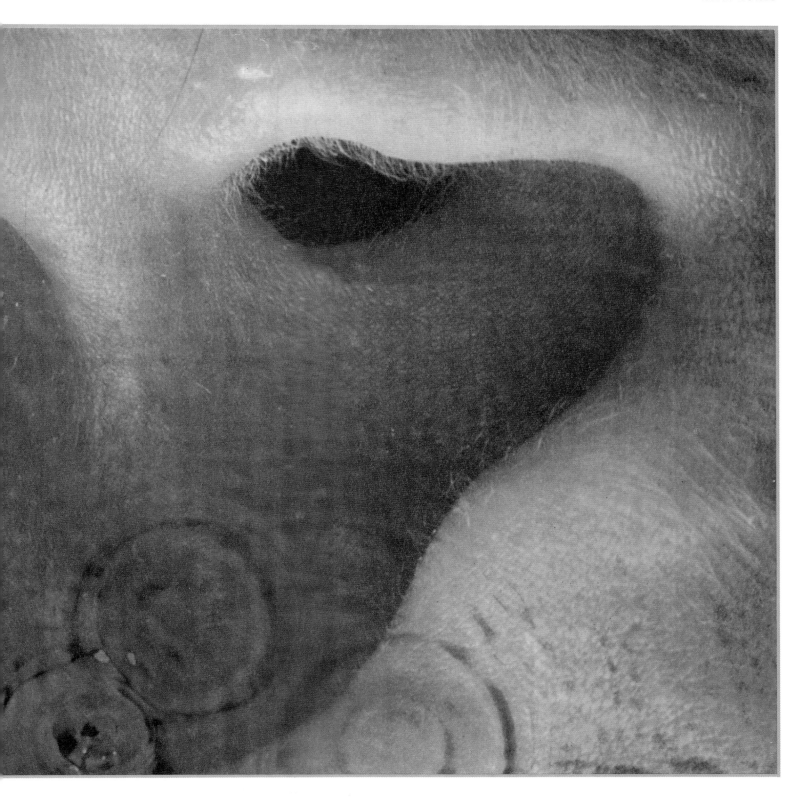

Rolling Stones Exile on Main Street

1972
Rolling Stone Records
America
Sleeve design by Jan Van Hammersveld and Norman Seeff
Photography and concept by Robert Frank

The cover image of this legendary Stones album was taken in 1950. Artist, photographer and filmmaker Robert Frank—whose 1958 photograph collection "The Americans" remains enduringly influential among photographers—met the band almost by accident. He visited the LA mansion where the Stones were working on a songbook with pop artist Jan Van Hammersveld, who had designed the Beatles *Magical Mystery Tour* album sleeve. Once installed as the designer of *Exile*, Van Hammersveld used Frank's shot, which is not a collage but the wall of a tattoo parlor somewhere on Route 66. The freaks—particularly the man with three balls in his mouth—seem entirely appropriate for an album recorded with various pharmaceutical aids in a rambling French mansion. The band name and album title were drawn by Jagger himself. The Stones were so impressed with Frank that they asked him to film their subsequent 1972 tour. The resulting film, *Cocksucker Blues*, as freakish as this sleeve, has never been officially released.

Alice Cooper School's Out

1972
Warner Bros
America
Sleeve design by Craig Braun, Wilkes &
Braun Inc.
Cover concept by Sound Packaging
Corp.

An album sleeve concept as outrageous as Alice Cooper's snake-baiting
stage act, *School's Out* was a multimedia experience. The year before,
designer Craig Braun had put together Andy Warhol's *Sticky Fingers* sleeve.
Clearly inspired by that three-dimensional groundbreaker, Braun designed
Cooper's sleeve as a school desk complete with a hinged lifting lid. To
prevent the lid from falling open and the vinyl falling out—and presumably
to avoid risking getting sued by the record company as he had almost
done with *Sticky Fingers'* zipper-scratching vinyl (see p. 30)—he designed
a pair of girl's panties in paper which stretched around the cardboard.
The desk lid is, of course, covered in schoolboy graffiti: in this case the
album title, initials of each band member and, ironically, the Warners logo.
Once opened, the desk reveals the inside contents of what a seventies
teenager's desk would hold: catapult, flick knife and comic featuring
Lovely Liberace.

1977
Harvest/EMI
England
Sleeve design by Storm Thorgerson and
Aubrey Powell, Hipgnosis

Pink Floyd Animals

For the cover of *Animals*, Roger Waters said he wanted a pig flying over Battersea Power Station, an abandoned 1930s coal-fired plant, the four chimneys of which still form an iconic part of the London skyline. Designer Storm Thorgerson commissioned a company in Amsterdam to build a forty-foot inflatable pig, and on December 2, 1976, an eleven-man camera team set out to film the shoot. Initially, a marksman was employed to shoot down the helium-filled pig if it broke free. They didn't use it on the second day as it was deemed an insurance risk and, inevitably, a gust of wind blew the pig away. Eventually, after a police helicopter and a Royal Air Force plane had failed to catch it, it was recovered from a field in Kent. They got the photo on the third day but the light was wrong, so Thorgerson had to superimpose the pig onto earlier pictures. The amount of sheer effort that went into this sleeve is hard to conceive in today's CGI-dominated design culture, particularly as most Pink Floyd fans probably have the CD version, on which the pig is barely visible.

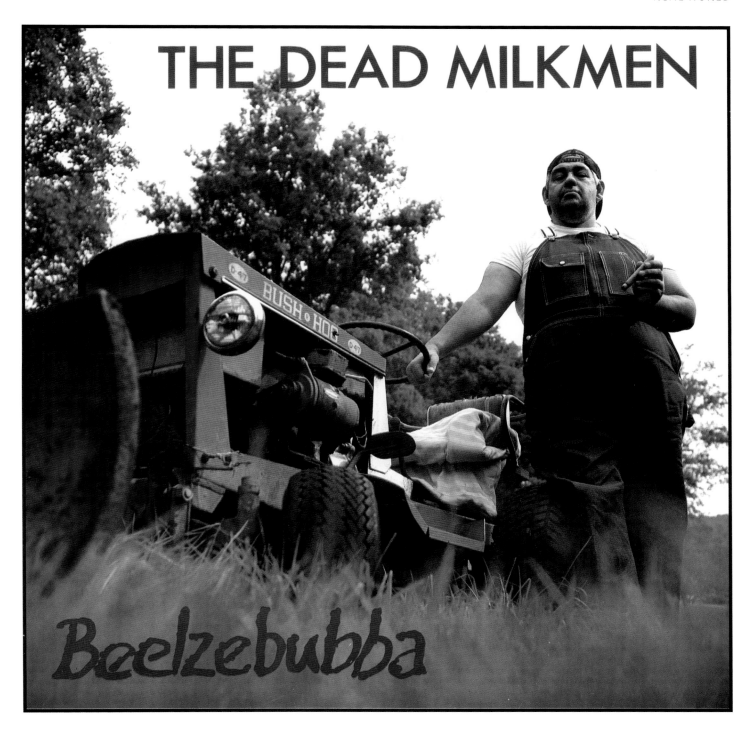

THE DEAD MILKMEN

Beelzebubba

1988
Fever/Enigma Records
America
Photography by Chris Coccia
Album Art © 1988 Dead Milkmen

⚠ The Dead Milkmen Beelzebubba

In truth, this cover is dreadful on purpose, and hopefully the Milkmen will appreciate the irony of being included in the "how not to design an album cover" category. The cover model is the father of one of the lead singers, and that's probably his tractor. Had the band name and title been left off, this could have been amazing, especially if it had been called *Bush Hog*. Sadly, the band had to include their name. The Philadelphian punk band (1983–1995) released this fourth album which contains their only MTV-generated hit single, "Punk Rock Girl." The band's influence can be seen on more successful and similarly witty pop-punk bands such as Bowling for Soup. Tracks on this album include "Bleach Boys," "Smokin' Banana Peels," and "Life Is Shit." Their next album (there were eight) was entitled *Metaphysical Graffiti*. They were funny guys.

The Wailers Catch a Fire

1973
Island Records
England
Sleeve design by Rod Dyer and
Bob Weiner
Art direction by John Hoernle

Island Records really went all out for Bob Marley and the Wailer's debut album. Label owner Chris Blackwell had been on a mission to make Jimmy Cliff a star prior to his "discovering" Marley, but Cliff had left the label before Blackwell could realize his ambition. When Blackwell met the Wailers he saw his second chance and put every effort into shaping their reggae sound for rock fans. The original artwork, too, is very much in the rock tradition and echoes similar three-dimensional sleeves that had been done for *Sticky Fingers* in '71 (see p. 30) and *School's Out* in '72 (see p. 267). Taking inspiration from the title track, this is a massive Zippo lighter, which flips out to reveal a wick and a flame, the vinyl providing the shape of a wheel which when spun, lights the wick. At the time, reggae was regarded by Island and all major record labels as being deeply misunderstood by rock fans. So, housing the album in something as demotic and familiar to them as a lighter was an attempt to give them something they instinctively recognized, while being a gimmick.

THE CURE

The Cure Three Imaginary Boys

1979
Fiction Records
England
Sleeve design by Bill Smith
Photography by Martyn Goddard

After this, the Cure's debut, came out with a track listing and artwork
unapproved by the band's self-proclaimed leader Robert Smith, Smith
took complete control over what all their subsequent artwork should
look like. As such, this is a bit of an anomaly in the Cure's canon of album
sleeves—which usually feature indistinct or blurred photos. Regardless of
Robert Smith's opinion, Bill Smith, art director at Polydor at the time, did a
fantastic job. Indeed, he said in an interview with *Arcade* magazine in 2009,
" . . . If I had to [choose] one of my [designs] it would probably be *Three
Imaginary Boys*. I think I nailed it with that one . . . the image . . . was to
look like a photo straight out of *Ideal Home* magazine circa 1967. And was
Robert really a lampstand?" Yes, the band was a trio at the time, and each
household object represented a different band member in a witty style. Bill
went on to design the cover for Cure's next album *17 Seconds*—as oblique
as this is clear. He would, in time, design sleeves for Kate Bush, Genesis
and Led Zeppelin.

STEREO FVS 9003

RURAL DELIVERY NO. 1
THE NEW LOST CITY RAMBLERS

Verve FOLKWAYS

TRACY SCHWARZ / MIKE SEEGER / JOHN COHEN

© Metro-Goldwyn-Mayer, Inc./Printed in U.S.A.

1965
Verve Folkways
America
Sleeve design by Ronald Clyne
Photography by John Cohen

The New Lost City Ramblers *Rural Delivery No. 1*

The New Lost City Ramblers formed in New York in 1958, at the height of the folk music revival. Members included Mike Seeger (brother to Pete and Peggy), John Cohen (who married Peggy Seeger) and Tom Paley. Dedicated to reviving the sounds of old American folk music, they played perfect imitations of songs from the seminal *Anthology of Folk Music* (Folkways) of 1952. Unlike contemporary folk revivalist movement acts such as the Weavers or the Kingston Trio, the NLCR refused to turn the 1920s and 1930s mountain music songs into pop tunes. John Cohen was also a photographer and filmmaker, and his image here was from one of his many journeys into the deep South and its rural heartland. There is an element of clarity about the image—it is as pure and unadulterated as the music the record contains. NLCR's unintentional romanticizing of the music was never intended to detract from the genuine poverty and grief of the areas that spawned the music. This photo shows a farmer working his land with a mule in the mid-1960s.

CRS 8003 STEREO

CURTOM

Featuring:
Seven Years
My Deceiving
Heart

THE
IMPRESSIONS
THE YOUNG MODS'
FORGOTTEN STORY

Buddah Records is a Subsidiary of Viewlex, In

1969
Curtom/Buddah Records
America
Sleeve design uncredited
Photography uncredited

The Impressions The Young Mods' Forgotten Story

Despite his undoubted songwriting talent and seminal influence on pop, Curtis Mayfield is still pigeonholed as the Superfly guy. Three years before that, Mayfield began the move away from his gospel-inflected love songs with this, the Impressions' twelfth album and the second on his own Curtom label. What marks this release was the new-found righteousness of Mayfield's lyrics on two tracks: "Choice of Colors" and "Mighty Mighty (Spade & Whitey)." His move toward social consciousness is reflected in the sleeve photograph of the three Impressions, sharply dressed in leather pea coats and peaked hats, posing by an archway. The previous album, *This Is My Country*, had pictured them beside a derelict building with guitars. It was the first move away from their one-time custom of happy smiling for the camera. Here they were, very much in the real world—like the Stones on *Out of Our Heads* (p. 22)—and looking like they were finally—after years of chasing prepackaged pop stardom Motown-style and in matching Mohair suits—keeping it real.

THE JAM / THIS IS THE MODERN WORLD

1977

Polydor Records

England

Sleeve design by Bill Smith

Photography by Gered Mankowitz

The Jam This Is the Modern World

The Jam's golden period was still a year away when their sophomore album was released in 1977. They'd already put out their debut earlier that year and it would take an album's worth of scrapped songs before they found their true voice with *All Mod Cons* in 1978. For now they were still exploiting what was left of the punk affiliation, which had swept them into the limelight. Thus we find them underneath the Westway—a freeway, from central London out west to Heathrow Airport, made famous by the Clash in their song "London's Burning." This alienating, sterile landscape was really the Clash's stomping ground and had nothing to do with the Jam, who hailed not from London but from suburban Woking. But clearly Polydor's art director Bill Smith wasn't going to let that get in the way of a good shot, ensured by hiring legendary Stones photographer Gered Mankowitz (see *Out of Our Heads*, p. 22). The band look genuinely thuggish despite, as a closer view reveals, Weller's homemade Mod top complete with arrows made of masking tape.

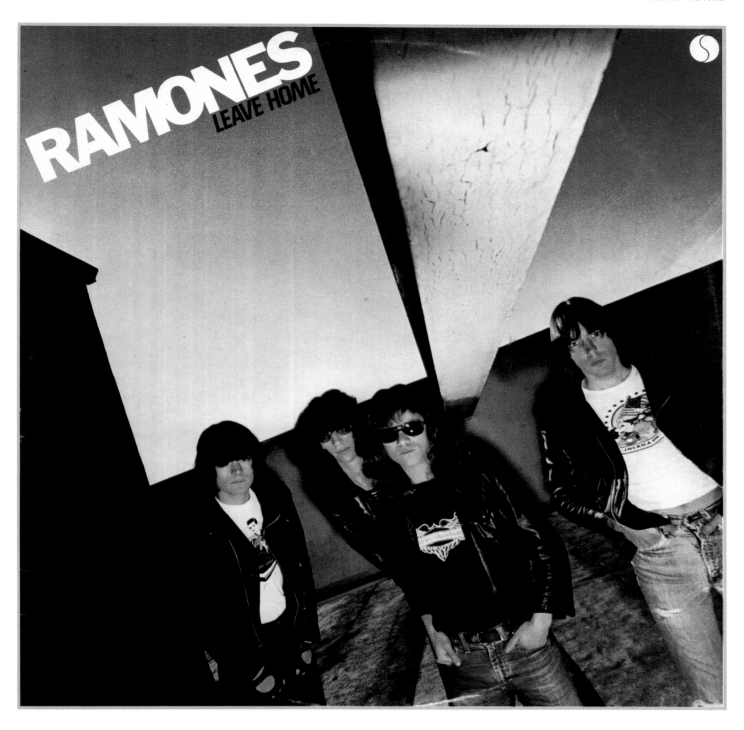

The Ramones Leave Home

1977
Sire Records
America
Sleeve design by Pat Chiono
Photography by Moshe Brakha
Art direction by John Gillespie

Despite Roberta Bayley's superb photo used on the cover of the band's hugely influential debut album, the Ramones turned to Moshe Brakha to photograph the follow-up. Although by this time a director of advertising commercials, and despite a Grammy Nomination for his Boz Scaggs' *Silk Degrees* artwork (see p. 74), Brakha was actually a big punk fan. His photo here takes Bayley's lead and gets the band all looking the same height (although, even with Joey at the back and leaning to the side, he is still taller than Tommy). But if the debut was a kind of Super 8 version of the band—grainy, black-and-white, romantic—this is video: colorized, bright and immediate. Like the band, the photo, with its angles defined by concrete cutting across the sky and the background still "grainy," is very much of the real world. The dramatic perspective of the shot evokes a sense of movement that echoes the album title.

Kraftwerk Autobahn

1974
Vertigo
Germany
Sleeve design uncredited

This is the sleeve of the English edition of Kraftwerk's debut album proper (see The Man Machine, p.168). The original German release featured a painting by Emil Shult, a lifelong friend of Kraftwerk main men Ralf Hütter and Florian Schneider. While Shult's German sleeve isn't bad (though far short of the standard of his later paintings), his involvement of lasting value with this album was in the cowriting of the title track—for which he is credited. The English artwork featuring the European motorway symbol is how most non-German speakers first discovered the album. Despite being uncredited—it was presumably done by the in-house team at Vertigo—the design has come to be regarded as a classic piece of album art. Indeed, designer Peter Saville (see p. 128) has described it as "a perfect example of beauty in the everyday, of realism and of subversion." The font is pretty damn good too.

UFO Phenomenon

1974
Chrysalis
England
Sleeve design and photography
by Hipgnosis
Tinting by Maurice Tate
Graphics by Richard Evans

UFO originated in London in 1969 and was named after the infamous underground (in every sense of the word) club which spawned many of the psychedelic acts that defined the era, among them Pink Floyd and Soft Machine. The band played fairly uneventful blues-based metal for the first four years and two albums of their existence, becoming popular in Japan and Germany in the process. Then, in 1973, they were joined by guitarist Michael Schenker who left the successful German metal band Scorpions to move to London, without speaking any English. They signed with Chrysalis after developing a harder-edged sound thanks to Schenker, and released this, their most successful album at that point. The cover bears little reference to the music, but is an interesting vignette of a suburban bungalow with a 1950s car in the driveway, a couple dressed in 1950s clothes, and a UFO hovering overhead. The scene is hand-tinted to give it an otherworldly feel, but the anonymity of the suburban street is perfectly represented. By far the best Hipgnosis cover created for UFO.

JOE JACKSON

LOOK SHARP!

1979
A&M Records
England
Photography by Brian Griffin

Joe Jackson Look Sharp

It is unusual for an album sleeve to focus on shoes—pop music is usually
looking at the stars rather than the gutter, after all. And footwear is
mundane. However, Brian Griffin's shot of Joe Jackson's new Densons
(the brand gets a credit) manages to define the album title: slick, neat,
ready for a night on the tiles. Jackson's boots are for more than just
walking. In an interview with *Rolling Stone* magazine, he said of the shoes:
"I'd just bought them the day before. Brian Griffin took maybe
one or two shots of them as part of an entire day spent doing more typical
portrait shots . . . the shot certainly wasn't intended to become the
cover but when we saw the contact prints, everyone liked the image." The
finished sleeve works well. In the way it makes a normal if slightly self-
conscious pair of shoes seem otherworldly, it has something of Barney
Bubbles about it. He was a designer with whom Griffin frequently worked,
and for good reason.

Roland Hanna Gershwin Carmichael Cats

1982
Polydor Records
America
Sleeve design by Blake Taylor
Photography by Pete Turner

Roland Hanna Gershwin Carmichael Cats

A classically trained pianist, Hanna (1932—2002) loved jazz, and for most of his adult life played with New York-based jazz bands including those led by Benny Goodman and Charles Mingus. In the 1980s he taught jazz at the Aaron Copland School of Music at Queens College in New York, but still found time to record occasionally. For this remarkable recording he led a band that included a number of star players, among them Chet Baker, Larry Coryell, George Mraz and Rufus Reid. The title reflects the music: songs by Gershwin, Hoagy Carmichael and from the musical *Cats*. The cover image is a remarkably straight but evocative photo of a rehearsal space floor, edged by the fluidity of dancers' feet and ankles. It is elegant, refined and very striking.

Lloyd Cole and the Commotions
1984—1989

1989
Polydor Records
England
Sleeve design by Michael Nash Associates
Photography "Diving Board, Salton Sea" by Richard Misrach

This is a greatest hits compilation—and its minimalism is certainly surprising. Michael Nash Associates has treated this sad and beautiful photograph with respect, subduing the title and artist name, allowing space for the appreciation of American photographer Misrach's image. Misrach specializes in images of man's intervention in the natural world. Like that other big name in postwar U.S. photographic art, William Eggleston (Big Star used one of his photos for their *Radio City* album), Misrach works in color. Either photographer's work would have suited Cole's bittersweet balladry.

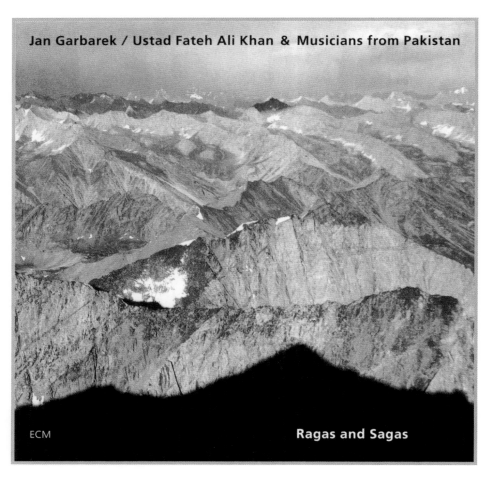

Jan Garbarek / Ustad Fateh Ali Khan & Musicians from Pakistan
Ragas and Sagas

1992
ECM
America
Sleeve design by Barbara Wojirsch
Photography by Herbert Maeder

Why did no one think of it before? If you're presenting a Western audience with music from another part of the world, why not show that part of the world in all its natural glory? This haunting aerial photo of Pakistani mountain ranges is elegant and awe-inspiring. It does not look like a travel ad—by virtue of the redeeming use of chiaroscuro and the absence of tourist cliches—and as such is all the more appealing. Norwegian sax player Garbarek fits his music perfectly around classically trained singer Khan and indigenous musicians to produce dreamlike sounds.

FLUKE · SIX WHEELS ON MY WAGON

1993
Astralwerks
England
Sleeve design by Michael Nash
Associates
Photography by Mathew Donaldson

Fluke Six Wheels on My Wagon

Who is Fluke? It's not important, and they would probably thank you for not asking. Despite the frequent use of their polished techno tracks for movies (*Matrix Reloaded*, *Sin City*), video games and commercials, plus the fact that they are still making music after fifteen years, Fluke remains pretty much anonymous. Key to all this is their extremely stylish artwork of which this, their sophomore album, is a key example. The title—referencing the old Western song—conjures up a romantic image of dusty trails and cowboys. The image here, of countless highly polished metal "wheels," which are of course wrench fittings commonly used in removing and securing automobile wheel nuts, brings a smile to your face. They can be mistaken for cookie cutters, too, and frequently are. You still have no idea what the music might be like, but you're fairly sure that this band is very much in the modern world.

the Crusaders - Those Southern Knights

1976
Blue Thumb Records
America
Art direction by Tom Wilkes
Photography by Ethan Russell

The Crusaders Those Southern Knights

Photographer Ethan Russell was used to working outdoors in the real world; he shot the Who's *Who's Next* cover, the Rolling Stones' *Get Yer Ya-Yas Out* and the Beatles' *Let It Be* sleeve, for instance. Tom Wilkes was also used to designing covers with complex concepts and images, often as part of Camouflage Productions with photographer Barry Feinstein (see p. 263 *Dr. John's Gumbo*, or the Who's *Tommy*). But what were they doing here? The image is beautiful, admittedly, and they clearly had a lot of fun doing it. However, sometimes a pun just isn't worthy enough of too much time, money and effort. This is such a case in point. The Crusaders were from the South (Texas, actually) and their music is full of the sounds of sultry southern nights. But dressing up in suits of chainmail to pose as drunken knights of the Crusades when all you have are the outfits and a beach is stretching it too far. At least most of the band look as if they're enjoying the scene, but you'd have to put speech bubbles above all of them saying "What the hell are we doing?" before this cover might work.

RUSH a farewell to kings

1977
Mercury
America
Art direction/Graphics by Hugh Syme
Photography by Yosh Inouye

! Rush A Farewell to Kings

If only the idiot in Elizabethan gear lolling and grinning maniacally on the throne had been left out of the image, this would have been a great cover. But instead of it looking like a post-punk statement on the death of deference, the destruction of civilization, and the ruination of the natural world in favor of capitalist expansion, it's a dumb, overstated and laughable image that says "fantasy." The title and image may well have been a comment on punk music's dissing of prog rock "kings" (Crimson, perhaps?). Designer Hugh Syme worked on pretty much every Rush album, came up with their star logo, and even played keyboards with them for a while. His work for other bands was not quite as "inspired" as it was with his fellow Canadians Rush, however. His design for Great White's *Hooked,* for instance (see p. 69), is almost as bad as this one and very similar to Whitesnake's *Lovehunter.* This was Syme's fourth Rush cover, but the first he art-directed. He got better at it—*Moving Pictures* is quite funny.

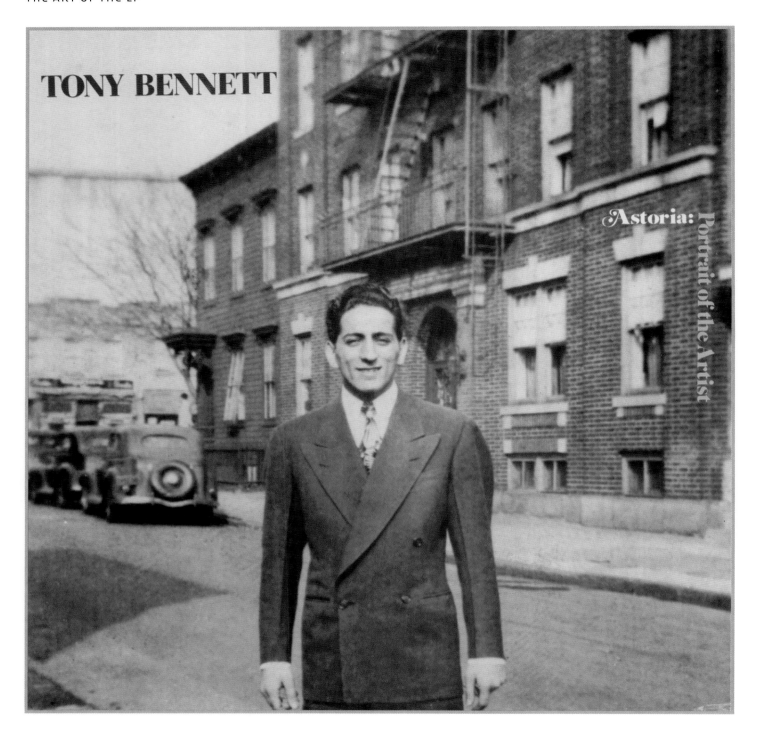

TONY BENNETT

Astoria: Portrait of the Artist

1990
CBS Records
America
Sleeve design by Josephine DiDonato
Photography by Ken Nahoum

Tony Bennett Astoria: Portrait of the Artist

Tony Bennett's star was really on the rise again as the 1990s began. He was one of the last performers from the golden age of the American songbook to still perform live, singing the great numbers of his youth to increasingly large and appreciative audiences. He was sixty-five when he recorded this album, and steeped in nostalgia, understanding that his new audience was too. So for the cover Bennett found a photograph taken of him in his hometown, the borough of Astoria, squeezed between the Triborough and Hell's Gates bridges in Queens, New York, from the days after he'd returned from serving in Europe in World War II. That went on the front. And for the back cover image he traveled to the exact same spot and had his photo taken again, forty-five years later. The building is the same, the cars are bigger, and so is the man himself. While the shy smile on the lean man in his double-breasted best suit looks like a young Robert De Niro, his older self looks just like Tony Bennett today.

WHEN DO THE BELLS RING FOR ME

A LITTLE STREET WHERE OLD FRIENDS MEET

THE GIRL I LOVE

IT'S LIKE REACHING FOR THE MOON

SPEAK LOW

THE FOLKS THAT LIVE ON THE HILL

SIDE TWO

ANTONIA

A WEAVER OF DREAMS/
THERE WILL NEVER BE ANOTHER YOU

BODY AND SOUL

WHERE DO YOU GO FROM LOVE

THE BOULEVARD OF BROKEN DREAMS

WHERE DID THE MAGIC GO

I'VE COME HOME AGAIN

Produced by Danny Bennett

CBS

1989
Capitol Records
America
Cover photography by Nathanial
Hornblower
Cover photo assistants Matthew Cohen,
Jeremy Shatan and Dominic Watkins

Beastie Boys Paul's Boutique

A landmark hip-hop album which, at the time of release, was particularly unloved. The Beastie Boys had exploded two years earlier with their frat boy rap album *Licensed to Ill*, and won a huge audience for their tongue-in-cheek stage shows. The debut album's artwork had been crassly adolescent with its jet plane painting, which on the back you discover has crashed into a wall. But there was an intelligence and a deep love of music in the trio, which emerged on *Paul's Boutique* and was aided by genius production team Dust Brothers and the brief window of no sampling laws. The sleeve shows Lee's Sportswear shop on 99 Rivington Street, where it intersects Ludlow Street in Manhattan's Lower East Side. The Paul's Boutique sign was hung for the shoot, but this is the Beastie Boys finally landing back in the real world. Eventually, the album got the respect it deserved. Until early 2007 the address housed a diner named Paul's Boutique in honor of the album.

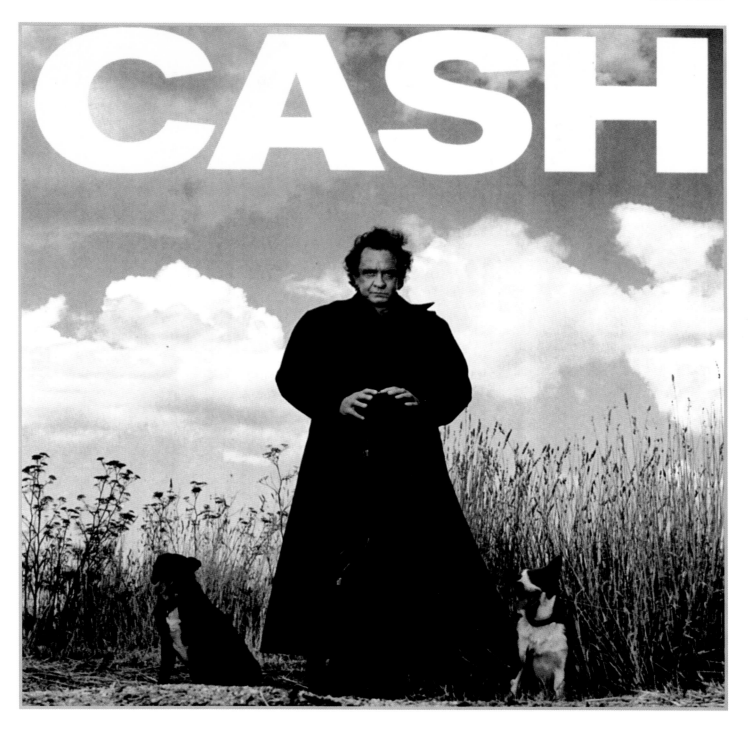

1994
American Recordings
America
Art direction by Martyn Atkins
Sleeve design by Christine Cano
Photography by Andrew Earl

Johnny Cash American Recordings

Toward the end of his long career and life, Johnny Cash became popular with a new generation of fans by embracing the real world: he was old and had made mistakes, and the songs he chose to record for a hip independent label after being dropped first by CBS (after twenty-six years) and then by Mercury (after ten) reflected that. His ex-son-in-law Nick Lowe wrote "The Beast in Me" for Cash, who recorded it with an acoustic guitar backing and included it on this stark, stripped-down and unadorned album. The cover photo, taken by a Brit on a commission from another Brit, the designer Martyn Atkins (who had worked closely with Peter Saville on Joy Division covers), shows Cash with his dogs—naturally one is black—in a scrubby field. His long black coat billows, and the photo taken from below attempts to make him look larger than life. "Cash" is written in the sky as if by God. Cash doesn't look frightening, though—he looks old and a bit tired, which he was. He wrote and recorded another seven albums' worth of songs for American, only four of which were released before his death, in 2003.

ESCAPE

While all forms of popular entertainment involve certain levels of escapism, there is a particularly strong element of escape in the founding songs of rock & roll. Chuck Berry in particular celebrated America's growing automotive culture in his mid-1950s songs. The kids in his song narratives were always "riding around in an automobile," celebrating the end of the school days and looking forward to . . . anything. The sheer exuberance and unbridled passion of early rock & roll songs were screams of release, of escape from the rigorous confines of what was to become known as "straight" society.

Watching Elvis wriggling his hips from the distance of half a century it's difficult to understand the moral outrage that this simple act had on civilization, but effect it certainly had. Each bump and grind by the former truck driver was a dance-step farther away from the dull monotony of driving trucks for him, and represented the shaking off of the chains of conformity for the generation of teenagers who watched in awe on their parents' television sets.

Elvis's first album attempted to capture his raw essence by showing a photo of the man in performance. However, as Frank Sinatra had demonstrated, the essence of escape for most people meant concrete objects, such as an airplane. Soon record companies began to put objects representing escape on their covers: cars, trains and planes, for example. Then the idea of escapist fantasies made its way onto sleeves.

What follows are some excellent examples of how to represent the idea of escape on an album sleeve—some concrete, others more implied by what they represent.

Frank Sinatra Come Fly with Me

1958
Capitol Records
America
Art direction by Frank Sinatra

More than fifty years after its release, this is still the most instantly recognizable Sinatra album cover of them all. Posters continue to be sold of the artwork (all marked "artist unknown"). On the rear of the sleeve of the original pressing, in small print it states: "Cover produced in cooperation with Trans World Airlines and featuring the TWA Jetstream Super Constellation." At the time, TWA had just won the battle for the skies with the British firm of de Havilland, whose Comet jet airliner had been the first of its kind to take paying customers across the Atlantic in 1952. By the late 1950s airline travel was becoming more affordable and the "jet set" of rich, famous and infamous who used planes to get around the globe fast were the subject of great media attention. Flying was glamorous. Sinatra was glamorous. His invitation to fly with him—and who could resist that wink?—is backed up on the album by songs that mention exotic locations, from "Autumn in New York" to "Blue Hawaii" and "April in Paris."

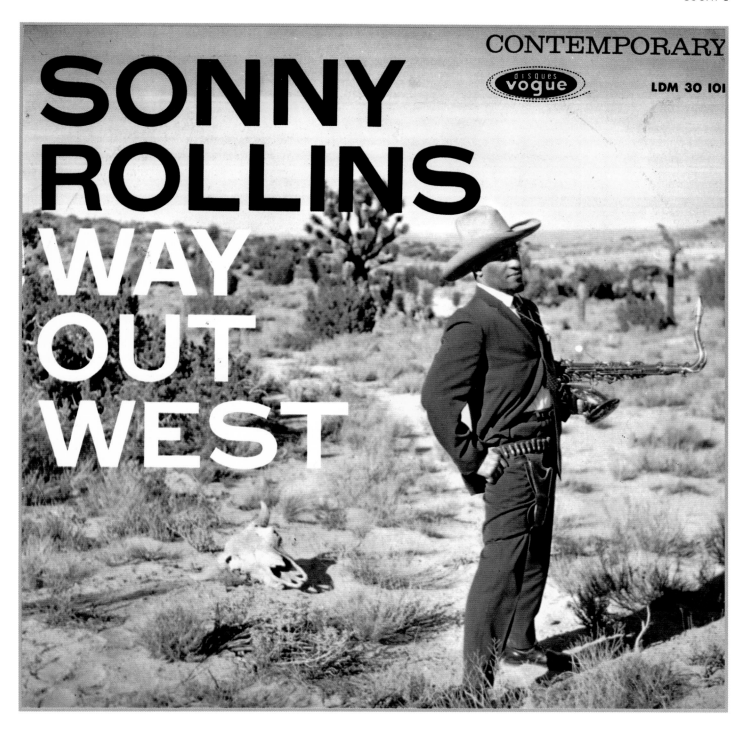

CONTEMPORARY

disques vogue

LDM 30 101

SONNY ROLLINS WAY OUT WEST

1957
Contemporary Records
America
Photography by William Claxton

Sonny Rollins **Way Out West**

It's difficult to overstate the ubiquity of Westerns and cowboys in mid-1950s America. Television and Hollywood were full of them, from John Wayne and Gary Cooper to the Lone Ranger and Hopalong Cassidy. Cowboy imagery was used to sell everything from candy to cigarettes. Country & Western music was increasing in popularity everywhere, not just in the West and Appalachians. New York—born Sonny Rollins and Pasadena-bred William Claxton, the photographer, were not men of the West. Indeed, the jazz Sonny plays here has no discernible Wild West theme or influence. However, the album takes its title from the final track, which was actually a reference to Rollins's traveling to LA to make the record at the company's recording studio. Making a light joke out of the title, Rollins donned the gear, they rode out of town to shoot the photo, and it makes for a fantastic, escapist fantasy cover. Note how the sax is held almost like a gun at his side.

CBS

Johnny Cash
Orange Blossom Special

Featuring
IT AIN'T ME BABE
ORANGE BLOSSOM SPECIAL
AMEN / THE LONG BLACK VEIL
DON'T THINK TWICE, IT'S ALRIGHT
THE WALL / YOU WILD COLORADO
MAMA, YOU BEEN ON MY MIND
WHEN IT'S SPRINGTIME
IN ALASKA (It's Forty Below)
ALL OF GOD'S CHILDREN AIN'T FREE
WILDWOOD FLOWER / DANNY BOY

1965
Columbia
America
Photography by Frank Bez

Johnny Cash Orange Blossom Special

From the moment Johnny Cash became famous, he was told that his peculiar, trademark rhythm sounded "like a train." Surprisingly, though, it took until 1960 for him to appear on an album cover with a train, and then it was in fancy dress. On *Ride This Train* Cash wears cowboy gear and is twirling the barrel of a Colt .45 pistol as a train rounds a track down below; the idea is that he's an outlaw about to rob the train, of course. Two years later, on the cover of *All Aboard the Blue Train*, Cash wears cowboy garb again, this time with the pistol holstered, rolling a cigarette, standing on a platform as a "blue" steam engine enters the frame behind him. It wasn't until this album that the idea of escape via riding a boxcar, long an American dream scenario—Jack Kerouac romanticized it in *On the Road* after traveling by that means in the late 1940s—was employed by Cash on an album cover. Photographer Frank Bez also shot *Playboy* centerfolds when not creating album covers for Columbia. Which was his escape, one wonders?

Merle Haggard and the Strangers I'm a Lonesome Fugitive

1967
Capitol Records
America
Sleeve design by Capitol Studio
Photography by Howard Risk

Country singer and cocreator of the Bakersfield Sound along with Buck Owens, Haggard really had been a lonesome fugitive: he twice absconded from juvenile detention centers in the 1950s and ended up doing three years in San Quentin jail on aggravated burglary charges. He was at the prison when Johnny Cash made one of his very public live performances there, and it so inspired Haggard he decided (so the story goes) to quit his life of crime and become a singer. When finally released, he entered a life of performing back in Bakersfield and made his way via a Vegas show to the big time with a hit single ("Sing a Sad Song") in 1964. His second album, *Swingin' Doors and a Bottle Let Me Down*, made #1 on the Country charts in 1966 and this, his third, made #3 a year later. The cover not only reminds people of his outlaw past but is also reminiscent of the opening credits of the hugely popular TV show of the time, *Fugitive*. During its opening credits an unjustly accused man played by David Janssen—to whom Haggard bears a passing resemblance—escapes along a goods train rather like this one.

THE ART OF THE LP

Cannonball Adderley Sophisticated Swing

1957
EmArcy/Mercury
America
Sleeve design and photography
uncredited

By the late 1950s jazz music was considered not only hip, but the height of sophistication. Blue Note had some challenging artists on their roster and their covers were deeply musical; of the artists, for the artists. Other artists whose music was slightly less challenging were being sold via the idea of social mobility in every form—see opposite. Smaller jazz labels knew that they needed to sell their music to non-jazz fans if they wanted to succeed, and that they also needed to sell "mobility," aspiration, and affluence. Adderley was also a Blue Note artist, but none of his covers for the label were ever as blatantly sexy as this: the rear end of the big red Mercedes would undoubtedly "swing" around corners. The driver's rear end is doing a fine job of showing how it might swing. Buyers—men, mostly—are invited to jump aboard with her in their dreams, and escape their troubles. At least, for as long as the album lasts.

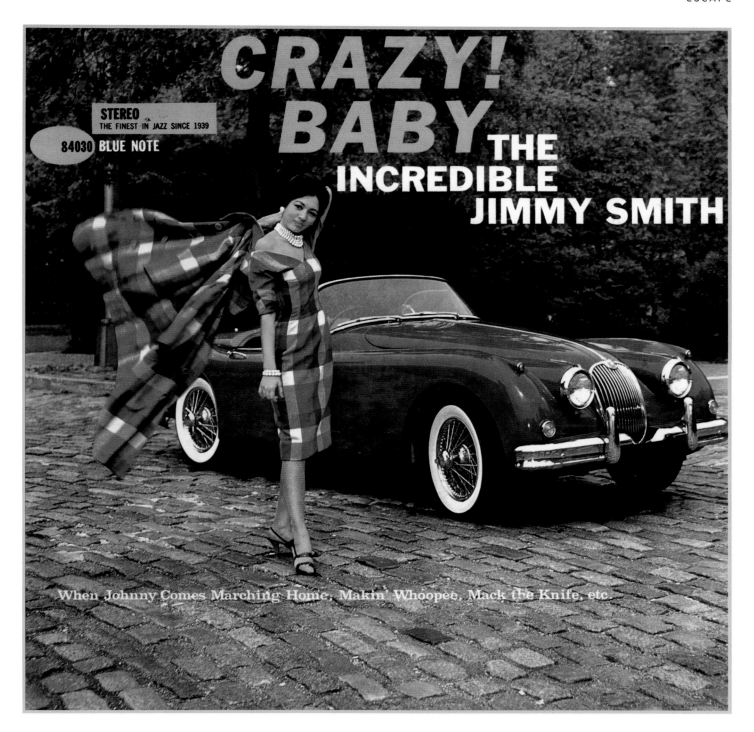

The Incredible Jimmy Smith Crazy! Baby

1960
Blue Note
America
Sleeve design by Reid Miles
Photography by Bob Ganley

There are many great Jimmy Smith sleeves—possibly more than there are great albums by the legendary Hammond organ player. Among the best are *Midnight Special* or *Back at the Chicken Shack*, both of which followed hot on this album's heels. But *Crazy! Baby*, his first album for the new decade, is interesting in that it didn't use the musician as cover star. Jimmy had been appearing on most of his Blue Note releases since his very first in 1956, but here he is dropped in favor of a girl and a car—the shibboleth of escapism since the early days of cinema. Of course it's not any old car, it's a British Jaguar XK150 and it's expensive (as well as fast). Perhaps label design chief Reid Miles thought Smith's music needed a fresh look for the new decade. The photograph is also exceptional in that it was not taken by Blue Note's usual photographer Francis Wolff, but by Bob Ganley. Cars were to become synonymous with Blue Note sleeves after this, and they were nearly all foreign (see p.296) and usually Jaguars. Other labels went for German cars (see opposite).

Donald Byrd Band & Voices A New Perspective

1963
Blue Note
America
Sleeve design and photography by
Reid Miles

The car is an English Jaguar E-Type, which had only been introduced to the world in 1961. It was a revolutionary and very fast car—low to the ground, sleek in a way that no car previously had been, with a throaty-sounding 3.8 liter, 6-cylinder engine under the long, deeply phallic hood. The car was truly the new perspective on automotives. Reid Miles's photo plays on the glassed-in headlamps and the long perspective that is needed to view the driver—Donald Byrd—leaning on the roof, the bump of the hood adding an extra curve to the shapes on show. Before long this car would become the symbol of the British Invasion when various bands—notably the Dave Clark Five—would be seen driving through the streets of London in one, the car making the cramped streets look even smaller than they were. The E-Type became an essential part of the culture of Swinging London. The Invasion happened the year after the release of this ground-breaking album, which mixes the voices of an eight-piece gospel choir with Byrd's trumpet, Kenny Burrell's guitar, Hank Mobley's sax and a wealth of other instruments.

GETTIN' AROUND
DEXTER GORDON
BOBBY HUTCHERSON
BARRY HARRIS
BOB CRANSHAW
BILLY HIGGINS

STEREO
THE FINEST IN JAZZ SINCE 1939
84204 BLUE NOTE

1965
Blue Note
Country
Sleeve design by Reid Miles
Photography by Francis Wolff

Dexter Gordon Gettin' Around

Tenor sax player Dexter Gordon (1923—1990) grew up in LA, the son of an MD who numbered Duke Ellington and Lionel Hampton among his patients. Dexter sat in with some of the Bop greats in the late 1940s after beginning with Hampton and then Billy Eckstine's band. He influenced and was in turn influenced by John Coltrane, and signed with Blue Note in 1960. Two years later Gordon moved to Europe and lived in Paris and Copenhagen, escaping both the drugs that had infested the jazz scene and the racism that plagued the whole country. In Europe he learned to ride a bike. This album was recorded during a trip back to the States in late 1964, and released in time for Christmas 1965. Not only is the cover shot remarkable technically, but the perspective manages to make the 6'6" Gordon look small, which was no mean feat.

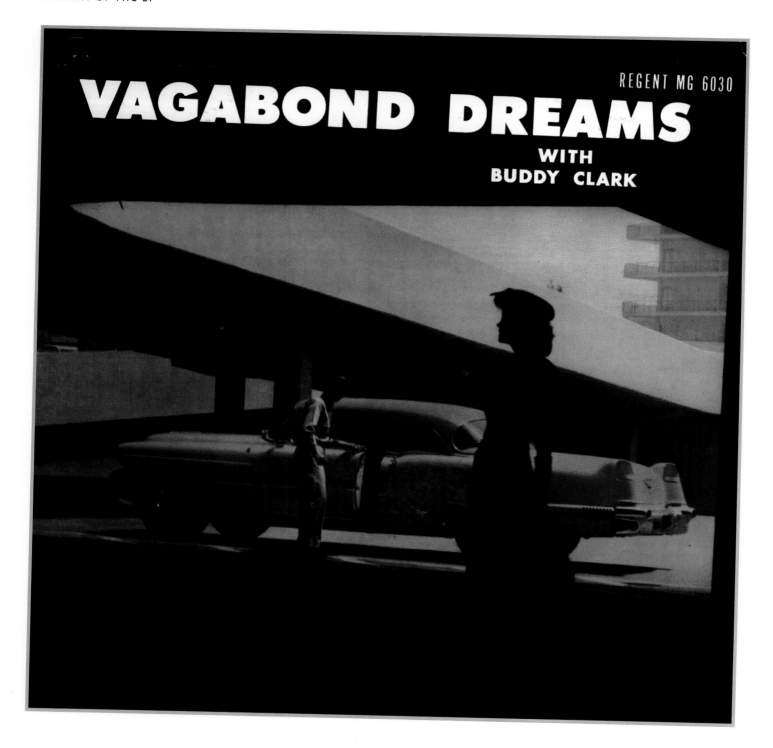

REGENT MG 6030

VAGABOND DREAMS
WITH
BUDDY CLARK

1955
Savoy/Regent Records
America
Sleeve design and photography
uncredited

Buddy Clark Vagabond Dreams

A crooner in the Bing Crosby mold, Clark (1911—1949) scored a couple of big hits in the late 1940s, the biggest being "Linda," which had been written by Jack Lawrence for the daughter of a lawyer named Lee Eastman. She grew up to become Mrs. Paul McCartney. Clark died in a small airplane crash, and his recordings were reissued at various times—several are still available today—though none was packaged as enigmatically as this one. The vast pink Cadillac door is being opened by a uniformed chauffeur for an elegantly dressed woman who looks like a catwalk model of the mid-1950s. Remarkably, the songs it contains are nostalgic while this sleeve is not at all; it represents the height of aspiration and escape from every drudgery for the working man of the time. The concrete city towers over everything, casting dark shadows, but her car sits in the glare of daylight. It's probably California; it's certainly a dream for any "vagabond."

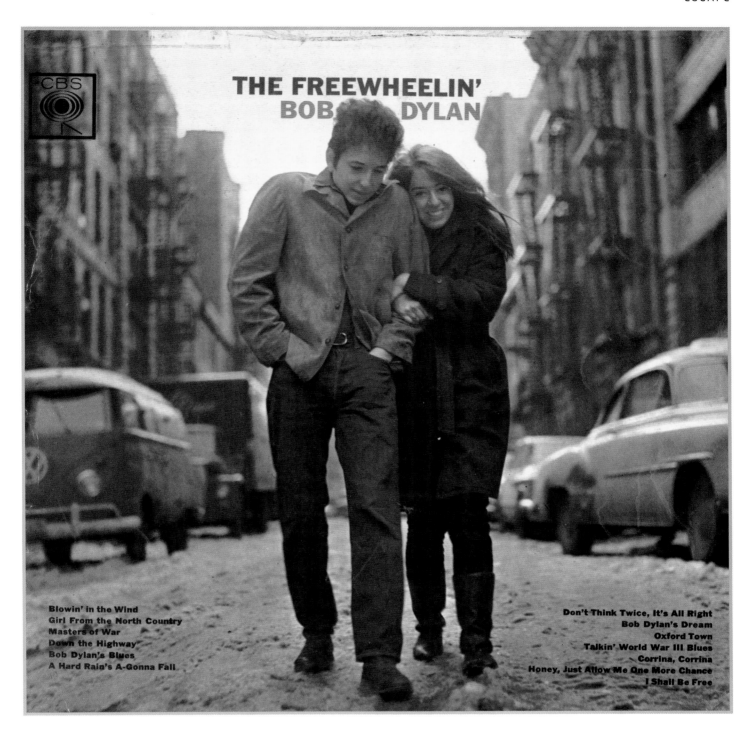

Bob Dylan The Freewheelin' Bob Dylan

1963
Columbia Records
America
Photography by Don Hustein

Originally taken for promotional purposes by CBS staff photographer Don Hunstein, this picture, like several others featured on Dylan sleeves, has become iconic. Suze Rotolo, the seventeen-year-old girlfriend of the nascent folk singer, warms herself against him as they walk through the snow on Jones Street and West 4th Street in Greenwich Village. The couple lived a few yards from where this picture was taken and you sense they can't wait to go back into the warm. Daughter of socialist parents, even at just seventeen Rotolo was extremely politically aware and had a profound influence on the young Dylan. For an impromptu shoot, Hunstein was really blessed: not only is the light excellent, picking out the youthful faces of the couple, but there is a VW Camper parked in the street—the van was to become a symbol of freewheeling escapism for the emerging generation of hippies in America. Dylan drew inspiration from the photo for parts of his "autobiography" *Chronicles*; in all the New York scenes he writes about from this period, there is snow. There's a lot of snow in *Chronicles*.

Simon & Garfunkel Wednesday Morning, 3 A.M.

1964
Columbia Records
America
Sleeve design and photography
uncredited

Paul Simon would of course go on to write the classic antithesis of escape, "Homeward Bound," at Ditton Railway Station near Widnes in Northwest England. That wouldn't appear until 1966, though. On a different railway platform two years earlier Simon posed with his partner Art Garfunkel for this, their debut album. The cover bears all the hallmarks of escapist youth: the hip young pair in smart suits and skinny ties, Simon with acoustic guitar strapped on, and the pair of them aching to get out and busk. To the right is the subway train, either speeding away or just arriving, letting us know that they are going places. But the picture is right at the bottom of the sleeve; the stencilled font uses more than half of the space, giving the composition the look of a flyer, informing us of when we can find this itinerant pair playing, in the wee hours of the morning—beatnik time.

Jefferson Airplane After Bathing at Baxters

1967
RCA Victor
America
Illustration by Ron Cobb
Album title by the Walking Owls

San Francisco's Airplane, after the pop success of *Surrealistic Pillow* and the hit single "Somebody to Love," took some more LSD, tuned up, tuned in and created five separate "suites" of music, each split into songs, for their follow-up album. They recruited *LA Free Press* illustrator Ron Cobb to create the cover art, and he took their huge tenement, bay-windowed house as inspiration for this idiosyncratic airplane. Helicopters and a jet circle above it, the city sits in the background, but that's all black and white. Only the Jefferson Airplane is colored—psychedelically colored, at that. The message is clear: the only escape from square life is with the 'Plane. Cobb went on to work in movies and became a production designer on, among others, *Star Wars* (1977), *Alien* (1979) and *Conan the Barbarian* (1982). In 1969 he designed the American ecology symbol using an *e* in an *o*, and it has become part of the American Ecology flag.

SIDE I
WASTED WORDS
SOUTHBOUND
RAMBLIN' MAN

SIDE II
IN MEMORY OF
ELIZABETH REED

SIDE III
AIN'T WASTIN' TIME NO MORE
COME AND GO BLUES
CAN'T LOSE WHAT
YOU NEVER HAD

SIDE IV
DON'T WANT YOU NO MORE
IT'S NOT MY CROSS TO BEAR
JESSICA

2637 103

Also available on cassette 3521 103

1976
Capricorn Records
America
Illustration and design by Jim Evans
Art direction by Diana Kaylan

The Allman Brothers Band Wipe the Windows, Check the Oil, Dollar Gas

This is not considered a genuine Allman Brothers album, and is composed of live recordings made over several years and released after the band had fallen apart through internecine arguments and drug abuse. Gregg Allman was busted on drug charges in 1976 and gave evidence against one of the band's tour managers in return for leniency from the authorities. The rest of the band (none of them Allmans) said they'd never work with him again. They were at the time a top live act, though record sales were falling. This excellent illustration of an old-time gas station perfectly captures the Allmans' all-Southern American touring band appeal.

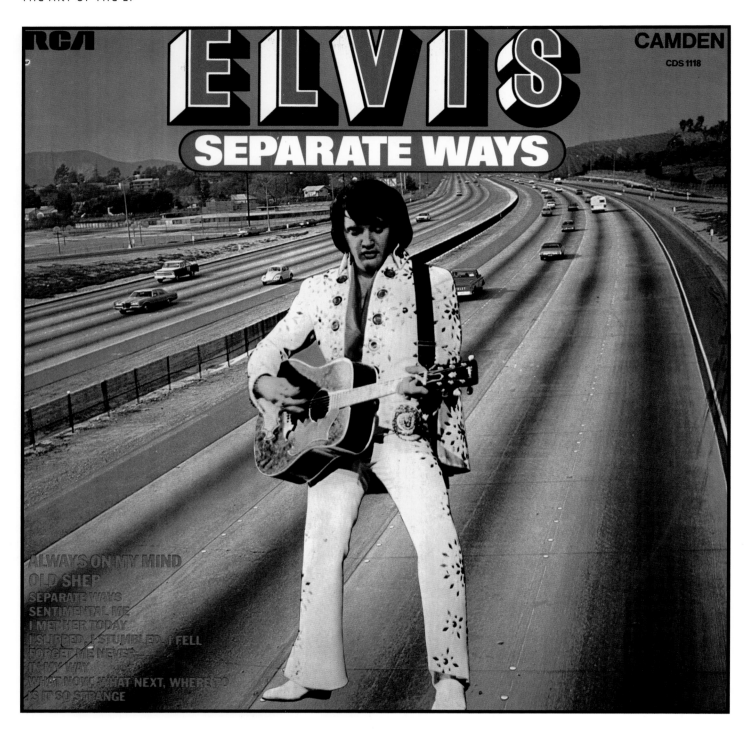

RCA

ELVIS

SEPARATE WAYS

CAMDEN

CDS 1118

ALWAYS ON MY MIND
OLD SHEP
SEPARATE WAYS
SENTIMENTAL ME
I MET HER TODAY
I SLIPPED, I STUMBLED, I FELL
FORGET ME NEVER
IN MY WAY
WHAT NOW, WHAT NEXT, WHERE TO
IS IT SO STRANGE

1973

Camden/RCA

England

Sleeve design uncredited

Elvis Presley Separate Ways

The Camden label was RCA's budget outlet, used for cheap compilations and reissues of music for declining artists. We must remember that by 1973 Elvis was considered pretty much a joke in rock & roll circles. His rhinestone-encrusted polyester jumpsuits were symbolic of the fake glitz of a Vegas entertainer, which is how he was then regarded. Elvis was still recording though, and new singles came out regularly. This album of mostly old material ("Old Shep" was recorded in 1956) was created around the hit single "Separate Ways," which had made #20 in the U.S. charts in 1972. The cover, wisely uncredited, is a complete mess. The best thing to be said for it is that at least Elvis stands in the middle of the highway of oncoming traffic so he doesn't look as if he's about to be run over. The six-lane highway—going in opposite directions, get it?—is presented in all its untinted glory, unlike the U.S. cover, which used the same cut-out of Elvis but on a hand-drawn color background of a highway disappearing between two green hills. Elvis is still presented as a giant, though.

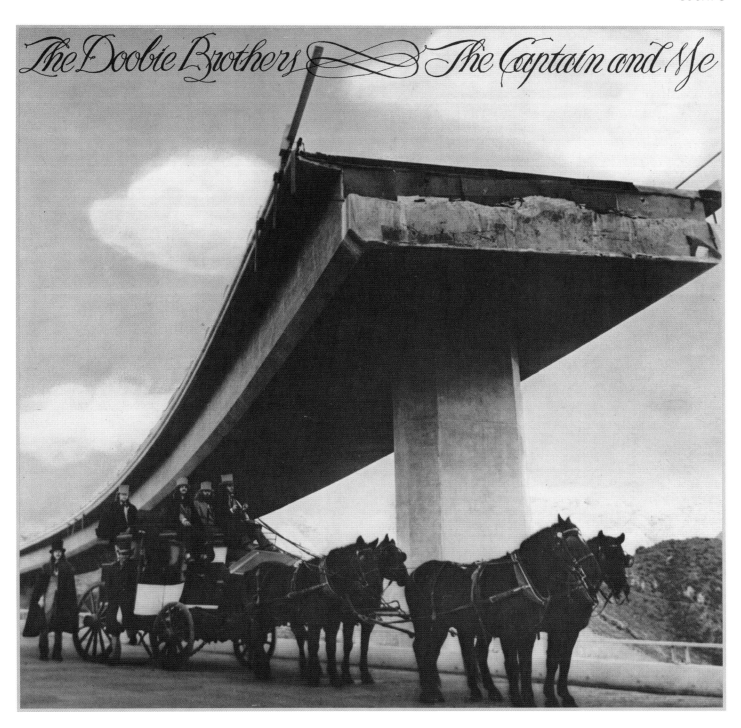

The Doobie Brothers The Captain and Me

1973
Warners
America
Sleeve design by John and
Barbara Casado
Photography by Michael and Jill Maggid
Art direction by Ed Thrasher

The Doobie Brothers The Captain and Me

In 1972 the Doobie Brothers had become enormous stars after the success of their second album *Toulouse Street*, and the singles from it, "Listen to the Music" and "Jesus Is Just Alright." Their first two albums had unremarkable covers using dull band pics. With a bigger budget, Warners design chief Ed Thrasher set up a shoot using clothes from the Warner Bros. film studio wardrobe department, an 18th-century stagecoach replica and photographers Michael and Jill Maggid. They took everyone (including band manager Bruce Cohen) out to a section of highway near Sylmar, outside LA, which had collapsed during a 1971 earthquake and hadn't yet been repaired. There were also a couple of coffins on the shoot, and a table with food, candlesticks and goblets. The band members are all seated at it in the inner sleeve photo. It was as far away from the Doobies' adopted Hells Angels beginnings as they could get. But it captured their old-world approach to their songs. Two years later the Maggids photographed the Doobies on horses for the cover of *Stampede*.

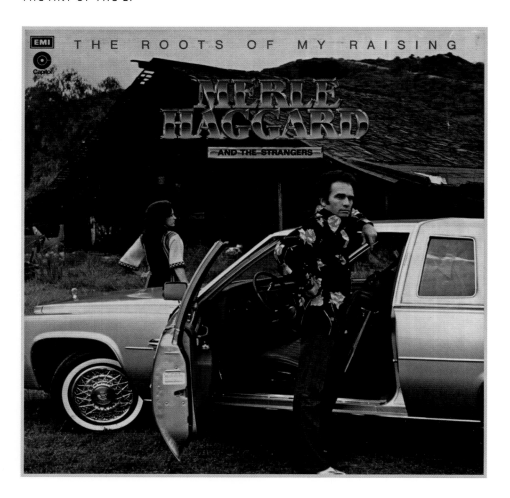

Merle Haggard and the Strangers The Roots of My Raising

1976
Capitol Records
America
Sleeve design by Richard Hurtado
Photography by Rick Rankin
Art direction by Roy Kohara

Merle escaped (see p. 293) and made it big. So he returned to the farm he was raised on in Bakersfield in his Cadillac, wearing fancy boots and with a gorgeous woman, to gaze at the shack in which he was raised (supposedly). It's the Great American Dream come true: despite bad beginnings anyone can escape poverty and make it, become rich, successful and famous. The car was an important symbol of American success and mobility, both social and actual, and the Caddy a pure American status symbol at that time. Merle is telling us that he escaped, but he ain't forgotten where he came from.

Delaney & Bonnie & Friends On Tour with Eric Clapton

1970
Atco
America
Sleeve design and photography by Tom Wilkes and Barry Feinstein for Camouflage Productions

The tour was, by all accounts, a wild and drug-fuelled romp across America. It's doubtful that everyone traveled in a Rolls Royce, which was a very British status symbol, as was Clapton at the time. However, the band leaders, husband and wife Delaney & Bonnie Bramlett, would have traveled with Eric, escaping the studio sessions in which both had made a living—he as guitarist, she as singer. The recording earned the Bramletts a contract with Atco (this was the first release with the label). The tour also included contributions from George Harrison. (Feinstein took the cover shot in 1966, and those are Bob Dylan's feet.)

Richard and Linda Thompson I Want to
See the Bright Lights Tonight

1974
Island Records
England
Sleeve design and photography
uncredited

After leaving Fairport Convention, Richard Thompson released his debut
album *Henry the Human Fly* to critical panning and poor sales. Now married
to Linda Peters, who had sung backing vocals on it, he recorded this with her
on a small budget in a short time. The gasoline crisis in the UK resulted in
limited vinyl supplies, so Island sat on it for a further eight months. Perhaps
they used this time to come up with the artwork. It is now acknowledged as
a classic that transcends its folk genre, partly because of some great tunes,
but also because of the sleeve, which echoes the distinct urban feel of the
title. The "sad stories" contained on the album are alluded to by the hastily
written text on bathroom mirror condensation—is it a leaving note? Or, like
the song on the album, an invitation?

1973
A&M Records
America
Illustration design by Maru
Photography by Jim McCrary
Art direction by Roland Young

The Carpenters Now & Then

This triple-fold-out sleeve is a slightly different take on the same theme as displayed by Merle Haggard's *Roots of My Raising* (see p. 306). Here the Carpenters are driving by their childhood home. The material differences are plain. The car—Richard's—is a Ferrari Daytona, one of the most expensive in the world. The house that they're driving by is on Newville Avenue in Downey, California. It's hardly a shack, though it is completely suburban. The album title came from the siblings' mother, and side two is devoted to a medley of pop hits from their youth. They look spookily unreal in the car, dressed almost identically. Yet the Ferrari is a potent symbol of escape from conformist beginnings, and they look happy to be not stopping.

peter gabriel

1977
Charisma Records
England
Sleeve design by Hipgnosis
Retouching by Richard Manning

Peter Gabriel 1 [car]

Kicking off his run of four eponymous solo albums, Gabriel's first after leaving Genesis is known as *Car*. Storm Thorgerson of Hipgnosis explained how the sleeve came about to Hypergallery. He was sitting in a cab in Trafalgar Square, "On the bonnet . . . sat myriad drops that were being shaken by the vibrating cab . . . I thought, 'That looks cool, can I duplicate it one day?' Which is how Peter came to be sitting, looking furtive in the front seat of my beloved Lancia Flavia which had been heavily dowsed with a garden hose . . . I feel that what makes this shot distinctive is the hand coloring (the blue) and the fact that each individual highlight was scraped clean with a scalpel by a very patient Richard Manning. This low-key portrait approach was a credit to Peter's modesty. He appeared similarly obscured in the next two albums in which the designs were more concerned with idea, mood, and evocation than with cosmetics and how good looking we made him. Don't get me wrong . . . he's not bad looking, is our Pete."

Side One
Moribund the Burgermeister
Solsbury Hill
Modern Love
Excuse Me
Humdrum

Side Two
Slowburn
Waiting for the Big One
Down the Dolce Vita
Here comes the Flood

All songs written by Peter Gabriel
and published by Run It Music/Ear Pieces, BMI,
except
'Excuse Me' written by Peter Gabriel and Martin Hall
and published by Run It Music/Ear Pieces,
BMI-WB Music Corp., ASCAP.

PRODUCED BY BOB EZRIN
for My Own Production Co., Ltd.

Allan Schwartzberg: Drums, Directories
Tony Levin: Bass, Tuba, Leader of BarBershop Quartet
Jim Maelen: Percussion, Synthibam, Bones and Barbershop
Steve Hunter: Full Frontal Guitar, Electric and Acoustic
Rhythm Guitar, Pedal Steel
Robert Fripp: Electric Guitar, Classical Guitar, Banjo
Jozef Chirowski: Frontal Keyboard, Barbershop
Larry (Wires) Fast: Synthesizers and Programming
Peter Gabriel: Voices, Keyboard, Flute, Recorder
with
Dick Wagner: Backing Voices; Solo Guitar
on 'The Flood' and end of 'Slowburn'
and
The London Symphony Orchestra ('Down the Dolce Vita')

Recorded and mixed at The Soundstage, Toronto
Additional recording at Morgan Studios, London,
Olympic Studios, London
Recorded by Brian Christian
with Robert Hrycyna, Jim Frank, Dave Harris, Rod O'Brien,
Robert Stasiuk, Keith Grant
Mastered at JAMF, Toronto, by George Graves
and Craig Richardson

Cover by Hipgnosis
Organisation by Tony Smith, Brian and Alex at Hit and Run
The L.S.O. Arranged and Conducted by Michael Gibbs

Atco Records
Division of Atlantic Recording Corporation
75 Rockefeller Plaza, New York, New York 10019
℗© 1977 Atlantic Recording Corporation   Printed in U.S.A.
Ⓦ A Warner Communications Company

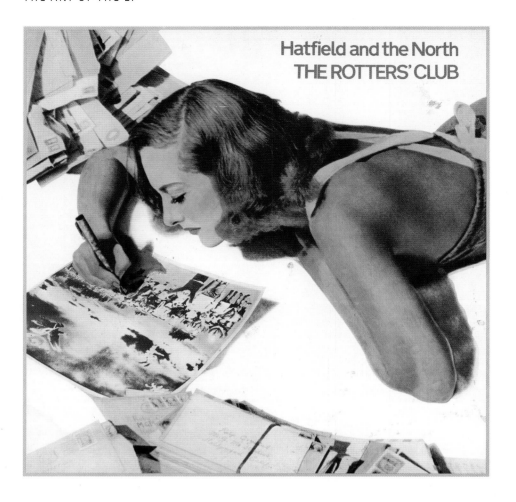

Hatfield and the North The Rotters' Club

1975
Virgin Records
England
Sleeve design and artwork by
Laurie Lewis

Long before he became a Eurythmic with Annie Lennox, guitarist and songwriter Dave Stewart was in this prog rock band which originated in Canterbury. This is their second album (of four). England in 1975 was in many ways still waiting for World War II to end and most people still held Hollywood films of the forties and fifties to be the height of sophistication and glamor. This cover appears to feature a Bette Davis look-alike, heavily tinted, coloring a black-and-white image of schoolkids, Edwardian gentlemen, and airborne cherubs in front of a cloudy sky, amid piles of unopened mail addressed to "Ruby Crystal, MGM Studios." The reverse displays the black-and-white photo in full.

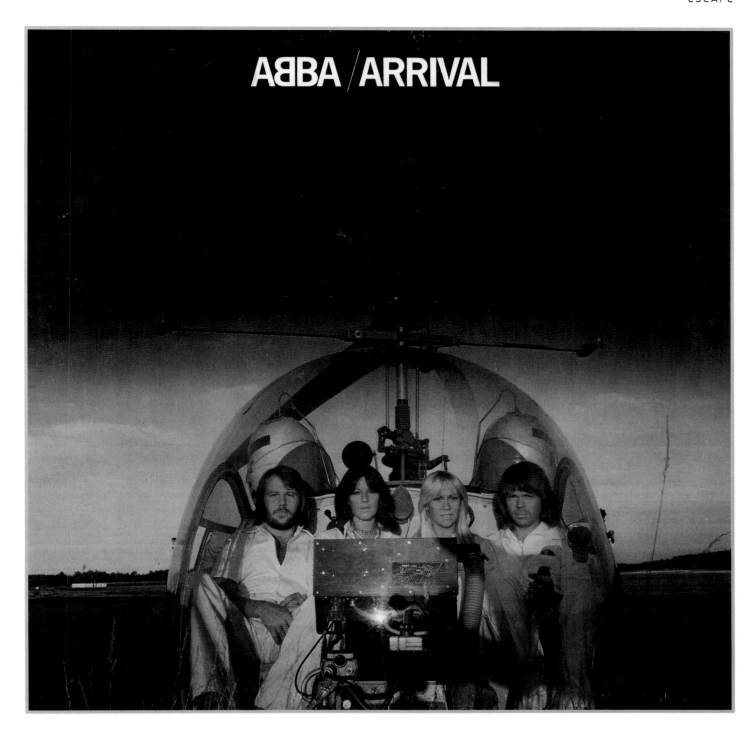

ABBA/ARRIVAL

1976
Epic Records
America
Sleeve concept, design and
photography by Rune Söderqvist and
Olga Lager

ABBA Arrival

A prescient album title if ever there was one, ABBA had already enjoyed
a couple of years of success after their Eurovision Song Contest winner
"Waterloo" in 1974. But it was in 1976 that they really arrived with this
fourth album, which contained the big hit singles "Dancing Queen,"
"Knowing Me, Knowing You" and "Money Money Money." This is the first
ABBA sleeve to show the group looking cool and also the first album to use
their logo. Now synonymous with the band, the reverse B logo was designed
by Rune Söderqvist and was first used on the "Dancing Queen" single
sleeve. Sitting in a beautiful Bell 47 helicopter, the band members look as
if they are finally living the high life, at least much more so than on their
previous album, where they sit drinking champagne in the back of a limo.

Sparks Propaganda

1974
Island Records
England
Sleeve concept and photography by
Monty Coles

Sparks had found success by moving from their native LA to London, signing to Island Records and making their version of glam rock. Their previous album, *Kimono My House* (featuring two geishas posing for the camera), often gets cited as one of the best sleeves ever, but this follow-up—their fourth album and released only months later in November 1974—is better. Not only do we see the visual identity of the band on the front cover for the first time (earlier albums had featured the whole line-up, but in reality Sparks is all about Ron and Russell Mael) but we get it in a characteristically unlikely style—a succession of shots featuring the brothers being kidnapped. It was taken just off Bournemouth on England's south coast and Australian photographer Monty Coles's cover shot perfectly captures the black comedy of the band's music.

Supertramp Breakfast in America

1979
A&M Records
America
Art direction and cover concept by
Mike Doud
Sleeve design by Mick Haggerty
Photography by Aaron Rapoport

Mike Doud's cover for this album won a Grammy for Best Recording Package in 1980. It's a complicated concept—downtown Manhattan recreated as a breakfast table (reminiscent of Maurice Sendak's illustrations in the classic children's book *In the Night Kitchen*), plus the Statue of Liberty recast as a waitress holding orange juice instead of the torch. It's just the sort of stoned idea a rock band would have but it has been executed beautifully. London-based Doud is best known for this and Led Zeppelin's *Physical Graffiti*, but he is hugely prolific and remains working to this day. The back cover photo of this album is worth examining too, as close inspection of the photograph of the band in the diner reveals each member reading his respective local British or Scottish newspaper. This would be an iconic sleeve regardless of the album's eleven million-selling contents.

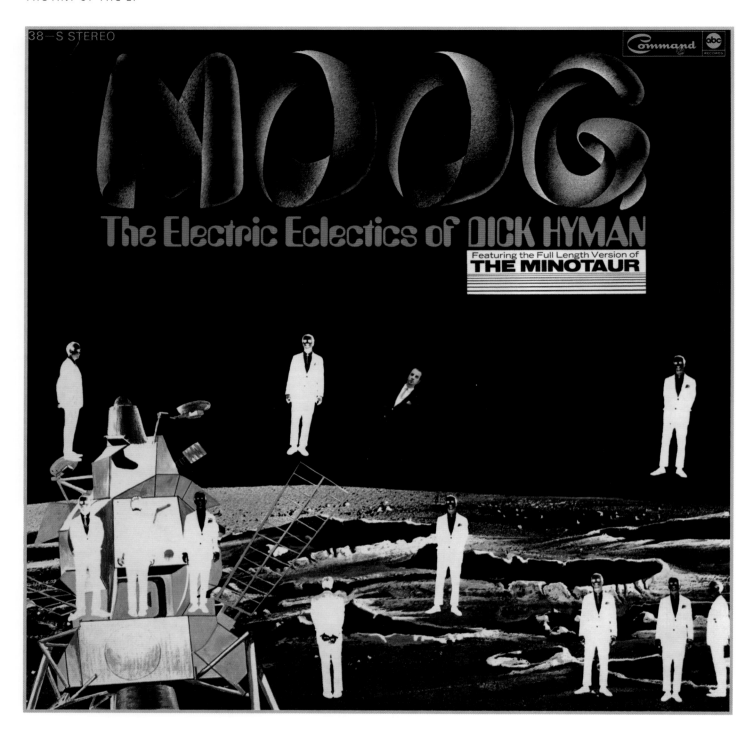

38—S STEREO

Command abc RECORDS

MOOG

The Electric Eclectics of DICK HYMAN

Featuring the Full Length Version of
THE MINOTAUR

1969

Command

America

Sleeve design by Byron Goto and Harry Epstein

Dick Hyman MOOG The Electric Eclectics of Dick Hyman

Or, Escape into the Future with Dick! What fantastic fun Dick Hyman had on Enoch Light's Command label. By the time of this release, the Moog synthesizer was being used by avant-garde composers and savvy pop performers alike, and the amazing array of sounds it could conjure were being utilized in many different and interesting ways. Here Dick chooses to play his own compositions for the Moog, including something called "Legend of Johnny Pot," which sounds like a kiddie's TV show theme, and a prog rock freak-out called "The Minotaur." The cover, featuring several negative-image Dicks floating on the moon (or distant planet), cashes in on the fad for all things related to space travel at the time. It worked, and Minotaur made the Top 40 singles charts when released, supposedly the first song completely composed and played on the Moog to do so.

Yes Relayer

1974
Atlantic
England
Sleeve illustration by Roger Dean

Artist, designer and architect Roger Dean doesn't admit to being a fantasy artist, but rather a landscape painter. His landscapes, most famously created for British prog rock band Yes, tend not to be of Earth, though. Dean's work is almost completely entwined with Yes albums and the band's guitarist Steve Howe has said that "There is a pretty tight bond" between his work and theirs. Yes's music is as futuristic and otherworldly as the art, and for this, their fifth album, the first since the departure of keyboard player Rick Wakeman, the rocky landscape includes three "warriors" on horseback (singer Jon Anderson's first band was named Warriors). It is far more contained than the space scene that was used as the cover for the band's previous double album release, *Tales from Topographic Oceans* (seen by many as the epitome of self-indulgent prog rock excess). The colors are muted, the snake almost invisible; it could just be an earthly landscape. Dean's cover art formed a tangible element of the escapism that the music hopes to encourage.

1975
Bronze Records
England
Sleeve painting by Ian Emes from an
idea by Teddy Osei

Osibisa Welcome Home

Almost thirty years after the *SS Windrush* had delivered scores of Afro-Caribbean nationals to England to live and work, racist elements in British society were still calling for them to be repatriated, or forcibly sent "home." A new political party, the National Front, campaigned on a policy of forced repatriation and attracted idiots who thought all black people came from Africa. Osibisa formed in London in 1969 and included Afro-Caribbean and expat African members; leader Teddy Osei was Ghanain. Their first three albums had covers by Roger Dean and Mati Klarwein. And then they did this, and it was all Osei's idea. It panders to the dumb notion of "home" for all black people being a jungle and was incredibly unwise.

Mickey Newbury Rusty Tracks

1977
ABC records
America
Sleeve design by Earl Klasky
Illustration by Joe Heiner (Star Studios)
Lettering by Bill Franks
Concept by Dave Willardson
(Star Studios)
Art direction by Earl Klasky,
Frank Mulvey

Although ostensibly a Country music singer-songwriter, Newbury is best known for his arrangement of three traditional American songs into *An American Trilogy* for Elvis Presley in 1972 (since covered by hundreds of others), and his songs do not fit neatly into any category. Newbury's solo singing career was never enormously successful, though many others had hits with his work. He was considered one of the original "Outlaw" country singers in Nashville in the 1970s, but that seems to have come as much from his friendship with Kris Kristofferson as anything else. Newbury was never a rebel like Haggard, Allan Coe or Jennings, and so on. He had a great ability to evoke an idea of America that appealed to the romantic—patriotic but realistic. The cover for this album conjures a sense of nostalgia by making the tone arm of an old-fashioned record player into an old train running through the record "tracks." It's almost hokey, yetaNewbury was far from a clichéd Country singer. He wrote emotionally challenging songs, usually suffused with a sense of longing, and always haunting.

1975
Mercury
England
Sleeve design by Hipgnosis
Drawing by Humphrey Ocean

10cc The Original Soundtrack

Manchester-born band 10cc was struggling on an independent label when it recorded this album, but Mercury was so blown away with the song "I'm Not in Love" that it signed the band on the spot. The album sleeve was designed (like many in this book) by Storm Thorgerson's company Hipgnosis, but unlike most of that company's artwork, it is a drawing rather than a photograph. The album title and many of its lyrics are cinematically inspired, so artist Humphrey Ocean has drawn the viewfinder of a cine camera with that classic icon of Hollywood, a cowboy, on its screen. The drawing stretches over the back and gatefold too. Ocean was the bass player in Ian Dury's band Kilburn & the High Roads at the time, and is now a well-respected painter with his work exhibited in the National Portrait Gallery in London.

1977

The Electric Record Company

England

Sleeve design by Michael Dobney

Illustration by Dan Pearce

Quantum Jump Barracuda

A British jazz–funk fusion band led by Rupert Hine, Quantum Jump had a strange history. In 1975 they released a single entitled "Lone Ranger" which was at first embraced by UK radio and then banned by it, and it failed to sell. Their debut eponymous album didn't do well, and this second was recorded just as punk was becoming the dominant musical force in their homeland. By the end of 1977 Quantum Jump had ceased to exist. But in 1979 the single of "The Lone Ranger" was rereleased and became an enormous hit. The band reformed but couldn't capitalize on the single's success, so split up again. Hine became a successful record producer, and copies of the band's two albums became collector's items. Comic illustrator Dan Pearce also drew the Welsh prog rock band Gryphon's covers, although they lacked the humor of this mini-epic tale of one woman's escape from a marauding fish truck.

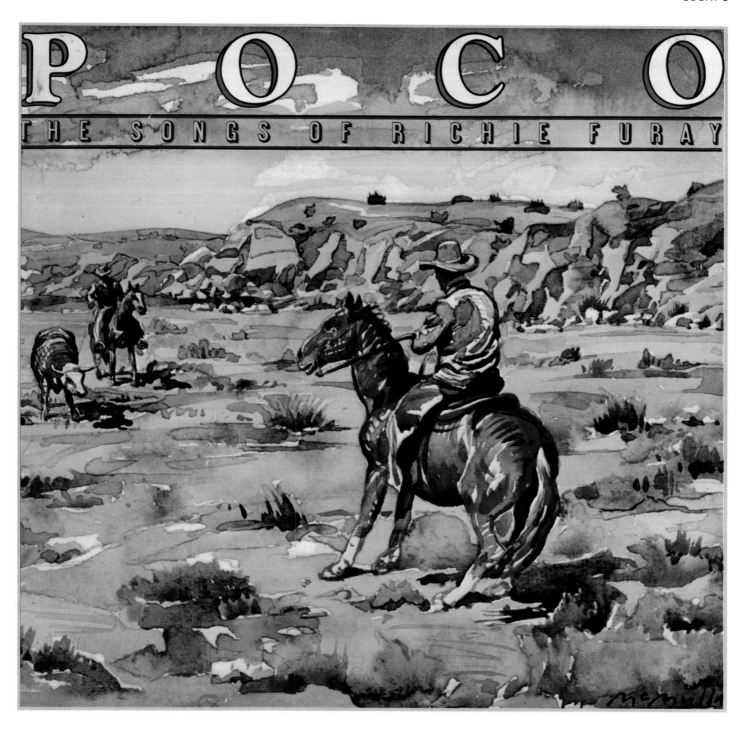

1979
CBS Records
America
Sleeve design by Paula Scher
Illustration by Jim McMullan

Poco The Songs of Richie Furay

Poco was one of the first and most successful country rock bands to form in the wake of Gram Parsons' trail-blazing work with the Byrds and the Flying Burrito Brothers. Led by former Buffalo Springfield members Richie Furay, Rusty Young and Jim Messina, along with George Grantham (the only member from the Midwest) and Randy Meisner (later of the Eagles), they released their debut album to critical acclaim in 1969. Their most successful album was the live recording *Deliverin'* in 1971, after which Messina left the band to be replaced by Paul Cotton. Three albums later Furay left the band too. Poco continue to play and Furay occasionally appears in concert with them. This compilation-release comprised of songs he wrote while with them employs the kind of artwork that Poco members grew up with, mythologizing the Wild West. It was released alongside *Songs of Paul Cotton*, which used a similar illustration of cowboys roping a steer. No other Poco albums had similar Western imagery, however, with only 1982's *Cowboys & Englishmen* using a cowboy on the cover.

Jackson Browne
Lawyers in Love

1983
Elektra/Asylum
America
Art direction and design by Jimmy Wachtel and Dawn Patrol
Photography by Matti Klatt

Despite first impressions, this cover is not an illustration, and not hand drawn nor computer generated. It is a photograph. That's a Mercedes coupé immersed in a water tank, sitting in front of a huge, hand-built and back-lit "sun," with apartments to each side painted to look like a city. The man in the car is a model; you can see him standing next to the Merc on the centerpiece of the vinyl. Amazingly, given how much this must have cost to set up and shoot, the inner sleeve contains no images from the session at all. Jimmy Wachtel also art-directed Joe Walsh's extravagant sleeve for *"But Seriously Folks . . . "* and was the king of such escapist, grandiose statements as album covers.

The Human League
Travelogue

1980
Virgin
England
Sleeve concept by The Human League
Design coordination by Angular Images
Colorization by Quicksilver

Before their high-gloss hits, The Human League was more experimental and left field. This was reflected in their artwork too—both on their debut *Reproduction* and on this, their second album, and the last before they went pop with *Dare*. The band gets credit for the artwork, which no doubt involved much sifting through photo libraries. The setting sun, highlighting the lone figure and huskies, gives a timeless romantic look to the sleeve, which is helped by the classic typography. Unlike the sleeve for *Dare*, this cover hasn't dated at all.

1974
Manticore
Italy
Sleeve design by Fabio Nicoli
Associates
Photography by Christine Spengler
Illustration by Terry Gough

Premiata Forneria Marconi The World Became the World

PFM became the world's best-known Italian prog rock band when they signed to Emerson, Lake and Palmer's label, following a support slot with ELP on the Italian leg of their tour in 1972. Their first English-language release, *Photos of Ghosts*, was issued in 1973, containing old songs with new English lyrics written by Peter Sinfield, ex of King Crimson. *The World Became the World* was a similarly concocted release, with Sinfield's new English lyrics replacing the original Italian words. The cover features a die-cut hole with ragged edges, and the island in the center is printed on the inner sleeve, the flip of which is printed with lyrics. The outside sleeve is a photograph of the sky, similar to one used on the cover of the Plastic Ono Band's *Live Peace in Toronto 1969* album. The island, a potent symbol of escape from the cares of the real world, is rendered almost as an 18th-century sketch as depicted by a shipwrecked sailor heading toward it.

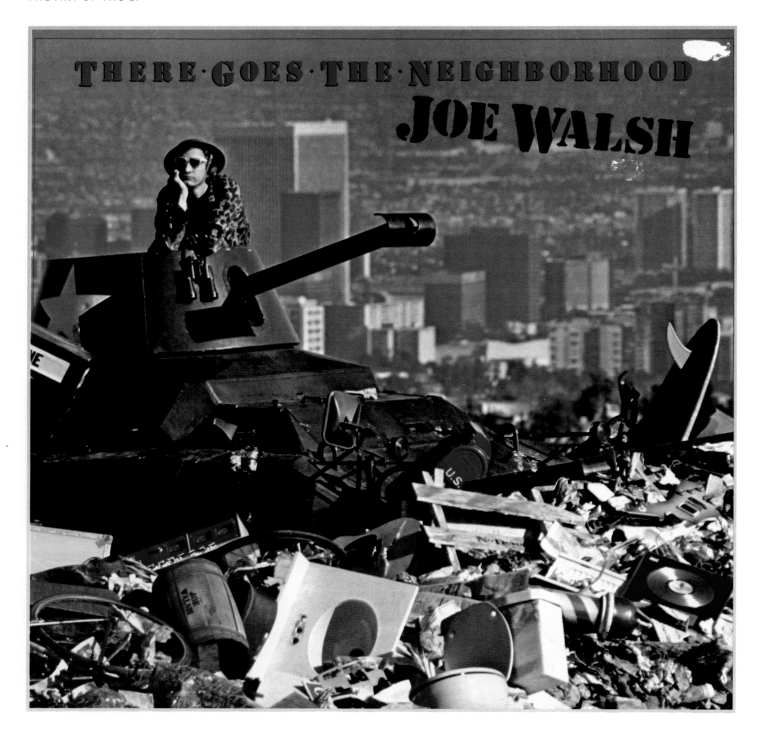

Joe Walsh There Goes the Neighborhood

1981
Asylum Records
America
Art direction and design by
Jeff Adamoff
Photography by Todd Andrews

Three years (and endless Eagles arguments) after the success of *"But Seriously, Folks . . . ,"* Joe Walsh's next solo album is most notable for its cover. The Eagles had split, and Joe was back to doing his own thing, though he wasn't happy with the way the split had gone. Some of the lyrics on this album talk about the Eagles management in not too kindly terms. Walsh was sick of double dealing and hypocrisy. The video for a single taken from this album, "A Life of Illusion," was filmed at the cover shoot, on a garbage dump, and shows how the set, designed to look as if the guitarist had blown up his own home, was built out of a garbage pile. Walsh is seen arriving and leaving the shoot in a limo after photographer Andrews and his crew created the right backdrop. The video completely undoes the effect of the cover, which is presumably what Walsh wanted. "There is no escape from the fictions that we employ to sell ourselves" is one possible interpretation. Another is that he really didn't want to have to make a video for the single.

326

1993
Food/EMI
England
Art & Craft by Stylorouge
"Mallard" painted by Paul Gribble

Blur Modern Life Is Rubbish

After the high-gloss pop art look of their debut release, *Leisure*, Blur's second album was very much a British affair: it focused on the decline of the UK while taking a perverse pride in it in much the same way as the Kinks had twenty-five years earlier. Rob O'Connor's design company Stylorouge had created the slick logo for the first album and must have worried about it not working with the distinct Festival of Britain typeface they use here. It works beautifully and the band was still using the logo twenty years later. The oil painting of the famous *Mallard* steam train would make for a rather flat unimaginative sleeve without the album title and font creating the irony. Indeed, this irony would develop for the next two Blur albums, reaching overkill with *The Great Escape*, after which the band stripped it back down and made the earnest, almost grunge-like, album entitled simply *Blur*—using a simple blurred image and the logo on the artwork.

POLITICS

Everything is political. All artists, when they create something to be subjected to public scrutiny, are making political statements. More often than not they are unaware of the political aspects of what they're doing, but that doesn't alter the fact that everyone has their own opinion on the meaning, intention and worth of any work of art that they consider.

Elvis was political in that he irrevocably altered the accepted view of societal norms of behavior and language, first in America, then in the world, with his music, hip shaking and lip curling. Bruce Springsteen's use of the American flag on the cover of his biggest-selling album has been subjected to several different interpretations (for ours, see p. 366).

Rock music confronted the norms of society, which ruled our world in many different ways. The great thing about an album cover was that even people who had no intention of listening to the music on the disc could and would be affected by the visual representation. That has led to many original covers being banned, of course—some are displayed in the following pages—but not until after the political message in the image has been disseminated via the media coverage it attracted.

And the media coverage is what album covers are all about: they need to grab the attention of the people most likely to buy the record; if they also impart a political message, then so be it.

On the following pages you'll find visual representations of anticapitalist sentiments, profeminist images, Black Power salutes, gender identity challenges, antidrug control propaganda and a few opaque, mixed political messages. Everything is political.

1975
Curtom Records/Warner Bros
America
Sleeve design by Lockhart
Illustration by Peter Palombi
Art direction by Ed Thrasher

Curtis Mayfield America Today

The fantastically named Ed Thrasher was instrumental in the so-called Big Idea artwork of the mid-sixties onward. He was the art director at Warner Brothers in LA from 1964 onward and moved away from the company's previously bland packaging, replacing it with some of the defining sleeves in this book (Jimi Hendrix's *Are You Experienced* and Joni Mitchell's *Clouds*, for example). Over in Chicago, by the late sixties Curtis Mayfield had noticed a change in the air and was developing a more socially conscious variation of his falsetto soul. This album, which came out three years after Mayfield's big breakthrough *Superfly*, is lyrically very clear about the irrelevance of the American Dream to African Americans. West Coast airbrush artist Peter Palombi created the amazing illustration, which reflects Mayfield's anger. It's also worth searching out Palombi's striking sleeve for Eddie Harris's *That's Why You're Overweight*, which he illustrated a year later.

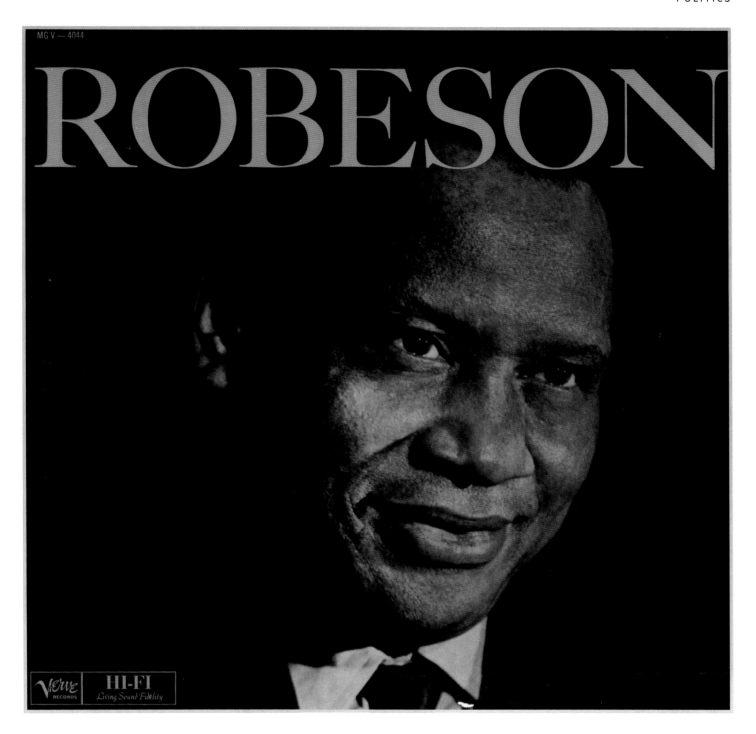

MG V — 4044

ROBESON

Verve
RECORDS
HI-FI
Living Sound Fidelity

Paul Robeson Robeson

1960
Verve Records
America
Art direction by Merle Shore
Photography by Robin Adler

Basso profundo singer Paul Robeson was considered a threat to America up until his death, at age seventy-seven, in 1975. A lawyer, civil rights and antifascist orator of very public profile, Robeson's FBI file remains the thickest ever compiled on an American entertainer. In 1960 this marvelously informal, smiling, close-up portrait was used on an album of gospel songs released barely two years after his passport had been returned to Robeson by U.S. authorities. In 1961, while on a tour of Soviet Russia, Robeson would "attempt suicide" and be hospitalized. The singer's son suggested that his father had been surreptitiously drugged by CIA operatives using LSD, which was then a tactic of the controversial MKULTRA program. After release from hospital in Moscow, Robeson traveled to the UK where he entered a private clinic and was given extensive electroconvulsive therapy. In 1963 he returned to America after spending almost two years undergoing psychotherapy in East Berlin. He never performed or recorded again. This was one of his last albums.

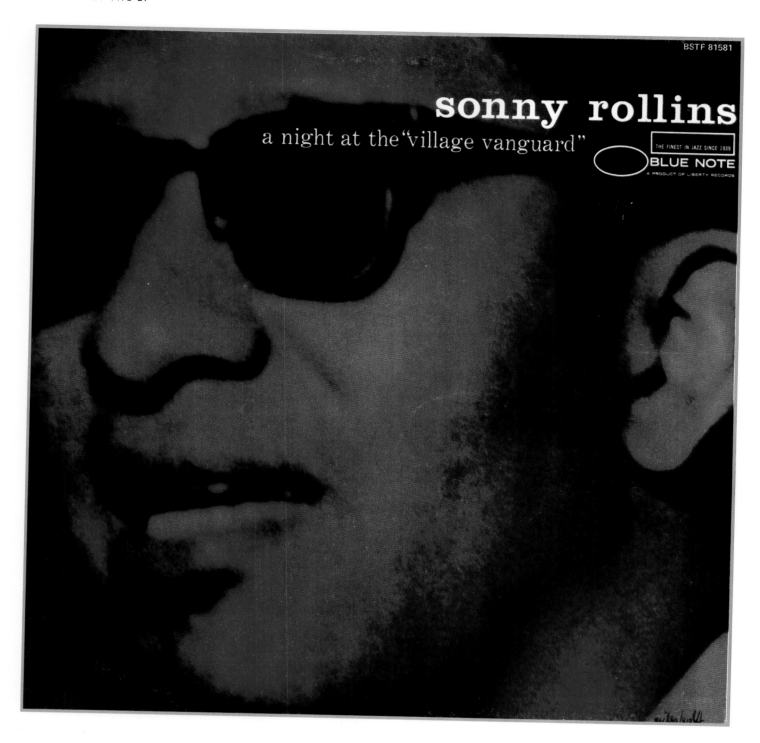

Sonny Rollins A Night at the "Village Vanguard"

1957
Blue Note
America
Sleeve design by Reid Miles
Photography by Francis Wolff

Reid Miles began his work at Blue Note in 1956, but his influence wasn't immediately apparent in sleeve designs for the company. Francis Wolff's photos had already been used on the company's releases and typographically they'd all been interesting, even groundbreaking. However, with this release Miles made his mark and a political point. He had already rendered jazz players in different, unnatural colors—John Coltrane in blue, for instance—and had used large portrait shots on covers. This was the first time he'd put such a large headshot so boldly on display, though. It was the first live recording to be made at the Vanguard (which opened in 1934) and it was Rollins's first recording as the leader of a live band. The photo printed with a red overtone is challenging, forceful (and the red runs the risk of suggesting Communist sympathies to hysterical elements in the country), and the dark glasses and thrusting appearance of Rollins all combine to create an almost sinister impression. The color of the sleeve negates the color of the sax player's skin and suggests danger.

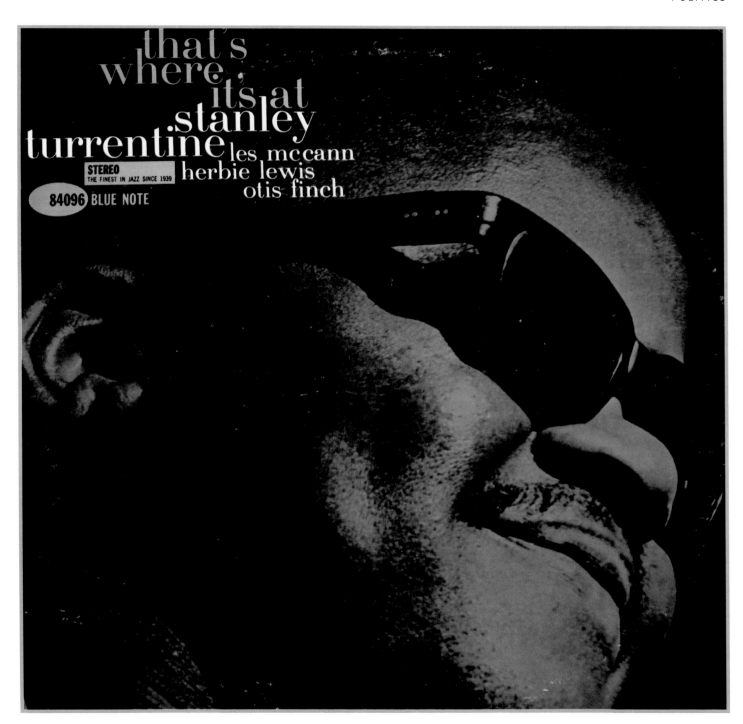

1962
Blue Note
America
Sleeve design by Reid Miles
Photography by Francis Wolff

Stanley Turrentine That's Where It's At

Five years after the cover opposite, Reid did it again, but differently. This time the color is blue, the face smiling. It's still a thrusting, full-on head shot with shades, surrounded by black borders; and it's still awe-inspiring. Turrentine wasn't as challenging a musician as Rollins—quite the opposite, in fact—but what he was attempting to do with jazz was almost as revolutionary. There had been a growing interest among white music fans in soul music (the sleeve notes here use the term "funk" for possibly the first time on record) and Turrentine (here on his only recording of the decade with soulful piano man Les McCann, who would score a worldwide hit in 1969 with his composition "Compared to What") mixed the rhythm and feel of the sound of Memphis, Detroit and his native Pittsburgh in his music. It wasn't what Blue Note or avid jazz fans were used to hearing, but it helped to bring even more people into jazz clubs, and break down the social and color barriers that were still very much in place in America in 1962, pre-Beatles and British Invasion.

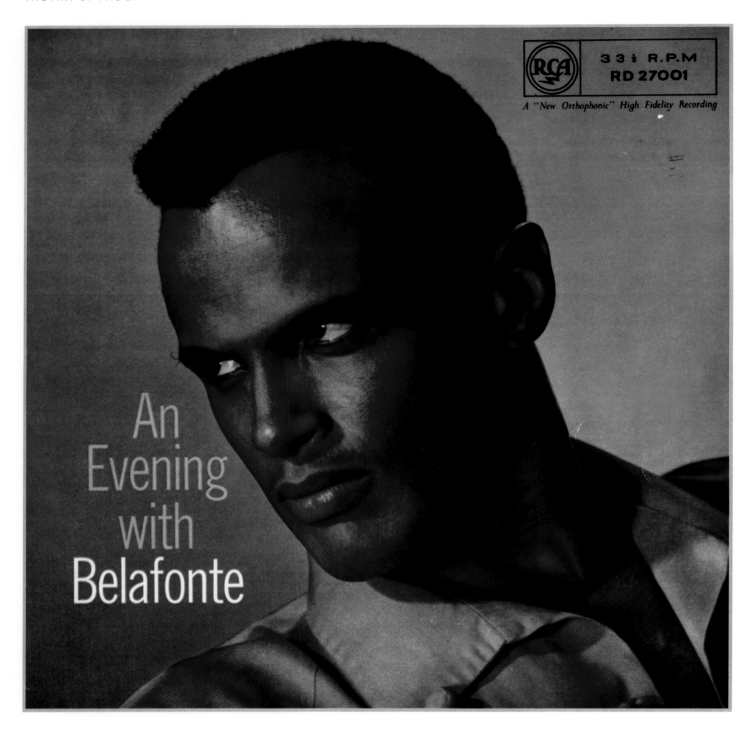

An
Evening
with
Belafonte

RCA 33⅓ R.P.M
RD 27001
A "New Orthophonic" High Fidelity Recording

1957
RCA Victor
America
Sleeve design and photography
uncredited

Harry Belafonte An Evening with Belafonte

The previous year Harry Belafonte had become world famous after
recording a novelty calypso song entitled "Day-O (The Banana Boat Song")".
Inoffensive, catchy and destined to be an eternal kids' song included
on endless compilations made just for the little ones, it introduced the
smiling, inoffensive entertainer to the world. The follow-up hit, a song all
about naughty children ("Mama Look at Bu-bu") was just as inoffensive.
And so Belafonte had already been welcomed into the homes of the white
supremacist-believing middle- and working-class homes of America
when he delivered this, complete with a non-smiling, heroic and damned
handsome portrait on the cover. Inspired by Robeson (see p. 331) and an
active civil rights campaigner, Belafonte played the entertainer game up
to a point, helping to erode ancient prejudices slowly, from the inside. It
was a brave move to use this image on the cover of the follow-up release
to *Calypso* (which had included "Day-O"). The album includes, among other
international folk songs, a version of "Hava Nageela."

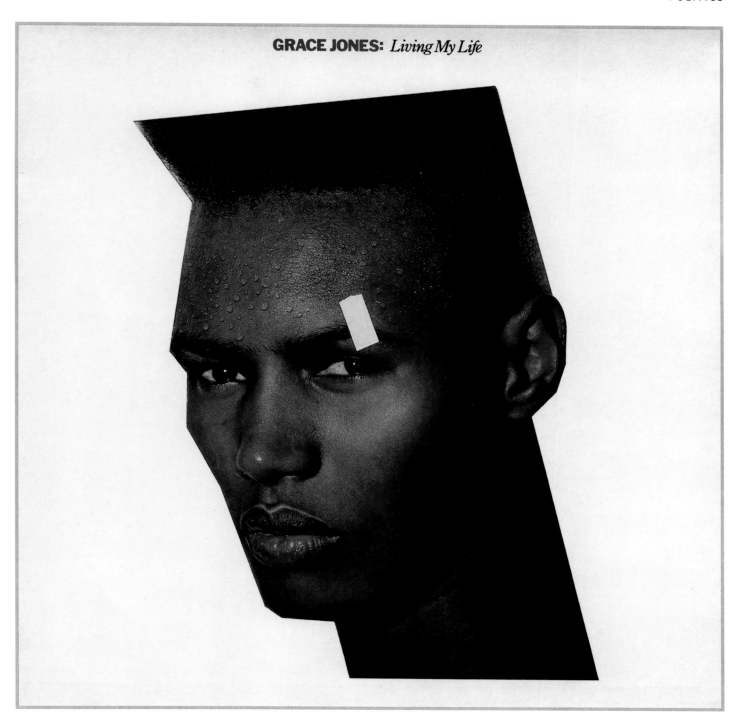

GRACE JONES: *Living My Life*

1982
Island Records
England
Sleeve design by Jean-Paul Goude and
Rob O'Connor
Photography by Jean-Paul Goude

Grace Jones Living My Life

Ex-model Jones had made a trio of disco albums in the late seventies and became muse to Andy Warhol in the process. However, crossover success eluded her. It was her relationship with French-born photographer and stylist Jean-Paul Goude that changed everything. The sexual and racial politics were clear: why should black women have to look ethnic, why should they even have to look female? Why can't they mix it all up? Goude's androgynous pictures and collages of Jones inspired Island Records boss Chris Blackwell to get her to listen to the emerging new wave music of the time and blend it with the music he instinctively understood: reggae. And so an odd mixture of avant punk (e.g., The Normal's "Warm Leatherette") was fused with backing musicians Sly & Robbie's tropical backbeat and Jones' imperious voice layered over the top. Producer Blackwell reportedly stuck one of Goude's shots on the studio wall and said to the musicians while creating the album, "Make it sound like that!"

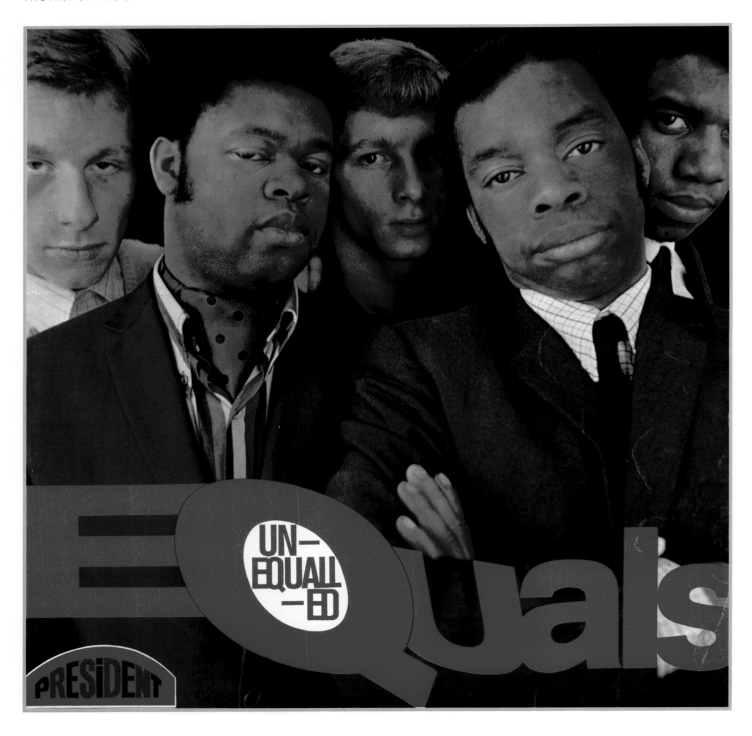

The Equals Unequalled

1967
President Records
England
Sleeve design and photography
uncredited

While there were regular collaborations between black musicians and white in the studio and clubs, there hadn't been a successful interracial pop band until the Equals came along. The songs might have initially been about love and similar teenage angst, but the Equals would also come up with "Police on My Back" (later covered by the Clash and Willie Nelson) and "Black Skinned Blue Eyed Boys." Singer and lead songwriter Eddy Grant, originally from Guinea, left the band after a collapsed lung almost killed him in 1971. He became a hugely successful solo star. The twin brothers Lincoln and Dervin Gordon, along with original members John Hall and Pat Lloyd, continued to perform as the Equals, although they didn't record again. The cover of this, the band's debut album, was a statement of intent: the brothers at the front, looking cool and hip, the five of them tight, together, a team. It led to countless other aspiring Mods forming bands with their friends, whatever their skin color.

Santana Greatest Hits

1974
Columbia
America
Sleeve design by John Berg
Photography by Joel Baldwin

After the worldwide success of *Abraxas* (see p. 106), Mexican guitarist Santana was a big star. The band's appearance at Woodstock had made them hippy darlings and the inclination of leader Carlos Santana to play long, intricate and improvised guitar solos endeared them to fans of the emerging prog rock scene. Santana then heard and became a fan of British guitarist John McLaughlin and his Mahavishnu Orchestra. The men became friends and Santana became a devotee of the same Indian guru as the Brit, Sri Chinmoy. The guru preached peace through meditation and universal love. When Columbia Records decided to cram the best bits of the first three Santana albums together following Carlos's dissolution of the original line-up in 1973, they took his new religious inclinations as inspiration for this simple and direct cover. The white dove of peace is clutched to the breast of a black man. There are no words or data on the front cover, just this striking and arresting image. The album was a huge hit. Joel Baldwin went on to become a top advertising photographer.

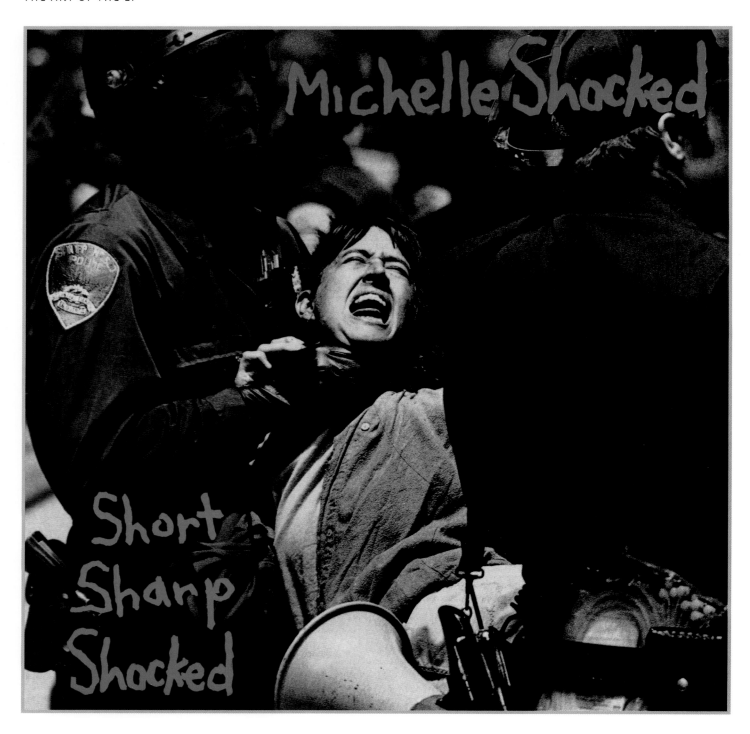

1988
Mercury/Cooking Vinyl
America
Sleeve design by Helen Namm
Photography by Chris Hardy/*San Francisco Examiner*

Michelle Shocked Short Sharp Shocked

Not many Texan singer-songwriters have used their arrest photo as a cover image on their major label debut release, but this shot of Michelle Shocked being restrained by police at a National Democratic Convention protest in San Francisco in 1984 is exactly that. *San Francisco Examiner* photographer Chris Hardy captured the moment and the paper ran it. Four years later, Shocked was a fast-emerging musical talent signed to a Mercury. Her low-fi debut, *The Texas Campfire Tapes*, had been produced and issued by a tiny UK label in 1986, to rave reviews in the UK music press. As is often the case, a major label listened up and signed her. This cover was partly an attempt on the artist's part to show her radical roots in the face of accusations of having "sold out." Although Shocked started as a protest folk singer, her first (of only two) hit single was a more personal song entitled "Anchorage," taken from this album. She went on to record a number of old American folk songs for Mercury, before entering litigation with them to get out of the contract. She succeeded, and now releases all her material on her own label.

Al Kooper You Never Know Who Your Friends Are

1969
Columbia
America
Sleeve design by Fred Lombardi
Photography by Don Hustein

Multitalented musician and singer Kooper played organ on Bob Dylan's first all-electric album; he formed the Blues Project which became Blood, Sweat & Tears and introduced Stephen Stills to Mike Bloomfield. Kooper also discovered and produced Lynyrd Skynyrd, and played on Stones, Who and Hendrix albums. Plus, he released some fabulous if underrated solo albums, of which this is the second. The cover shows U.S. state police breaking up a student demo, the title in dripping blood adding extra feeling to the title. It was happening all over America at the time: U.S. cops beating kids with clubs, shooting them with rubber—and soon live—bullets.

Mark Stewart As the Veneer of Democracy Starts to Fade

1985
On-U Sound
England
Sleeve design by Mark Stewart
Photography uncredited

Originally from Bristol, UK, Mark Stewart had formed the uncompromising punk band Pop Group in 1978. They produced a unique blend of reggae, punk, jazz and free-form sounds. They had an extreme anarchist political view, which was clearly derived from Stewart. After Pop Group split, other members formed a pop band (Pigbag) and a jazz outfit (Rip, Rig & Panic), while Stewart became more extreme both politically and musically. Mixing dub sounds with electronic beats, his distorted vocals swell through the sound clash, chanting anticapitalist rants. Exactly what you'd expect from a record with a cover like this.

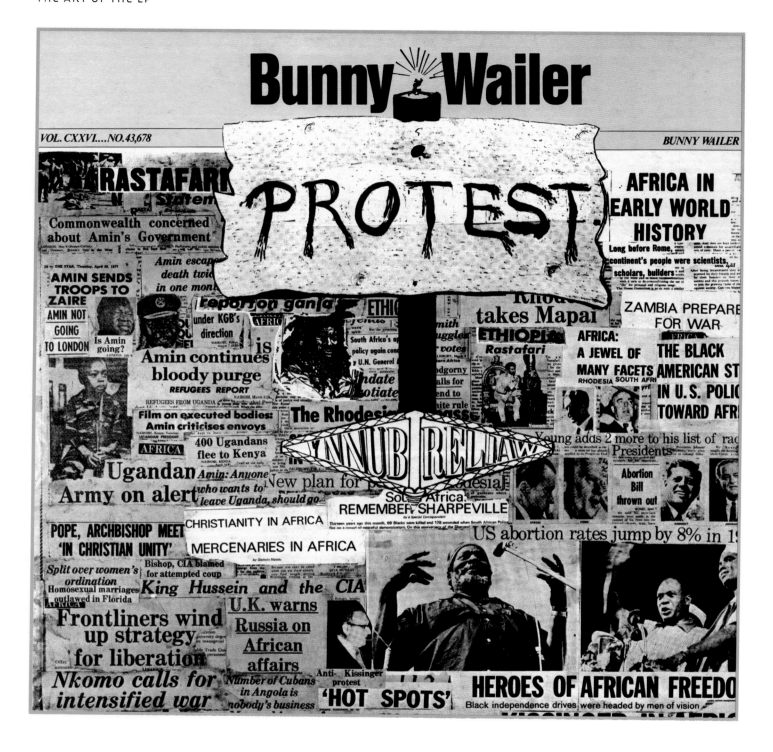

Bunny Wailer Protest

1977
Island Records/Solomonic
England/Jamaica
Sleeve design uncredited

This incredibly simple yet shocking idea was used on the original Jamaican release of Bunny Wailer's second solo album and kept for the UK and world release. Bunny Wailer grew up in the same home as Bob Marley, his father having formed a relationship with Marley's mother when both were young boys. They formed the Wailers together with Peter Tosh in the 1960s and became the most influential and successful musical trio in Jamaican music in the early 1970s. After leaving the Wailers as they came to be seen more as Marley's backing band in the mid-1970s, Bunny began recording his own, Rasta-inspired, politically infused songs. His debut release, *Blackheart Man*, includes a who's who of the great Jamaican reggae musicians of the day, including Tosh, Aston Barrett and Robbie Shakespeare among others. The clippings displayed on *Protest* are from a variety of newspapers and bear reports on African and American events, the style of the design possibly inspired by the cut-up and "blackmail" graphics then being employed on punk records.

The Mighty Diamonds Stand Up to Your Judgement

1978
Channel One Recordings
Jamaica
Sleeve design and illustration
uncredited

Jamaica in the 1970s was rife with political struggle, which provoked assassinations, kidnapping and riots. Still under British colonial rule (the law courts in particular were answerable to the UK justice system), the head of state today is England's Queen Elizabeth II. In the 1970s the country was run by white politicians, and the prime minister, Michael Manley, was biracial. Manley was the fourth to hold the position, and was the son of the nation's second prime minister, Norman Manley (1955—1962). His opponent, Edward Seaga, was a Boston-born white man. The parties of both men waged a bloody war during the 1976 elections, leading to a state of emergency to be installed. Manley won that election, but lost four years later after more violent confrontations between his People's National Party and Seaga's Jamaican Labour Party. The Mighty Diamonds, a close-harmony trio who took dancehall into roots reggae, were making an antiviolence statement with the cover. "Death to everyone," chants each crudely drawn character, until the final one simply says "death. . . ."

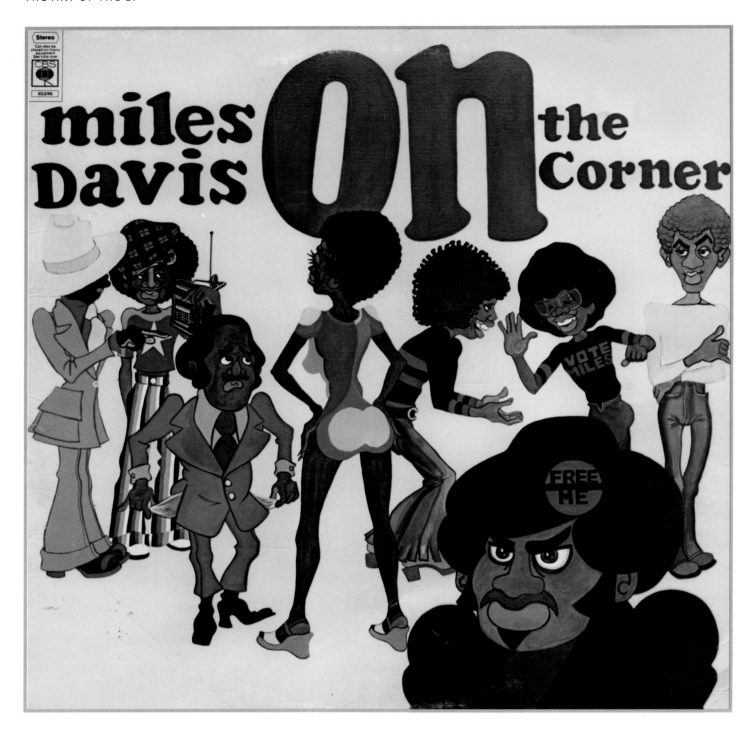

Miles Davis On the Corner

1972
Columbia
America
Illustration by Corky McCoy

By the time of this release, it looked as if Davis's jazz fusion, or "New Directions in Music" was really working commercially (see *Bitches Brew*, p. 107 and *Silent Way*, p. 213). Still with Teo Macero as producer, Davis was beginning to take things further, citing avant-garde composer Stockhausen as an influence. Previous album *Live-Evil* had used another Mati Klarwein dreamscape as cover art but now Miles wanted to connect with a younger, more socially conscious black audience and asked former roommate and cartoonist Corky McCoy to design something that they'd like. His depiction of a "typical" street corner shows poverty, political awareness, prostitution and plenty of attitude. But the public just didn't get it and it didn't sell. Perhaps fans objected to what they saw as racial stereotyping, though it was more likely that, again, Davis's music was ahead of its time. Still, it's a great sleeve and McCoy would go on to design several more for Davis. Columbia's six-CD box set released in 2008 recreated it in a three-dimensional metal case.

The Mothers of Invention Weasels Ripped My Flesh

1970
Bizarre
America
Cover concept by Frank Zappa
Art direction by John Williams
Painting by Neon Park

Artist Neon Park is best known for his work with Little Feat (see p. 161). However, before he met them he was asked by Frank Zappa to create this cover for his band the Mothers of Invention's seventh album in four years. Zappa had seen Park's work for the Family Dog poster company in San Francisco and liked it, so he called Park to ask him if he could produce something based on the cover of a magazine called *Man's Life*, which featured an illustration of a man in a river, being attacked by weasels. Park's resultant artwork is a damning and witty indictment of American consumer society. A smiling executive type uses an electric shaver in the shape of a weasel, and smiles while making the sound of the razor, just as the model in a contemporary Schick electric razor ad might do. A little discomfort while doing one's patriotic duty—to consume—is nothing as long as one does that duty, is the message. Park met then member of the Mothers, Lowell George, while working on the sleeve and they became friends. The rest is illustrated history, as they almost say.

Funkadelic One Nation Under a Groove

1978
Warner Brothers
America
Art direction by Ed Thrasher
Illustration by Pedro Bell

This cover has echoes of the American flag being raised on Iwo Jima, and the album tracks are printed on the new, Funkadelic nation's flag (reading like a manifesto). This is a clear and deliberate call to arms. Or rather, a call to dance. George Clinton was the blissed-out, fabulously attired, groove-master central of a shifting musical collective known as Funkadelic. And he wanted to rule a country, so he set about creating a new nation, one in which color of skin meant nothing as long as you could dance. The album, Funkadelic's tenth, came as a 12" LP plus a 7" EP, and it became the band's biggest hit record to date, making #16 on the Billboard Hot 200 album chart. Funkadelic hadn't changed the world much with *America Eats Its Young* (see p. 347), nor had they found people obeying George's mandate to *Free Your Mind . . . And Your Ass Will Follow*, but with *One Nation*'s title track making it into the UK Top 40 charts, people did want to get down just for the funk of it. The "so high" and "so low" lines have been used several times since in different songs by numerous artists.

STEREO

Music for Peace

Mary Lou Williams ... and her friends

Mary Lou Williams and her Friends Music for Peace

Pianist Mary Lou Williams (1910—1981) had rejected jazz music, from which she had made an increasingly good living for twenty years, in 1954. She converted to the Roman Catholic faith and refused to perform live until Dizzy Gillespie and a priest persuaded her to return to music. With a Roman Catholic priest as manager, Mary Lou wrote and recorded religiously inspired music, helping other musicians to find gigs and a (religious) voice for themselves on her own label, Mary Records. In 1969 she wrote "Mary Lou's Mass," as *Music for Peace* came to be called. Illustrator David Stone Martin (1913—1992) had made his name creating illustrations for jazz covers in the late 1940s and through the 1950s before creating hand-drawn covers for *Time* magazine in the 1960s and 1970s. The symbol that Martin has created here had become synonymous with the then prevalent hippy movement in America, although it was actually the logo for the British Campaign for Nuclear Disarmament, and was created in 1958 using the semaphore symbols for *N* and *D* by British graphic designer Gerald Holtom.

1970
Mary Records
America
Sleeve illustration by
David Stone Martin

1971
Tamla Motown
America
Sleeve design by Katherine Marking and
Alana Coghlan
Photography by James Hendin
Art direction by Curtis McNair

Marvin Gaye What's Going On

In 1970 Marvin Gaye was the brightest star in Motown's firmament, having
scored the company's biggest hit single ever with "I Heard it Through the
Grapevine" the previous year. Even so, when he demanded artistic control
for his future recordings, label owner Berry Gordy was loath to give it to
him, especially after hearing "What's Going On," describing it as the worst
song he'd ever heard. Gordy stalled on releasing the single, eventually
letting it out with no publicity. The song, demonstrating Gaye's newfound
social conscience, partly affected by the death of his former recording
partner Tammi Terrell in 1970, was a huge hit. Gordy asked for more such
songs. The album includes "Mercy Mercy Me (The Ecology)" and "Inner
City Blues (Make Me Wanna Holler)," among others. Motown photographer
Hendin's shot of Gaye standing in the rain amid the wreckage of an
abandoned children's playground has an almost holy air. Gaye gazes into
the middle distance as if he can see the future, and it's not good. The
close-up photo echoes those on Blue Note covers from two decades earlier.

Funkadelic America Eats Its Young

1972
Westbound Records
America
Cover concept by George Clinton and
Ron Scribner
Illustration by Paul Weldon

The first album to include bassist Bootsy Collins as a member of the
Funkadelic collective, this is a truly political funk album. As with many of
his peers at the time, band leader George Clinton had developed a social
conscience that danced to a funk beat, and this album showcases his
ability to get across political slogans with a stomp. The title track disses
America big-time and the cover design perfectly suits it. Messing with the
dollar had been done before, but never as big as this. The Statue of Liberty
is feeding off a handful of babies, her mouth red with their blood. Yet
things were often not as straightforward as they could be with Funkadelic
and the album also contains songs about sex as well as one number
("Biological Speculation") that seems to be about ecological disaster.
Canadian graphic artist Weldon, who created the dollar, also drew the cover
for Rush's debut album, on which the band's name explodes out in the style
of a superhero comic.

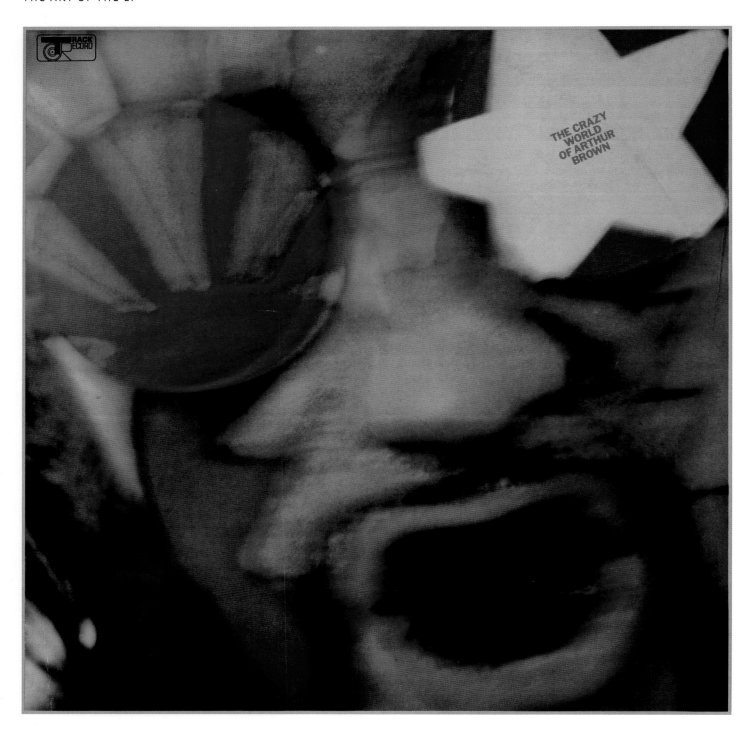

THE CRAZY
WORLD
OF ARTHUR
BROWN

The Crazy World of Arthur Brown
The Crazy World of Arthur Brown

1968
Track/Atlantic
England
Sleeve design by David King
Photography by David Montgomery

This fantastic piece of psychedelic action art manages to make the idea of consuming hallucinogenic drugs look both exciting and terrifying. Arthur Brown wasn't crazy and he wasn't particularly political either, but he was an activist in the war on the "straight world" waged by hippies in the mid-1960s. His live shows included flaming headdresses, nudity, screaming, wild dancing and loud, loud rock & roll. Arthur wanted no limits put on what he could and couldn't do, and damn the consequences. A good twenty years before Michael Jackson was disfigured by his hair catching fire during the filming of a cola advertisement, Arthur's hair caught fire during a live performance and he was saved by members of the audience who dowsed the flames with their beer. The show carried on as if it were a planned part of the action.

Fanny

Mothers Pride

1973
Warner Brothers
America
Sleeve design by Rod Dyer, Inc.
Photography by Leandro Correa

Fanny Mothers Pride

As the feminist movement gained impetus and its influence spread
throughout the Western world, feminist authors, poets and filmmakers
began to get their work noticed and produced. The rock & roll world was a
far more difficult barricade to storm, however, being run and supported
by unreconstructed and essentially adolescent males (emotionally if not
actually). In the early 1970s, if women appeared on stage at rock & roll
concerts they would invariably be wearing very little and shaking their
asses at the crowd. There were a few successful female singer-songwriters
and vocalists, but the only all-female groups that existed were vocal
groups; Fanny changed all that. It was the first hard rocking all-female
band where the members played their own instruments, wrote their own
songs and did not show off their bodies for an audience's titillation. Led
by sisters Jean and June Millington, they signed to Reprise in 1969. This was
their fourth studio album (of five). The disturbing baby doll with stars in its
eyes is a subtle and clever play on chauvinist expectations of the band.

1973
Mercury Records
America
Sleeve design by Album Graphics, Inc.
Photography by Toshi Asaka

New York Dolls *New York Dolls*

With the exception of David Bowie, glamorous, androgenous rock & roll never really happened in the United States. So even if on the face of it today the New York Dolls look a little comical and kind of like Bowie's band the Spiders from Mars, their adoption of this look was very brave. They outraged fellow New Yorkers, so imagine how it was in the rest of the country, particularly the conservative Midwest. There is an endearing attention to detail with the styling here, made clear on the album credits, which list, "Hair by Shin," "Makeup by Dave O'Grady." Despite that, as was often the case at the time, only a couple of members of the band look comfortable with the part they're playing, that of degenerate, possibly homosexual, guys in drag. Yet it helped to empower gender-challenged transvestites everywhere to flaunt their stuff while also opening up conventional society just a little more to the idea that nonconformity was everywhere—and attractive.

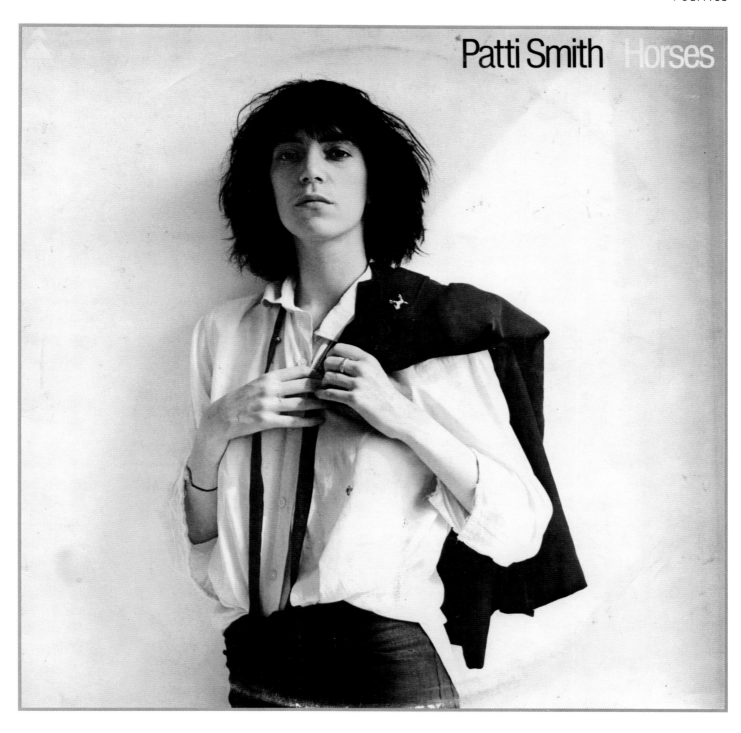

Patti Smith Horses

1975
Arista Records
America
Photography by Robert Mapplethorpe

Patti Smith Horses

Like Dusty Springfield in 1964 (see p. 216), Patti Smith was having nothing to do with how female singers were normally depicted on sleeves. Arista Records boss Clive Davis had given Smith complete control over her image and so she used her ex-boyfriend Robert Mapplethorpe to take the photo for the cover of her debut major label release. Mapplethorpe used his boyfriend Sam Wagstaff's New York apartment because the light was so good. Patti bought a suit in Saks Fifth Avenue especially for the picture but made no special effort to tidy her hair or apply any makeup. She nonetheless looks astonishing—sexy, intelligent and righteous. Almost a feminist statement in itself, the resulting picture was hated by her record company but it went on to define her image while striking a blow for female rockers who didn't want to have to bare their bodies or conform to sexual stereotypes in order to sell their music.

1981
Statik Records
America
Sleeve design by Winston Smith/Fallout
Productions and Jello Biafra

Dead Kennedys In God We Trust, Inc.

Jello Biafra's Dead Kennedys were always the most satirical of American punk bands. Their names, the songs and the imagery used were all employed to make people think, laugh and then think again. Here is Christ crucified on a collage of U.S. dollar bills, the title in—what else—gold, the font echoing that of the Federal Reserve's own print style. It's aimed at the hypocrisy of America, the religious right and moral majority who in Ronald Reagan had their own sheriff in the White House. Designer Winston Smith's name is taken from George Orwell's nightmare vision of a totalitarian future, *1984*. His work was used on several releases from the Alternative Tentacles label in San Francisco, and has also appeared on a Green Day album, *Insomniac*. Sometimes referred to as an EP because the eight songs on it are so short, this was in fact the band's second album and included DK classics "Nazi Punks Fuck Off"—the single version of which made #31 on the UK singles chart—and "We've Got A Bigger Problem Now."

Killing Joke Killing Joke

1980
EG Records
England
Sleeve design uncredited

It's amazing to think that agit-rock band Killing Joke actually released their debut album on EG Records, home to art school rock society such as Roxy Music, Brian Eno and King Crimson. His fellow labelmates were the sort of musicians you can imagine KJ singer Jaz Coleman wanting to destroy. Killing Joke's aggressive hardcore sound was a major influence on the alt-rock scene, which grew throughout the eighties on both sides of the Atlantic and reached its commercial apex with Nirvana—who KJ accused of stealing their song "Eighties" for "Come As You Are." Killing Joke's artwork reflects Coleman's hoarse, angry vocals and the band's industrial rock. Possibly achieved via the commonly used eighties method of degenerative photocopying, this picture of figures climbing over a wall could be any one of a number of scenarios, but the message is plain: it's anarchy out there and we are at the center of it.

The Contortions Buy

1979
Ze Records
America
Cover by Anya Phillips

New York jazz punks the Contortions were led by saxophonist and singer James Chance. Part of the now legendary "No Wave" scene, they were managed by Chance's girlfriend Anya Phillips. A New Yorker, she cofounded the city's famous late seventies hangout the Mudd club. Phillips was a fashion designer as well as a professional dominatrix. She came up with Chance's 1940s suit and tie look, as he admitted: "She more or less came up with the look that I have stuck with since then." The bikini in the picture is one of her bizarre creations and while it reveals lots of flesh, the torn appearance provokes unease: has it been ripped in an attack? It manages to be both antimaterialistic and antisexist, alienating and compelling. Phillips died of cancer in 1981.

Liz Phair Exile In Guyville

1993
Matador Records
America
Sleeve design by Liz Phair & Mark O
Photography by Nate Kato

Anyone who has heard "Fuck And Run" will know that Phair's debut album was controversial largely because it deals with relationships in a frank, unflinching way. But the artwork was controversial too. What is she saying here? It was created with fellow musician Nate Kato from post-grunge band Urge Overkill. He was filming her miming to one of her songs in a photo booth and asked her to take her shirt off. As Phair says, "Then I brought out the product . . . and he was like, 'This is the album cover! This is so nineties!' And he cropped it all up for me and I thought that was really cool." It's definitely nineties but perhaps in an exploitative way, as with photographs in nineties guy magazines such as *Maxim*.

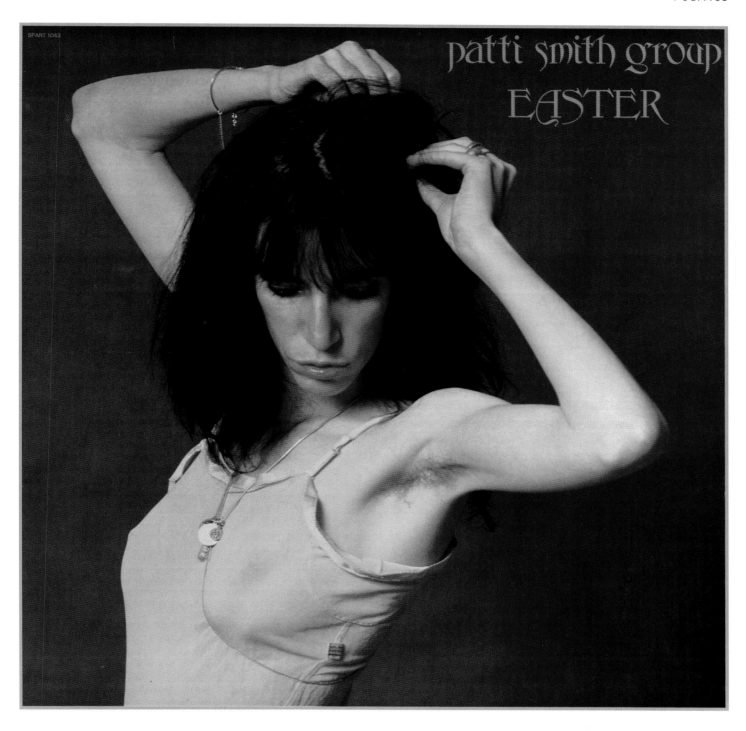

SPART 1043

patti smith group
EASTER

Patti Smith Easter

1978
Arista Records
America
Photography by Lynn Goldsmith

Three years after her groundbreaking debut (see p. 351) and its follow-up *Radio Ethiopia*, Patti Smith returned with this. It turned out to be her most commercial album, mainly because it contained "Because The Night," a song she cowrote with Bruce Springsteen and which became her first big hit single. For the cover shot here Smith used Lynn Goldsmith, a photographer and film director. Goldsmith's photograph of Smith achieves a similar effect to that of Mapplethorpe's three years previously: it makes a bold feminist statement in that Smith shows that she is not interested in makeup or shaving her underarm hair, while at the same time she looks sexy. The photo was also the first and almost only time that Smith used a color shot on a cover. In the 1980s Lynn Goldsmith signed to Island as Will Powers and had a big hit in Britain with "Kissing with Confidence."

1979
Island
England
Sleeve design by Bloomfield/Travis
Photography by Pennie Smith

The Slits Cut

In some ways the sleeve of the Slits' debut album overshadows the fact that it is a good record. A good record in a truly great sleeve. Like John-Paul Goude's Grace Jones photos, this is a shot which contains a proto-feminist message: just because they are women with their breasts out doesn't mean that they are there to be objectified. There is also something witty and playful in Pennie Smith's picture, suggesting that the band actually isn't posing at all but has been caught on camera just messing around in the garden. Smith's iconic *London Calling* photograph of Paul Simonon smashing his bass (see p. 11) and many of her other photographs have a similar natural feel, despite being taken in contrived situations. The album title could be a comment on the cover pose, as if they're acting at being "Amazons," the legendary female warriors of ancient Greek myth. Or it could be a deliberate misspelling in reference to the band's name. The Slits had always played with conventional masculine ideas of femininity; they used to perform wearing men's underwear over their outer clothes.

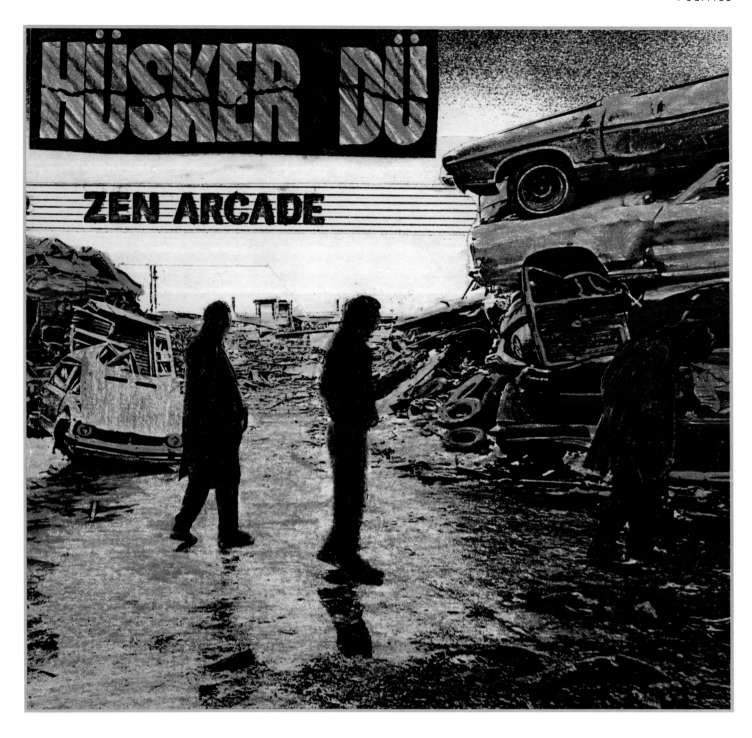

Hüsker Dü Zen Arcade

1984
SST Records
America
Artwork by Fake Name Graphics
Photography by Mark Peterson

Although not as overtly political as either the Dead Kennedys or Black Flag, hardcore trio Hüsker Dü from Minneapolis had politics that were more personal. Singer-guitarist Bob Mould spent eight years with the band writing emotionally raw love songs (this album contains a two-minute thrash entitled "I Will Never Forget You" on which he repeats the title with increasing harshness as the song speeds to an end) but never admitted that he was gay. Drummer and co-songwriter Grant Hart is also gay but it was never a defining element of the band's music or identity. Zen Arcade, a double album recorded in forty-five hours and the second to be put out by Black Flag's Greg Ginn's SST, is a concept album about an adolescent's problematic coming of age. The cover, shot in an auto junkyard is elegantly morose, the harsh hand-tinting lighting up the dark, wet scene. That it's an auto junkyard lends the political angle: so many autos sit in states of disrepair, rusting, piled precariously on top of one another. It's a metaphor for the state of Hüsker Dü world and the decaying American dream.

BLACK FLAG III

FAMILY MAN
A SPOKEN
WORD/INSTRUMENTAL RECORD

1984
SST Records
America
Sleeve art by Raymond Pettibon

Black Flag Family Man

Greg Ginn's Black Flag was the first true American hardcore band. They
formed in California in 1977 (originally as Panic) and extolled the UK punk
scene's do-it-yourself ethos. Ginn set up SST to record bands like his who
made fast, complex, dissonant music and who sang about politics from
an anarchist angle. The band's name and logo was developed by Raymond
Pettibon with Ginn, his brother (Raymond changed his name). The black flag
was the anarchist ensign—if there could be such a thing. This is the band's
third album, the second to use a Pettibon illustration on the cover, and
the first to have one side composed almost entirely of spoken word pieces
read by the singer and author Henry Rollins, who joined BF in 1981. The other
side is composed entirely of instrumental pieces. The cover references the
assassination of JFK (in the date) while lampooning the "straight" world of
mother, father and two children representing "normality" in traditional U.S.
society. Pettibon would draw a nun grasping a naked male leg for their next
album cover, but it was almost comical and not nearly as shocking as this.

Sonic Youth Goo

1990
Geffen
America
Sleeve design by Kevin Reagan
Illustration by Raymond Pettibon

Sonic Youth came from the other coast from Black Flag and the Dead Kennedys, and they began slightly later (1981), yet their concerns were pretty similar. The political, both federal and personal, concerned the New York quartet just as much as it did the hardcore bands of the West. Sonic Youth's sound was not as fast or buzzing either, taking their inspiration from Patti Smith, Television and John Cage in a typically New York art-rock style. By the time they had signed to major label Geffen and released this, their debut for the company, Sonic Youth had developed a following through the release of six albums (two with SST). *Goo* proved to be their most successful release, partly because of Pettibon's typically subversive artwork, the title of which is printed in the top right of the sleeve. The scotch tape was designer Reagan's addition, in an attempt to make the big, rich record company look cheap.

....THE TUBES...........................REMOTE CONTROL.....

1979

A&M Records

America

Sleeve design by Michael Cotten and
Prairie Prince

Photography by Jim McCrary

Art direction by Roland Young

Cover coordination by Chuck Beeson

Cover concept by Jeff Ayeroff

Vidi trainer built by Dave Mellott and
Michael Cotten

The Tubes Remote Control

The Tubes formed in 1975 in San Francisco with a healthy amount of
cynicism and humor. The debut album, *The Tubes*, was produced by Al
Kooper (see p. 339) and included what would become their theme song,
"White Punks On Dope." The song was a satirical anthem deriding their
middle-class following, but that didn't seem to bother their fans, who
increased as each album was released, and each new, theatrical stage
show concocted (though that may also have been because they employed
more and more scantily dressed women for their shows and brought in
S&M themes). The cover for this, the band's fourth studio album, apes the
Who's *Tommy*, an idiot brought up and thriving only on TV. The cover was
an epic construction, involving various band members (Prairie Prince and
Michael Cotten) and the creation of the TV as baby-feeder—that's a bottle
with a rubber nipple on the side of the screen. Unfortunately their lavish,
expensive and hugely theatrical live shows were never well supported by
album sales and they had to scale back by the mid-eighties.

Nirvana Nevermind

1991
Geffen
America
Sleeve design by Robert Fisher
Photography by Kirk Weddle

When one of Nirvana frontman Kurt Cobain's heroes had signed to Geffen (see Sonic Youth, p. 359), it was OK for Nirvana to sign too. Only it wasn't. This album and the enormously successful single from it, "Smells Like Teen Spirit," made the band the biggest in the world briefly, and that damaged the already shaky psyche of Cobain. This plaintive image of a very young baby following the dollar through water is symbolic not just of America's kids in general, caring only for money and what it can buy, but also for Nirvana. The underwater baby was swimming for the first time (proving that we can all swim but many have it frightened out of us) and the dollar was on a hook provided by Cobain, both physically and conceptually.

1978
EMI Records
England
Sleeve design by Cookie Key
Photography by Trevor Key

X-Ray Spex Germ Free Adolescents

X-Ray Spex singer Poly Styrene (real name Marian Joan Elliott Said; she is the daughter of a dispossessed Somalian aristocrat) wrote witty caustic lyrics that gave punk an early female voice. Her songs "Oh! Bondage Up Yours" and "I'm A Cliché" remain classics of the genre. This was their first and only album, a sizeable hit in the UK. The cover is inspired by the title song, a keyboard-driven hypnotic ballad about being a cleanliness-obsessed teenager and an antimaterialistic anthem decrying the unnaturalness of factory-produced, sterile products made to make us not smell human. The band in their test tubes—unnatural, inhumanly produced; in-vitro fertilization was in its infancy at the time—wear trademark DayGlo shirts and socks (the band's previous hit had been "The Day the World Turned DayGlo") and, despite the potential for the whole thing to collapse in comedy (think of Spinal Tap trying to get out of their on-stage pods), it works remarkably well. Photographer Trevor Key also photographed various Orchestral Manoeuvres in the Dark album covers, for designer Peter Saville.

Aimee Mann I'm with Stupid

1996
Geffen
America
Artwork concept by Aimee Mann
Photography by Kate Garner
Art direction by Gail Marowitz
Design by Aimee Mann & Gail Marowitz

Aimee Mann, a Virginia-born singer, was living in London during the early nineties when she made this. Instead of phoning Oasis and Blur to help out with the recording, though, Aimee prudently opted to work with Squeeze main men Glen Tilbrook and Chris Difford as well as recently departed Suede guitarist Bernard Butler and Rutle Neil Innes. The artwork concept was around even while she was recording it and photographer Kate Garner makes it work fantastically well. What parent hasn't used fridge magnet letters to spell out adult messages? Mann's often painful examination of fractured relationships and conventional gender roles is made visually accessible here and the design is arguably better than that of later album *The Forgotten Arm*, for which she and Gail Marowitz won a Grammy Award.

GIL SCOTT-HERON   REFLECTIONS

1981
Arista Records
America
Sleeve design uncredited

Gil Scott-Heron Reflections

Gil Scott-Heron is the daddy of all clued-up hip-hop and rap music. But it wasn't really until this album that he got a sleeve worthy of his radical street poetry. Early artwork had simply featured him looking serious or, from the mid-seventies onward, had been obsessed with attempting to illustrate his lyrics about apartheid in South Africa, Ronald Reagan's foreign policy and the plight of African Americans. Here, while the title is again taken literally, instead of going off into a mess of conceptual pictures (like, for example, 1975's *From South Africa To South Carolina*), visual references to his words are contained within the sunglasses, and kept in black and white. The composition looks great and the politics are hard hitting. Inside the shades look out for, among other things, Klansmen, Reagan, Billie Holiday, Miles Davis and the Statue of Liberty. The message is clear: Gil Scott-Heron is a man of color, but he sees a black-and-white world reflected back at him.

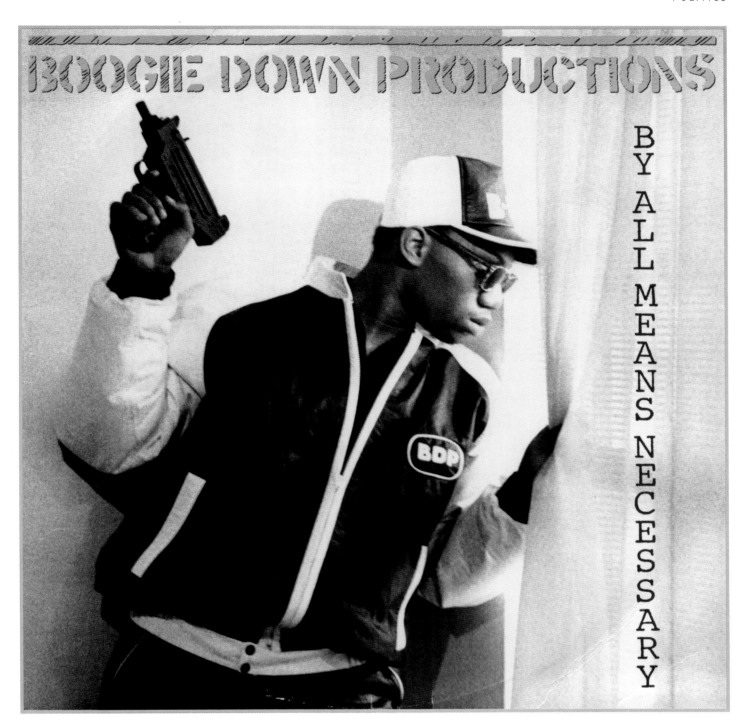

BOOGIE DOWN PRODUCTIONS

BY ALL MEANS NECESSARY

1988
Zomba/BMG Records
America
Photography by Doug Rowell

Boogie Down Productions By All Means Necessary

The album title and the pose are all taken from Malcolm X. The pose, of BDP founder KRS-One, is a modern updating of a black-and-white image of Malcolm X as he peers through net curtains, holding an M15 rifle, although Malcolm wore a suit and tie. The quote was "We want freedom by any means necessary. We want justice by any means necessary. We want equality by any means necessary." Not only the clothes and gun were updated; though the pose, light and angles are all pretty correct. This is the second album by the outfit, who had lost a founding member the previous year in a shooting when Scott La Rock Sterling was killed in the Bronx. He had made some musical contributions to this album before his death, but following it, his erstwhile rap partner KRS dropped his former gangsta image and adopted the new moniker of Teacher, and began rapping against violence as a means to any kind of suitable end. Malcolm might have agreed.

Sly & The Family Stone There's a Riot Going On

1971
Epic
America
Sleeve design by John Berg
Photography by Steve Paley

Set against the context of Black Power and anti-American feeling due to the country's involvement in Vietnam, a photograph of the U.S. flag (taken by Epic A&R director Paley) becomes a complex and powerful message. Stone was inspired by Marvin Gaye's *What's Going On* to change his album title from its original name *Africa Talks to You*. But Sly's intentions were typically unfocused and apolitical; he originally wanted suns instead of stars on the flag, because, as he says in Miles Marshall Lewis's book on the album, "There are already too many stars in this world."

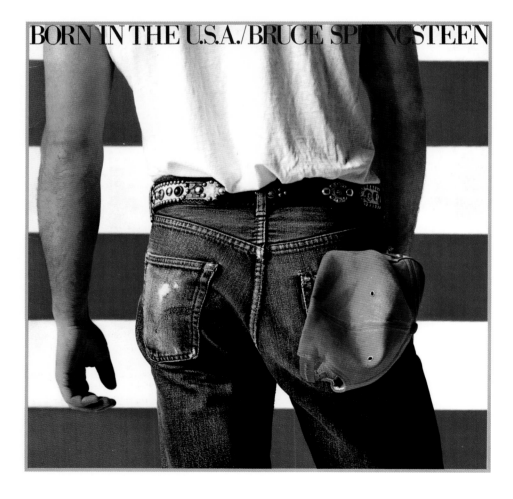

Bruce Springsteen Born in the U.S.A.

1984
Columbia
America
Sleeve design by Andrea Klein
Photography by Annie Leibovitz

Springsteen's biggest-selling album was frequently misunderstood as a gung-ho celebration of all things American, which is precisely why it sold so well. But of course the lyrics to the title track (a massive hit) revolve around a Vietnam vet not being able to get a job on his return to his homeland. Celebrity photographer Annie Leibovitz's now iconic cover shot of Springsteen's Levi's-clad rear only fueled the idea that the album was celebrating America. His blue collar outfit of jeans, white T-shirt and baseball cap combined with the stripes of Old Glory is much less complex than the album's themes and can be read positively or negatively.

The Black Crowes Amorica

Apparently taken from a 1976 United States Bicentennial issue of *Hustler* magazine, the cover for blues rockers Black Crowes' third album was not intended to make any political point about the state of the Union. Or was it? Certainly some record stores reacted badly to it and Def American was forced to black out the offending image. But what's so different about this crotch shot with its tuft of pubic hair pointing out and, say, the sleeve to *Country Life* (see p. 66)? Pubic hair is similarly on display on Roxy Music's cover which also, arguably, suggests masturbation. The difference is of course the flag. This was America, not "Amorica." It's an oddly old-fashioned protest statement really, one that could easily have been made in 1969 to illustrate the protest to Make Love, Not War; except that it would have been banned before leaving the printers in the sixties, for fear of offending the factory workers who would have to handle the sleeve during production of the album.

1994
Def American
America
Sleeve design by Janet Levinson
Art and art direction concept by Chris
Robinson and Janet Levinson

DEATH

This is the end, beautiful friend. And in the end . . . Rock music in all its many forms has always been fascinated with mortality. In 1956 Elvis recorded "Old Shep," a maudlin old song about a dog who stays faithful to his deceased master. In 1986 Slayer released *Reign in Blood*, the multimillion selling "heaviest album of all time" according to one music magazine, the first track of which is entitled "Angel of Death."

Between "Old Shep" and *Reign In Blood* there are a multitude of death-obsessed, dark-side exploring records that have been contained within suitably wreath-like covers. All the imagery we associate with death, ghosts, the spilling of blood, devil-worship and angels has been employed in one form or another as album cover art.

In the pages of this final chapter you'll see some disturbing images, and some that are laughable in their attempts to shock by displaying some kind of Satanic worship. It is perhaps inevitable that as music, from jazz and rock to rap and metal, has sought to stretch the boundaries of what is considered bad taste, that all areas of once taboo topics are covered.

While blatant sexism and depictions of graphic sexual activity are not acceptable, they were nonetheless more prevalent by the early 1990s than they had been before. Likewise, bad language had lost much of its power to shock. Yet shock is what much rock, rap and metal music seeks to do. The question is, then, what was left to do in order to shock?

The answer is to exploit the last taboos remaining in the largely Christian Western world, those of death and Satanism. Which is what many of the sleeves in this chapter do. It's not all doom and gloom, however. Many attempts at shocking are shockingly funnily, whether intentional or not.

1963
United Artists Jazz
America
Sleeve design by Gauna-Douglas
Photography by Toni Frisell

Bill Evans Jim Hall Undercurrent

This astounding underwater photo (entitled "Weeki Wachi Spring, Florida") was taken by New York socialite and World War II camerawoman Toni Frisell in Florida in 1947. The ethereal, elegant image full of foreboding, symbolic of death, dying and burial at sea has appeared on four different covers (this was the first). Frisell began as a fashion photographer, and learned her trade as an apprentice to Cecil Beaton. In 1942 she took shots of women and African American airmen in service for use in recruiting back home. Bill Evans (1929—1980), the sparse, elegant and drug-addicted pianist, had begun his career as sideman, most notably as pianist on Miles Davis's *Kind of Blue* ('59). His first solo album in 1956 featured the track for which he's best known, "Waltz for Debby." Two live albums recorded with his trio in 1961 made him a big jazz name. This album, recorded with just guitarist Jim Hall, is a true classic of the genre. The mood of the cover is reflected in the mood of the music. This is the gatefold; there is also a single sleeve that has the title and artists' names in an "underwater" font on the front.

Last Kiss

josie

J. FRANK WILSON
and the Cavaliers

TELL LAURA I LOVE HER
ONLY THE LONELY
THAT'LL BE THE DAY
YOUNG LOVE
SCHOOL DAYS
OVER THE MOUNTAIN
SEA OF LOVE
KISS AND RUN
SPEAK TO ME

1964
Josie/Jay-Gee Records
America
Sleeve design and photography
uncredited

! J. Frank Wilson and the Cavaliers Last Kiss

So much is wrong with this cover that it's hard to know where to begin. The title track was the only chart hit for Wilson and the Cavaliers, in 1964. It is a macabre song about a real car crash that occurred in 1962, near the author's home in Georgia. In it three teenagers were killed, among them a sixteen-year-old girl who had been on a date when the car she was in collided with a truck. The inclusion of the similarly death-themed "Tell Laura I Love Her" suggests that Wilson was attempting to corner the death record market. In the photo here a young girl, eyes closed, lies limp against a tree, presumably dead, while an older man looks as if he's strangling her, but is holding her head still while he kisses her breathless mouth. The font used in the title implies speed (nice touch) while an odd dotted line (cut here?) frames the action of the photo. A different font and color displays the band name, yet another font displays the album tracks. It's a mess. The final line of the cover notes says of J. Frank, "His idol is the late and great Buddy Holly." Wilson died in 1991, of "prolonged alcoholism."

SONGS FOR SWINGIN' SELLERS

mono

PARLOPHONE
LONG PLAYING 33⅓ R.P.M. RECORD

WANTED

SONGS FOR SWINGIN' SELLERS

1959
Parlophone
England
Photography by Ken Palmer

Peter Sellers Songs for Swingin' Sellers

It would be nice to think that the portable Dansette record player in the photo here is playing J. Frank Wilson's *Last Kiss* (see previous page). Actor, comedian and writer Peter Sellers had a streak of cruel humor and this cover, unusual for the time in that it doesn't feature a huge image of the star, just that Wanted poster on the tree, perfectly reflects that. The inclusion of the spurs adds a comical Western element, and makes it somehow more "normal," since TV and movie viewers were used to seeing bad guys strung up in the countless shows and movies that proliferated at the time. Plus, the opening track on the record is entitled "You Keep Me Swinging." The album is partly Sellers' knocking the growing rock & roll and pop culture abroad in England at the time, made more interesting by the fact that it's produced by future Beatles producer George Martin, and partly a shameless cash-in on his popularity as a radio and movie star. The track "So Little Time," in which Sellers interviews an ex-army colonel who has gone from dealing horses to managing rock & roll stars, is brilliant.

History of Otis Redding

1967/8
Polydor/Atco
England
Sleeve design by Paragon Publicity
Photography by Paul C. Acree Jr.

Otis Redding History of Otis Redding

How could they have known? This compilation album was put together, packaged and released mere weeks before Otis Redding's death in a small airplane crash. The great soul singer had recorded "(Sittin' On) The Dock of The Bay" just three days before he died in the icy waters of Lake Monona, Wisconsin, along with four members of his band, the Bar-Kays. The poignant irony of that song has helped it become his signature tune. This compilation, though, features hits from the first three years of his remarkable career, including "I've Been Loving You So Long," "Mr Pitiful" and "Respect." The cover photo of this UK edition of the album is almost medieval in its symbolism: the singer rides horseback, looking over his shoulder as he follows a sunlit path into the woods from which he will never return. The trees are bleached to an almost ice-like stillness. The photo was taken on Redding's ranch in Georgia. The original U.S. release of the album used a naive drawing of the singer and multicolored type instead of this photo.

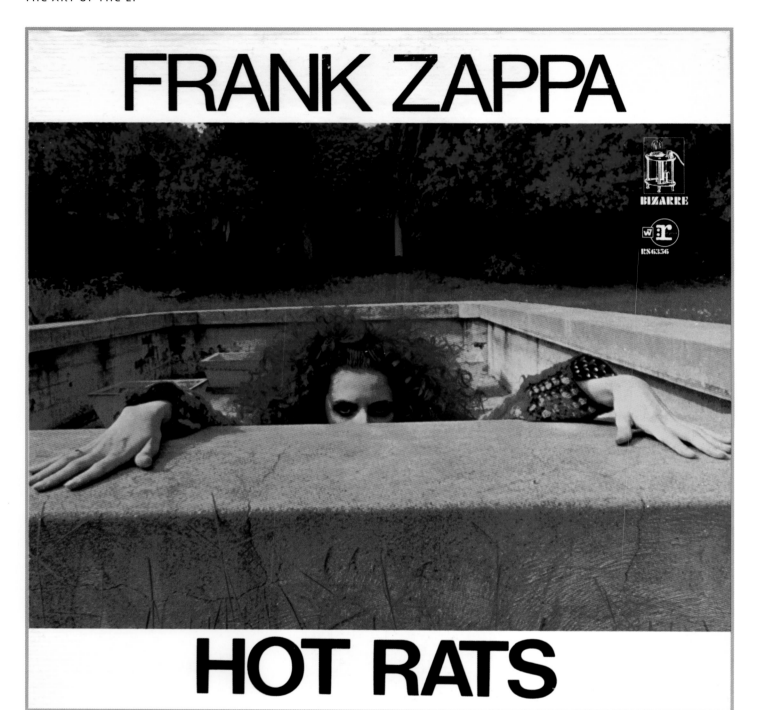

FRANK ZAPPA

HOT RATS

BIZARRE

RS 6356

1969

Bizarre Records

America

Sleeve design by Cal Schenkel

Photography by Andee Nathanson

Frank Zappa Hot Rats

For almost forty years this cover photo was incorrectly attributed to regular Zappa collaborator Ed Caraeff. However, it was actually Andee Nathanson (then Cohen), the cover star's roommate, who took this remarkable shot. Andee and Christine Frka (Miss Christine of the GTOs) found a deserted LA mansion and decided to shoot a few frames of Christine in the empty pool. Miss Christine had been a nanny to Zappa's children before joining Pamela Des Barres and three others to be transformed by Zappa into the GTOs. Andee handed her shot, with its ominously red, gold and bleached hues, and Christine seeming to crawl from a grave, to Zappa. He then passed it to designer Schenkel with instructions to use it as his next cover. Cal assumed it was by Ed because Zappa's covers usually were. Andee's life story is fascinating, but Christine's was tragic. Originally from San Pedro she died of a drug overdose in a motel room in 1972, having supposedly spent a year in a bodycast to correct a bent spine. Before then, though, she put Alice Cooper into his trademark eyeshadow and dressed him in a feather boa.

Original Soundtrack Recording of
Catch My Soul

1973
Metromedia/RCA
America
Sleeve design by Norman Moore/Rod Dyer, Inc.
Photography by Leandro Correa/Rod Dyer, Inc.

Original Soundtrack Catch My Soul

Although British born, Jack Good was an early innovator in rock & roll TV who spent most of his professional life in America. In the UK he developed the first British rock music TV shows and persuaded Gene Vincent to wear black leather (which is where Elvis got the look). In America he produced a range of TV shows, the most famous of which was *Shindig!* He wrote columns for teen mags, produced a TV special with the Beatles in 1964, and helped to make rock & roll TV groundbreaking. In 1969 he created a rock musical based on Shakespeare's *Othello—Catch My Soul*—and promptly took the lead role (as Othello) despite being Caucasian, in the London production (which also included P. J. Proby as Cassio). In 1973 a movie was made of the play featuring Richie Havens as Othello, Tony Joe White as Cassio, and Delaney & Bonnie. This is the soundtrack for that film, the songs mostly written by Tony Joe White (many with Good). The cover would appear to be for another movie, one about a black Christ, but that's Season Hubley as Desdemona in the statue's arms. It's a terrific and powerful image.

1984
Atlantic
America
Photography by Mark Weiss Studio
Art direction by Bob Defrin

❗ Twisted Sister Stay Hungry

Before anyone points out the obvious, yes, it is meant to be funny. Except, as with art director Bob Defrin's other Heavy Metal "joke" cover, AC/DC's *If You Want Blood You've Got It* (see p. 27), it isn't funny, it's tacky. Twisted Sister took inspiration from Alice Cooper, makeup tips from transvestites, and riffs from a hundred other metal bands and made a bit of a splash with this record. Amazingly, it sold triple platinum in America and made #15 on the Billboard Hot 200 album chart, and is still their most successful release. It spawned their only Top 30 hit single, "We're Not Gonna Take It," the video for which is claimed to be the cause for the formation of the Parents' Music Resource Center, although it's hard to see why. For the cover Defrin has lead Sister Dee Dee Sneider attempting an impersonation of a zombie, but instead looking like a vaudeville tramp showgirl. It's nowhere near as witty or impressive as the sleeve opposite. Nice logo though.

Harry Nilsson Son of Schmilsson

1972
RCA
America
Photography by Michael Putland
Graphics and lettering by
Peter Agapiou

After ten years and six albums, Harry Nilsson finally became a star with the release of *Nilsson Schmilsson*—the title a play on everyone's inability to spell or even pronounce his last name—in 1971 and the international hit single from it, "Without You." That album made #3 on the Billboard charts and RCA, who had supported his often eccentric wishes and released all his albums, even the soundtrack to a kids' story about a boy with a pointed head, entitled *The Point* (and it did make #25 on the U.S. album charts), wanted a follow-up. Harry supplied it, after demanding and getting a film crew to make documentaries about every song recorded, which remains unreleased. *Son Of Schmilsson* made #12 on the album charts but despite recording an album with John Lennon (see p. 193), Nilsson never sold as many records again before his death from heart failure in 1994, at age fifty-three. This cover has the singer as Dracula and is a response to the comments made about the cover of *Schmilsson* that he looked "half dead." The photo is by Brit Putland, a Rolling Stones–favored photographers.

Alice Cooper Killer

1971
Warner Brothers
America
Sleeve design by Alice Cooper
Photography by Pete Turner
Boa constrictor: Kachina

Johnny Lydon, when still Rotten, declared this the greatest rock album of all time, and Jello Biafra (of the Dead Kennedys) covered one of its tracks, "Halo of Flies." Marilyn Manson stole everything he shows from Alice. Today he's everyone's favorite old rocker, but back in 1971 Alice and his band of gothic glam rockers were regularly booed off stage by hippies, and for good reason—Cooper described the band as being the nail in the coffin of hippy. The Velvets' debut album cover used a banana because there was a myth that smoking their skins made you high. Alice used this photo of a boa (not his famous Yvonne) because it is a menacing symbol of death. People didn't do that on major record labels in 1971. The childish scrawl predates the use of child killers in horror movies by a good five years; the almost lustrous color can easily be described as "blood-red." The follow-up LP is a genius piece of packaging (see *School's Out*, p. 267), but this is more immediate and thrilling.

378

Blue Öyster Cult Some Enchanted Evening

1978
CBS
America
Cover concept by Hillary Vermont and
Marty Pekar
Painting by T. R. Shorr

The band is most famous for the hit single "(Don't Fear) The Reaper,"
released in 1976 and taken from their fifth album, *Agents of Fortune*. While
they had developed a considerable live following in America, their first
three studio albums had failed to make any real impression on the charts.
Their fourth LP was a live recording (*On Your Feet Or on Your Knees*, 1975)
and made #22. *Agents of Fortune* reached number 29 on the Billboard
Hot 200, but its follow-up, *Spectres*, only got as high as #43. So in 1978
they released this, another live album recorded at various venues across
America and England, and used a cover painting of the Grim Reaper on
a horse, in case people had forgotten who Blue Öyster Cult were. It's a
very fine and now clichéd rock & roll visual, copied by and inspiring many
subsequent metal album covers. It didn't help sales enormously though,
only making it to #44, despite containing a six-minute version of "(Don't
Fear) The Reaper."

Black Sabbath Black Sabbath

1970
Vertigo
England
Sleeve design and photography by Keef

Recorded in a couple of days, Black Sabbath's debut is perhaps not their best but it certainly laid down much of the law for the heavy metal genre, with its preoccupation with death and the occult. Bass player Geezer Butler was a big horror film fan so presumably he had some input into this spooky front cover design. It features a depiction of the 15th-century Watermill at Mapledurham, situated on the River Thames in Oxfordshire, England. The ghostly figure dressed in black robes standing there is an actress hired for the shoot by Vertigo Records' in-house designer "Keef" Macmillan (who also photographed Bowie's *Man Who Sold the World* cover). She may not represent death but must have done a good job of unsettling the more pharmaceutically affected Sabbath fans, particularly as the album was released on Friday, February 13. Look closely and—supposedly—she's holding a black cat. The mill went on to be used in the 1976 film *The Eagle Has Landed*.

Golden Earring To the Hilt

1976
Polydor Records
England
Cover concept by George Hardie
Cover design and photography by
Hipgnosis
Retouching by Richard Manning

Dutch rockers Golden Earring had reached the Top 20 singles charts around the world with "Radar Love" in 1973. They had been the first Dutch band to tour the United States in 1969, and released their debut album in 1965. This is the band's eleventh album release, but the first to employ the talents of Hipgnosis for the cover art. The gatefold sleeve reveals two more images of the moustachioed elderly man in similarly dangerous situations to this, as does the rear face of the sleeve. Exactly why the old man is being murdered in a Penelope Pitstop fashion isn't exactly clear, but it's great fun. Surprisingly, there are no images of naked or semi-naked females to be seen anywhere on the sleeve, unlike in the work that Hipgnosis did for other European rock bands of the time (particularly the Scorpions). Golden Earring went on to make thirteen more studio albums, release eight live albums and countless compilations, and were still gigging and recording more than forty years after they first formed.

1983
Warner Brothers
America
Art direction by Richard Seireeni and
David Jellison
Illustration by Margo Zafer Nahas
Photography by Raul Vega

Van Halen MCMLXXXIV

It's an angel, with a forelock, smoking a cigarette. The cigarette is held in the manner of a seasoned jailbird between the middle two fingers (in order to be able to create a fist quickly if needed, and to hold onto it should someone try to steal it). The Roman numerals (for 1984) and Van Halen typeface are reminiscent of a gravestone inscription. The cigarette packet inscription should read something along the lines of "smoking can severely damage your health" or even "smoking kills." In some parts of the United States the album cover was stickered over in order to remove the offending image—of the cigarettes. It was the band's sixth album, and their most successful, providing them with a #1 single ("Jump"), for which they're still largely remembered. The album went on to sell over eight million copies, reaching #2 on the Billboard album chart. Who said death doesn't sell?

Violent Femmes Violent Femmes

1983
Slash Records
America
Sleeve design by Jeff Price
Photography by Ron Hugo

Most of the songs on Violent Femmes' debut were written by singer Gordon Gano while he was still at school in Milwaukee, Wisconsin. Many of them, including "Blister In The Sun," "Add It Up," and "Gone Daddy Gone," have become classics of their kind, possibly because of his adolescent and morbid view of the world. Add to this his yelping voice and the scratchy folk punk that bassist Brian Ritchie and percussionist Victor DeLorenzo supply, and the overall impression is one of feral youth discovering the evil that men do. As such, Jeff Price's artwork is perfect: what is the barefoot child in Ron Hugo's photograph looking at? For newcomers to the Femmes—which most of course were—the name of the band was also extremely relevant to the sleeve: there is a sense of unease, of potential violence and death here. Gano's songs imply and describe much violence and anger, urgency and unevenness. Which is what this image of threatened innocence suggests.

·CLOSER·

1980
Factory
England
Sleeve design by Peter Saville and
Martyn Atkins
Photography by Bernard Pierre Wolff

Joy Division Closer

It's difficult to disconnect this sleeve from the context in which Joy Division's second and final album was released. Ian Curtis, the band's singer, committed suicide in May when the album was originally scheduled for release. It was delayed until July but the artwork still became the source of much controversy, with many people suggesting that Factory was exploiting Curtis's death to market the band. The image is a photograph of the Appiani family tomb in the Cimitero Monumentale di Staglieno in Genoa, Italy—one of the biggest cemeteries in Europe. The photograph of Demetrio Paernio's sculpture was taken just one year earlier, by celebrated French photographer Bernard Pierre Wolff. But it isn't just about the photo, it is Saville's contextualization that was ground-breaking. The juxtaposition of the classical imagery in the context of a rock band along with stark lines and understated graphics inspired many record sleeves during the eighties, but none came as near to perfection as this.

THE WANNADIES

BAGSY ME

1996
Indolent/RCA
England
Sleeve design by Lars Sundt
Photography by Irmelie Krekin

The Wannadies *Bagsy Me*

It's a decidedly odd image in combination with the band name and album title. If you didn't know that the Wannadies made mellifluous power pop with lovelorn lyrics you might be forgiven for thinking that they were obsessively morbid. Hailing from Skellefteå in northern Sweden, the Wannadies had made three albums prior to this but they were now signed to UK label Indolent and were swept up in the Britpop scene that was raging at the time. They didn't let that distract them, however, and continued to use Swedish designer Lars Sundt for their artwork. Sundt was the designer and co-owner of highly influential Swedish magazine *Pop*. The cover concept, which extended to all the band's singles at the time, was to feature beautiful girls who had suddenly fallen asleep. Another shot featured a waitress asleep at a lunch counter. It was an ambitious idea which, because of the band's name, got frequently misinterpreted. The ultimate misfortune befell them when Princess Diana died just before they rereleased surefire hit "You & Me Song." Radio dropped it because of the band's name.

Thin White Rope In the Spanish Cave

1988
Frontier Records
America
Sleeve design by Wendy Sherman
Art by Stephen Blickenstaff

Comic book illustrator Stephen Blickenstaff specializes in drawing zombies and monsters and plays the drums (and theremin). His ghoulish art has graced covers for the Cramps and They Might Be Giants as well as TWR and others. He'd previously drawn the cover of their second album, *Bottom Feeders* (1987). This is by far the best, though. It's a bit of a mystery why pirates haven't made more of a visual impact in rock & roll than just Johnny "Shakin' All Over" Kidd and Bow Wow Wow. After all, they were desperate, romantic, death-defying outlaws who wore cool eye patches. The gruesome pirates on this cover predate the SFX of *Pirates of the Caribbean* and Johnny Depp's channeling of Keith Richards by a good ten years or more. It didn't help Thin White Rope (another William S. Burroughs—inspired name; this a phrase he used to describe semen) though. After two more albums the band split, in 1992, having never made it big.

386

1987
Noise International
America
Sleeve design uncredited
Illustration by Lawvere

❗ **Rage Execution Guaranteed**

Who ever said that Germans have no sense of humor? These heavy metal Germans clearly do. At least, one hopes they do. This is an appallingly naive piece of cover art, and compared with the work opposite seems especially so. The grinning skull in a 1920s-era Chicago gangster-style suit is such a cliché that it should have been banned in the 1950s. Even the logo is dull, and almost lost in the mess of the whole. The glittering ring on the hand of the executed corpse is quite nice, though. Formed in northern Germany in 1984, Rage plays speed-metal thrash overlaid by screaming, doom-laden lyrics. The band exhibits a deeply cynical casuist thrust, their non-conformity to secular ideals or moral precepts unique in its brilliantly argued contradictions, most notably on their track "Wake Me When I'm Dead." This is the second of eighteen Rage albums to be released at the time of writing.

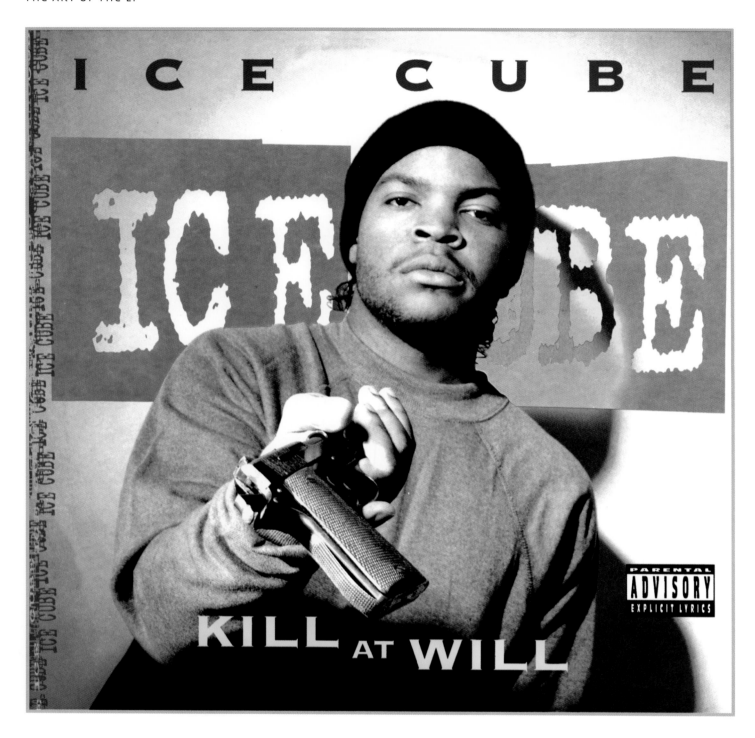

Ice Cube Kill at Will

1990
Priority Records
America
Sleeve design and photography
uncredited

Any other self-professed gangsta rapper would be holding the gun handle and pointing it at the buyer, but Cube (born O'Shea Jackson in 1969) is handing the buyer the gun, instead. The title and the pose do not display Cube's suicidal tendencies; rather they are his statement regarding the prejudices and preconceived ideas that the majority of the rap music—buying public—predominantly white and male—had about gangsta rap at that time. This was something of a preview for his longer *AmeriKKKa's Most Wanted* album and follows on from where he left off with N.W.A. (see opposite). While it's easy to misread both his intentions—both here and on his apparently sexist, macho-posing music, which followed—the only rapper with a degree in architecture was trying to get through to people by talking their talk, making them think without blowing their brains out. The proffered gun could just as easily be to a rival rapper or gang member, the use of the word "will" a suitably Malcolm X-style reminder that no one makes us do the things we do, nor should they. It's all about free will.

This
Record contains
explicit language.
It should not be
played in the
presence of
minors!
BRLP 562

PARENTAL
ADVISORY
EXPLICIT LYRICS

"NIGGAZ4LIFE"

1991
Ruthless/Priority Records
America
Art direction by Kevin "Design"
Hosmann
Photography by Peter Dokus

N.W.A. Niggaz4life

By the time that this third and final album was released, N.W.A. had ceased
to be a musical or political power. The politics had come from Ice Cube—who
left in 1989—and the credible beats from Dr. Dre, who was already working
with a host of other rappers and who left N.W.A. the same year this was
released. Despite that, this album made #1 in the Billboard album charts,
helped no doubt by the censorship debate that raged around the rappers'
use of the *N* word, their antipolice stance and the rumor that the cover
image was taken at a real murder scene. That seems unlikely, given the
quality of lighting used here and the very convenient fact that all of the
police officers are white while the corpses are clearly black. Obviously the
image is manipulated, and the band members superimposed, but there's
something about the clear lines and composition of the main image that is
too perfect to be a "snap." It is a powerful visual, though, which highlights
the commonplace incidents of death on the streets of America before TV
series such as *Homicide* and *The Wire* were aired.

1986
Music for Nations
America
Cover concept by Metallica and
Peter Mensch
Illustration by Don Brautigam

Metallica Master of Puppets

In a 1988 interview Metallica singer James Hetfield described the title track from their third album as being primarily about drugs, "How things get switched around, instead of you controlling what you're taking and doing, it's drugs controlling you." Metallica's lyrical themes, like those of many metal acts, deal with the less pleasant aspects of life and very often confront humans' ultimate fate. Indeed there is a song on their previous album, *Ride the Lightning*, called "Creeping Death." The artwork here was conceived by the band with their manager Peter Mensch, and is far from ambiguous. Endless rows of identical headstones, each one overgrown and presumably unloved, and above the headstones the band's logo, attached by guy wires to the graves. The logo had been established with their debut album, the amusingly entitled *Kill Em All*. With its distinctive stainless steel sheen and exaggerated letters *M* and *A*, it's one of the most enduring rock logos around. It'll outlive the band for sure.

Slayer Reign in Blood

1986
Def Jam Records
America
Sleeve design and artwork by
Larry Carroll

In the mid-1980s heavy metal got faster, louder and more Satanic—mostly as a result of the success of this, Slayer's breakthrough (third) album. At a time when black American males began to glorify their subculture in rap, with the sexist and violent gangsta rap being the "hardcore" end of the genre, white disaffected American males began to listen to thrash metal. With its death-obsessed, blood-and-guts-spouting lyrics and extreme visuals that usually contained sexist acts of violence or arcane devil worship, it's easy to patronize the sub-cult as being eternally adolescent; yet its effects have been profound. The cover of *Reign in Blood* by Larry Carroll—a political cartoonist for the *New York Times* and *Village Voice*, among others—creates a vision of Hell in which the devil in goat form sits in a throne carried by Slayer members. Apparently one band member disliked the sleeve, but after another showed it to his mother and she pronounced it "disgusting," they knew they had something. It is now held to be one of the best heavy metal covers of all time by various metal magazines.

Elliott Smith
Elliott Smith

1995
Kill Rock Stars
America
Photography by J. J. Gursa

Texan singer-songwriter Smith (1969—2003) said of his second album that he "personally can't get more dark" than this. It is an acoustic record with songs about drugs and losing his girlfriend; some are almost positive but mostly in a restrained way. The falling figures on the cover eerily presage the victims of 9/11 and perhaps reflect the singer's own sense of falling. Apparently future suicides often have dreams of flying in which they fall from a height. Smith killed himself, by stabbing himself in the chest, in 2003 after an argument with his girlfriend. An autopsy found prescribed antidepressants and ADHD medication in his blood stream, at prescription levels. No note was found.

Opeth Morningrise

1996
Century Black
America
Photography by Tuija Lindstrom
Layout by Timo Ketola

Swedish metal band Opeth has proven to be one of the most inventive and interesting of the wave of death metal bands to emerge from Europe in the 1990s. The trio's songs, written by singer and guitarist Mikael Akerfelt, have become mini-epics with key, time and thematic changes more reminiscent of early 1970s prog rock bands, and lyrics generally more thoughtful than those of the usual metal acts of the same ilk. For this, their second album, Akerfelt wrote a song to his recently deceased grandfather ("The Night and the Silent Water") and chose a black-and-white photo of the Palladian bridge in Prior Park, Bath, England as the very suitable cover image. It looks like a mausoleum; the water could be the Styx. All very restrained and refined.

rage against the machine

1992
Epic
America
Art direction by Rage Against the
Machine and Nicky Lindeman
Photography by Malcolm Browne,
Associated Press

Rage Against the Machine Rage Against the Machine

This sleeve could just as easily have been in the politics section: RATM
singer Zack de la Rocha is one of the most overtly politicized musicians
around, campaigning for and even testifying at the UN on behalf of death
row-accused Mumia Abu-Jamal, as well as supporting the Zapatista
movement of Mexico. However, the sleeve for this, their debut album,
features an award-winning photograph by Malcolm Browne of Buddhist
monk Thich Quang Duc self-immolating and burning to death in Saigon
in 1963. The monk was protesting against Vietnamese president Ngo Dinh
Diem's administration for oppressing the Buddhist religion. De la Rocha
must have admired the power of the picture, which helped persuade then
U.S. president John F. Kennedy to withdraw support for the Ngo Dinh Diem
regime. De la Rocha's idealism was met with disappointment when, despite
several #1 albums, the band failed to change the world. However, in 2007
the singer was still calling various U.S. presidents "war criminals."

INDEX

BY DESIGNER

PICTURE CREDITS

10 RCA Starcall; 11 top RCA/US/Sony; 11 bottom Epic; 12 Charly/Specialty/US; 13 Rockstar; 14 Roulette Records; 15 Charly; 16 Capitol; 17 EMI; 18 Columbia; 19 Track Records; 20 Columbia Archive Recordings; 21 Island Records; 22 Universal Records; 23 top Track Records; 23 bottom CBS Records; 24 A&M Records; 26 Capitol; 27 Atlantic Records; 28 Warners; 30 Rolling Stone Records/Universal Records; 31 Elektra; 32 Columbia/US/Sony; 34 RSO Records; 36 Epic; 37 Elektra; 38 Bronze; 39 Epic/CBS Records; 40 Vertigo; 41 Paisley Park/WEA; 42 Sire Records/ US/Warners; 43 Enigma/Capitol; 44 Illegal Records; 45 Def Jam Records, CBS Records/US; 48 Geffen; 49 Liberty/US; 50 Jaro International; 51 Sugar Records; 52 Capitol; 53 Columbia; 54 Command; 55 Reprise Records; 56 Brunswick; 57 Music For Pleasure; 58 Trojan; 59 RSO/Polydor; 60 Liberty/US; 62 Mercury/US; 64 Swan Song; 66 Island Records/UK; 67 4AD; 68 Phonogram; 69 Sunburst Records; 70 Chrysalis; 71 Atlantic; 72 Elektra; 73 Hannibal Records; 74 CBS Records; 75 Island Records/UK; 76 Pickwick Records; 77 Phillips; 77 Elektra /US/ Warners; 78 Harvest/ EMI; 80 Harvest/EMI; 82 Rough Trade; 83 Nude; 84 EMI; 85 A&M Records; 86 Warner Chappel/ UK; 87 Island Records/UK; 90 Blue Note/US/EMI; 91 Blue Note/US/EMI; 92 Victor/Prestige; 93 Columbia/US/Sony; 94 Brunswick Records; 95 Columbia/Sony/US; 96 Reprise Records; 97 Verve/ US; 98 top "Brunswick"; 98 bottom Allegro; 99 RCA/US/Sony; 100 Liberty; 102 Command Records; 103 Island Records; 104 Verve/US; 105 RCA/Victor; 106 Columbia/Sony/US; 107 Columbia; 108 Warners; 110 Atlantic Records; 111 Harvest/EMI; 112 CBS Records; 113 Brother/Reprise Records; 114 Reprise Records; 115 Tamla Motown; 116 Warners; 117 Phonogram; 118 Virgin/UK/EMI; 119 Sire Records; 120 top Radar Records; 120 bottom Vertigo; 121 top Radar Records; 121 bottom Stiff Records; 122 Sire Records/Warners; 123 Harvest/EMI; 124 top United Artists; 124 bottom Virgin; 125 EMI; 126 Ember; 127 Island Records/UK; 128 Factory/UK/London/Warners; 129 Factory/UK/London/Warners; 130 Island Records; 131 Island Records; 132 Stiff Records; 133 RCA; 134 Mute; 135 Mercury; 136 top 4AD; 136 bottom 4AD; 137 top 4AD; 137 bottom 4AD; 138 Warners; 139 Creation/Sony; 140 Capitol Records; 141 Matador; 142 Fontana/Phonogram; 143 Angel Records; 144 CBS Records; 145 Sub Pop; 148 Colgems; 149 Karma Sutra; 150 Abnak Music Enterprises; 151 Warners; 152 Atlantic; 153 EMI Records; 154 Virgin Records; 155 Vertigo; 156 EMI Harvest/UK; 157 ABC Records/US; 158 Casablanca; 159 Atco; 160 Warners; 161 Warners; 161 Warners; 162 CBS Records; 163 Columbia/US/Sony; 164 Charisma; 165 Chrysalis; 166 Epic; 167 Sire Records/US/Warners; 168 EMI; 169 Island Records/UK; 170 Gull Records; 171 top Epic/US/ Sony; 171 bottom EMI/UK; 172 Hannibal; 173 Elektra; 174 Virgin; 175 Columbia; 176 Tamla Motown; 177 Def Jam Records; 180 Prestige/Fantasy jazz; 181 Sony/US Columbia; 182 Parlophone/UK/ EMI; 183 top Parlophone/UK/EMI; 183 bottom Colgems; 184 Radarscope/ Warners/US/Charly; 185 Polydor/UK/US; 186 Mercury; 187 Atlantic; 188 Atlantic; 189 RCA Victor; 190 Universal Records; 191 Fantasy Liberty Records; 192 Warners/US; 193 RCA; 194 Atlantic; 195 Columbia; 196 Mercury; 197 Mercury; 198 Virgin; 199 Rolling Stone Records/UK/ Virgin/EMI; 200 RBS Records; 202 Charisma Records; 202 United Artists; 203 Swan Song; 204 CBS Records; 205 Dedicated Records; 208 Pye Records; 209 Verve/US; 210 Clefe; 211 EMI/US; 212 Atlantic/US/Warners; 213 Columbia; 214 RCA/US/Sony; 215 Rocket Records; 216 Philips/UK; 217 Atco; 218 Elektra Records; 219 Capital World Record Club; 220 Track/Polydor; 221 RCA; 222 Island Records/UK; 223 Embryo/ Atlantic; 224 Polydor; 225 MGM; 226 RCA/UK/Sony; 227 Nothing/Interscope/US; 228 Monument Records; 229 Harvest; 230 CBS Records; 232 Disc-rest Records/Warners; 233 Blue Sky/CBS Records; 234 RCA/UK/Sony; 235 Astor Records; 236 Warners; 237 Columbia/US/Sony; 238 Virgin/ UK/EMI; 239 Blast First!; 240 Elektra/Asylum; 242 Cold Chillin'/Reprise Records; 243 Def Jam Records, CBS Records/US; 244 Tommy Boy; 245 Elektra; 246 Elektra; 247 CBS Records; 248 One Little Indian; 249 EMI; 250 Paisley Park/Warners; 251 RCA/Artista Records; 254 EMI Harvest/ UK; 255 Blue Note; 256 Capitol Records; 257 Columbia; 258 Capricorn Records; 260 RCA Victor;

261 Polydor; 262 A&M Records; 263 Atco; 264 Harvest/EMI; 266 Rolling Stone Records/Universal Records; 267 Warners; 268 EMI Harvest/UK; 269 Fever/Enigma Records; 270 Island Records/UK; 271 Polydor; 272 Verve Folkways; 273 Curtom/Buddah Records; 274 Polydor; 275 Sire Records; 276 Vertigo/Germany/EMI; 277 Chrysalis; 278 A&M Records; 279 Polydor; 280 top Polydor; 280 bottom ECM; 281 Astralwerks; 282 Blue Thumb Records; 283 Mercury; 284 CBS Records; 286 Capitol Records; 287 American Recordings; 290 Capitol US/EMI; 291 Contemporary Records; 292 Columbia; 293 Capitol Records; 294 EmArcy/Mercury; 295 Blue Note; 296 Blue Note; 297 Blue Note; 298 Savoy/Regent Records; 299 Columbia; 300 Columbia; 301 RCA Victor; 302 Capricorn Records; 303 Capricorn Records; 304 Camden/RCA; 305 Warners; 306 top Capitol Records; 306 bottom Atco; 307 Island Records; 308 A&M Records; 309 A&M Records; 310 Charisma Records; 311 Charisma Records; 312 Virgin Records; 313 Epic; 314 Island Records; 315 A&M Records; 316 Command; 317 Atlantic; 318 Bronze Records; 319 Bronze Records; 320 ABC Records; 321 Mercury; 322 The Electric Record Company; 323 CBS Records; 324 top Elektra/Asylum; 324 bottom Virgin; 325 Manticore; 326 Asylum Records; 327 Food/EMI; 330 Curtom Records/Warners; 331 Verve Records; 332 Blue Note; 333 Blue Note; 334 RCA Victor; 335 Island Records/UK; 336 President Records; 337 Columbia; 338 Mercury/Cooking Vinyl; 339 Columbia; 339 On-U Sound; 340 Island Records/Solomonic; 341 Channel One Recordings; 342 Columbia/CBS Records/Sony; 343 Bizzarre Records/US/Rykodisc; 344 Charly/UK; 345 Mary Records, The Mary Lou Williams Foundation, Inc.; 346 Tamla Motown; 347 Westbound Records; 348 Track/Atlantic; 349 Warner Brothers; 350 Mercury/US; 351 Arista/Sony; 352 Decay/Manifesto; 353 EG Records/UK/Warners; 354 Ze Records; 354 Matador Records; 355 Arista Records; 356 Island Records; 357 SST Records; 358 SST Records; 359 Geffen/US; 360 A&M Records; 361 Geffen/US; 362 EMI; 363 Geffen; 364 Arista Records; 365 Zomba Records, RCA/Sony; 366 top Epic/US/Sony; 366 bottom Columbia/US/ Sony; 367 Def American; 370 United Artists Jazz; 371 Josie/Jay-Gee Records; 372 Parlophone/ UK/EMI; 373 Polydor/Atco; 374 Bizzarre Records/US/Rykodisc; 375 Metromedia/RCA; 376 Atlantic; 377 RCA; 378 Warners; 379 CBS Records; 380 Vertigo; 381 Polydor; 382 Warners/US; 383 Slash Records; 384 Factory; 385 Indolent/RCA; 386 Frontier Records; 387 Noise International; 388 Priority Records/US; Island Records/UK; 389 Def Jam Records, CBS Records/US; 390 Music For Nations; 391 Def Jam Records; 392 Kill Rock Stars; 392 Century Black; 393 Epic

ACKNOWLEDGMENTS

Thanks go to my very lovely wife, Robyn, who waived all familial duties while I wrote this. Also thanks to my good neighbors Steve and Mandy Jesner, who let me pilfer many of the sleeves you see here from their quietly impressive vinyl collection. And, lastly, thanks to Mal, not just for asking me to help write this book but also for allowing me to write about all the sleeves that used to grace my bedroom walls.
Ben Wardle

Thanks to Michael Fragnito, vice president and editorial director at Sterling, for commissioning this book and agreeing to its unique system of categorizing album covers. Thanks also to the record companies who commissioned the artwork for the covers included in this book, and to the artists they commissioned—if we haven't included your name, then please get in touch and we will correct that in future editions. A big thanks to Mike Muller for supplying a good number of the covers that we didn't already own and couldn't easily find (Jah Rastafari!), and of course thanks to Ben, for not arguing too much over the choices made in the final cut. Finally, thank you, Essential Works, for being so essential.
Johnny Morgan